D0892036

Women in the Holocaust
Volume 1

WOMEN

IN THE

HOLOCAUST

A COLLECTION OF TESTIMONIES
VOLUME I

Compiled and Translated by
Jehoshua Eibeshitz
and
Anna Eilenberg-Eibeshitz

WOMEN IN THE HOLOCAUST

Edited by Fayge Silverman

FIRST EDITION
First Impression — July 1993

Published by
REMEMBER
705 Foster Avenue
Brooklyn, N.Y. 11230
(718) 692-3900

ISBN 0—932351—44-1 (Casebound Edition)
SBN 0—932351—45-x (Softcover Edition)

Printed in the U.S.A.

TABLE OF CONTENTS

INTRODUCTION

❖

The thought of writing a work on the subject of women in the Holocaust was born and stifled over twenty-two years ago.

One morning in 1981, when I was living in Kiryat Ata in Chaifa, my telephone rang. It was a woman, a member of a *kibbutz,* who told me that she had heard of my work in Holocaust research and wished to discuss an "urgent" matter with me. I invited her to come to my house, but she politely refused, suggesting instead that we meet in a neutral place, without the presence of "other faces," as she put it. I later understood why she wished, for her own peace of mind, to remain in an anonymous surrounding.

We met in a cafeteria in Chaifa. I had anticipated a short visit, an hour at the most, perhaps; but it continued for a full seven hours and would have lasted much longer if not for my weariness.

The woman had a strong urge to unburden an emotional load, a secret which had nested in her conscience for many years now, dogging her day and night. She had reached a point where she could not carry it alone and felt she must share it with someone who would understand her. She requested that I publish her story without using her name. "Just call me Miriam," she said.

I myself had suffered cruelly at the hands of the Nazis and had heard countless tales of horror through my work as a chronicler of human experience in the Holocaust; and yet this woman's tale was so brutal that I could not bring myself to commit its details to paper.

The story began in a town in the Carpathian mountains in Hungary, where "Miriam" had been raised in a sheltered religious environment. When the Germans invaded in 1942, she was twelve years old. That spring all the Jews in the area were deported to Auschwitz, and at the first "selection" Miriam was separated from her parents and relatives.

Miriam was a rare beauty. The Germans ordered her out of the line and brought her to a barracks known in Auschwitz as the "House of Dolls," where she was kept for almost eight months. She and all the other young girls in that house were used for the most licentious purposes, kept alive solely to satisfy the base instincts of several sadistic and bestial Nazis.

She had kept her secret deep inside her all these years. But now something totally unanticipated had happened, intensifying her need to speak: her own son was dating a German girl! What if he married her? What if the girl was the daughter of one of the many murderers who had so sadistically abused her?

During those seven hours Miriam told me innumerable details of her bitter experiences in the "House of Dolls." I was convinced that I had already plumbed the abyss of Nazi savagery, but this story shocked me to the depths of my being. I knew in my heart that the world must be told about what the Nazis did to our Jewish daughters, yet my dilemma was painful. How could I describe the indescribable — how could I print the unprintable?

I returned home broken and torn inside. The ensuing days gave me no peace. In the end I decided that I would collect and publish authentic stories of the Jewish woman's struggle during the Nazi regime: stories of their heroic behavior and of their role as guardians of the Jewish family in the face of a living death.

My wife Hedva, of blessed memory, who was my literary advisor and critic, was skeptical of the project and advised me not to touch such a terribly sensitive topic. She was of the opinion that no man would ever understand the plight faced by the Jewish woman during the greatest tragedy in our history. On her urging I shelved the idea, leaving it concealed in a not-too-distant corner of my mind; but fate had its own design.

After my dear Hedva was abruptly taken from me, I decided to perpetuate her memory by writing a book about her. Indeed, throughout the forty years of our life together, there had been many events worthy of record; but I found that such an undertaking was beyond my emotional strength. Even now I cannot bring myself to put down on paper all that is in my heart. Maybe the reason lies in the fact that one needs a great deal of time and distance to create a perspective on a person in whom so many priceless qualities were concentrated.

Yet I could not rest; I felt that I owed her something. After much reflection I decided to bring back to life the dormant project of many years and to publish an anthology of stories of women in the Holocaust. Perhaps I would never truly understand the scope and depth of their plight, and yet I was reminded of words that I had read in the diary of Emanuel Ringelblum, the well-known historian and keeper of the underground archives during the Holocaust: "The historian of the future who will write about the events of our days will have to devote a special page to the Jewish woman and her place in this war. The Jewish woman has assumed a special chapter in Jewish history. In the abyss of darkness she was a pillar of strength and courage."

My hope was that in each of these accounts of the woman's courage, wisdom, self-sacrifice, and moral fortitude, a part of my Hedva's character would be represented; and that the preservation of the woman's testimony could provide us with a model of the enormous depth and strength of the human spirit.

Jehoshua Eibeshitz

PREFACE

The testimonies gathered in this anthology are personal experiences and observations of women who survived the darkest period in Jewish history. Their stories form a powerful chronicle of enormous suffering, unwavering strength, and remarkable perseverance in the face of disaster.

The woman's role in the Holocaust is particularly poignant. Many historians and witnesses have testified to the fact that her bravery during the war surpassed the man's and that she endured suffering better. The woman's work load was greater, especially in the ghettos, for she was subject to the same forced labor as the man, and yet she was still responsible for her home and family. Women frequently became the sole family providers if their husbands or brothers wore beards and sidelocks and could not afford to be seen in the streets. Often they performed their duties in great peril because of the decrees imposed by the Germans on pregnancies and birth. They also played an important part in the underground resistance because no physical proof of Jewishness could be discerned upon them, a danger to which the men were constantly subject.

The heroism of these women is intensified by the fact that most of them were young girls at the time of the war, and one who bears this in mind will read the stories in an entirely different light. The Holocaust precluded any semblance of a normal childhood. It created adults who were adolescent only in terms of chronology, children of twelve and fourteen who found themselves in positions of responsibility unimaginable to their teenage counterparts of today, unthinkable to the average citizen of any peacetime society. They stood guard outside ghetto homes where organized prayer was taking place; they cared for younger siblings in cases where their parents were either imprisoned or dead; they ran life-saving errands on roads patrolled by German soldiers; they worked in the underground as couriers and relief agents. Although their testimonies have been given with adult hindsight, the wise judgment, courageous endurance, and emotional maturity they exhibited in times of crisis are an awesome tribute to a group of children-women whose insight and abilities far exceeded their years.

The testimonies not only pay tribute to the women themselves, they are also a potent weapon against two stubborn myths. The first of these is the preposterous notion maintained by some professed historians that the Holocaust never took place at all. The validity of personal testimonies as objective historical data has long been disputed, but no one can challenge their value as eyewitness proof of the Holocaust — and of its brutal severity. The twenty women in this book have different stories to tell, but there are common threads running through all of them that sharply outline their authenticity. The dovetailing of many of their descriptions, including everything from emotional impressions to the details of entry procedures in the concentration camps, is striking and powerful.

The second myth dissolved by personal testimonies is the still-prevalent notion that the Jews during the Holocaust went "like sheep to slaughter." This accusation is very painful to survivors, regardless of whether it is asked out of ignorance or insensitivity, and it can only be answered by the survivors themselves. Only they, who took part in and witnessed the heroic spiritual struggle of the inmates in the ghettos and concentration camps, can testify that such allegations have no basis in fact.

Current political slogans such as "Never again" are somewhat misleading in terms of their suggestion that perhaps the Jews really could have stood up to their oppressors the first time around. However, a little research into Nazi strategy, which was well in motion years before the outbreak of the war, will elicit the utter unfeasibility of any mass, organized physical resistance. As the war opened, the Jews were systematically uprooted from their homes by the combined means of force and deception. They were then relocated to large cities, where they were concentrated in ghettos which had been created for the express purpose of entrapping them. These communities were then sealed off, and their residents were deprived in stages of food, radio and written communication with the outside world, religious freedom, adequate housing, heat, and medical care, and the most basic of sanitary and health provisions.

Any resistance was effectively quashed by a calculated campaign of random terror. Many Jews were arrested, thrown into prison, and tortured for minor infringements of the new plethora of anti-Jewish legislation — or for no reason at all. The ghetto inmates were also subjected to brutal forced labor. They could be snatched off the streets at any time and sent to clean stables, scrub city streets, and perform other types of menial and degrading tasks. Some were sent to work sites outside the city, from which they returned battered and broken; many never returned at all, and their families had no idea what had become of them.

In the second, more "settled" stage of ghetto life, the Germans enforced compulsory labor in a network of workshops — most notably in Lodz — which produced goods for both German civilians and the military. The workshops gave the Jews the temporary illusion of protection from deportation, for those not working were considered useless and were the first to be sent away; but they furthered weakened the constitution of the laborers, who worked long hours with little food. The ghettos themselves, in short, were a calculated agent in the liquidation process, for they quickly fell prey universally to the rapid spread of disease, exhaustion, and death.

Each of the large ghettos was situated near a major railway line, convenient conduits to the last stopping place in the Final Solution. Through a series of methodical deportations, the Jews were gradually emptied into the concentration camps, from which escape was almost entirely impossible. A few individual attempts were successful, but most of the escapees found that there was virtually no place to run; the Nazi grip on Eastern Europe was orderly and airtight. In some of the testimonies that follow, one can get a clear sense of the paralysis that arrested the Jewish communities in this process of relocation, a combination of physical enervation and disbelief that cauterized any collective attempt at organized defense.

And yet, in spite of the enormity of the catastrophe, it would be a gross mistake to think that there was no resistance.

The resistance did exist on a physical level, in fragmented but fierce components, of which the Warsaw ghetto uprising is the most famous episode. The resistance movement itself was a highly controversial one. Many were of the opinion that it endangered people unnecessarily, for German retaliation was swift and brutal; innocents could be killed in reprisal for the activities of their relatives or friends, entire towns wiped out as punishment for the actions of a few people. On the other end of the spectrum were those who believed strongly that a resistance was crucial. They felt that even though the prospects for success were bleak — and in many cases non-existent — there was no telling how many people might be saved by coordinated efforts, and that the possibility outweighed the risk.

Scores of people, many of them in their teens, actively participated in the underground. They carried out their missions in the cities, in the forests, and even in the camps, where hundreds of prisoners performed sabotage by damaging aircraft parts and other products in the factories where they worked, or by destroying money and valuables in the sorting kommandos in order to keep them out of German hands. Men, women, and children alike participated, and although their efforts yielded narrow results from the German perspective, their effect on Jewish morale cannot be overestimated. Young fighters such as Chavka Raban-Folman ("The Liaison Agent") and Mala Zimetbaum ("Escape from Auschwitz") were among many who helped to preserve the precious sense of self-worth of countless Jews and to bring them aid and comfort, even as they stood on line to the gas chambers.

However, to define the resistance only in terms of its physical aspect would be to overlook its true significance. The twenty stories in this book are a keen testimony to the depth of the spiritual struggle kept alive by women in the Holocaust — women of vastly different social strata and divergent educational and religious backgrounds, who were nevertheless united in their fight to retain their Jewish and humanitarian values.

These young women were instinctively aware of the very basic Jewish principle of freedom of choice. They understood that restrictions and walls could limit their physical movement but not their mental or moral freedom; and so, with great self-respect, they exercised their choices even in the most horrendous circumstances.

The spiritual resistance manifested itself in many forms. One of the first of these was the drive for education. Again and again in the testimonies the theme of self-education arises, the recognition by the youth of the ghetto of the all-important need for nourishment of the mind and spirit. These young people actively organized learning circles and underground schools once the Jewish schools in the ghetto were closed by the Nazis, and the hunger for learning was universal among them. Several of the testimonies that follow pay tribute to teachers for whom the women held a profound reverence — teachers who not only transmitted information but who provided them with the resources to understand and endure the great tragedy of their own suffering.

Sara Selver-Urbach ("A Brief Spring") tells of the exhausting treks that she and her friends made along the icy winter roads of the Lodz ghetto for the privilege of studying with Miss Zelicka, their adored mentor. In her shabby, unheated apartment, they sat huddled together in their coats among the pans placed beneath the leaking roof, and absorbed their teacher's words: "Miss Zelicka infused us with a love of the Bible, uncovering its treasures for us and interpreting it as though it had been written especially for us. In particular she demonstrated to us the relevance of the Scriptures and their implications in our own days . . . Miss Zelicka forged a link between us and our past to help us better understand the present and to give us the capacity to believe in a future." These girls did not require a roll book or a grading system to motivate them. They were well aware that their souls and not their bodies were responsible for their survival, and they turned their attention to the cultivation of their precious inner resources.

The spiritual resistance did not cease in the ghetto. The young women continued to exercise their moral freedom even in the black terror of the death camps, where cultural and prayer groups were organized under the watchful eye of their overseers, where poetry was written, where Sabbath candles were lit in secrecy, where pocket *siddurim* were kept and treasured — where faith flourished among the observant and non-observant alike.

Even in the final hour, the women did not relinquish their right of choice. Many of them found the courage to demonstrate that even if one is aware that he is walking to his death, there still remains to him to choose the manner in which he will walk. Testimony is given of the eleven-year-old girl who asked her mother not to debase herself by begging mercy of a Polish policeman but to accept her death sentence in dignity; of several young underground activists who, rather than allowing themselves to be led meekly to the gallows, chose instead to shout words of encouragement to their fellow prisoners even as the nooses were being lowered over their heads.

Chava Bronstein, a prisoner in the Reinikdorf camp in Germany ("The Engineer"), succinctly articulates the feeling of many young women who resolved not to allow the Germans to gain control over the innermost chambers of their souls: "I marched in my torn coat and wooden clogs, and I trembled from the cold. I was fourteen years old then, and I was hungry and humiliated, yet I thanked G-d for being strong inside. The Germans, hoping to crush my faith through the evil hand of degradation, instead succeeded in strengthening my belief in the Almighty. I looked and actually saw the hand of Providence in many events."

To such moral heroism as this the survivors in the following pages give testimony.

Fayge Silverman
EDITOR

A NOTE ON THE TRANSLATION

Women in the Holocaust was originally published in several volumes in Israel, and although it was intended for a general audience, the nature of the testimonies assumes some basic knowledge of the Holocaust on the part of the reader. Those who are not familiar with this period of time are advised to read the preceding introduction, which provides some minimal background on the Jewish situation during the war.

All of the testimonies have been translated from the Hebrew original. The problem of maintaining the integrity of an original language in translation is well known, and very often it is virtually impossible to find literal equivalents for words or expressions. An attempt has been made to adhere as closely as possible to the Hebrew version and to maintain the authenticity of the emotional tone of the testimonies. Adjustments in syntax and description have been made for the needs of the English-speaking public and, where necessary, historical background information has been added.

A glossary is provided to explain several foreign words and expressions which appear frequently in the testimonies. It is interesting to note that many of these words were used by the Jews of the Nazi era not in their literal sense, but rather as part of a unique jargon which grew up around the horrors of the regime. The prisoners in the concentration camps in particular had a special and often cynical argot. One example would be the word "organize," which meant to obtain, always at great risk, a needed item — whether it was a bit of medication or an extra piece of bread for a sick inmate. The word "steal" was not used by the prisoners, for to steal what the Nazis had already stolen from them was blatantly illogical. Such usage has been left intact to as great an extent as possible in the narratives.

Women in the Holocaust is intended mainly to be a collection of deeds and not a collection of biographies, and therefore the length and depth of the testimonies vary considerably. This is due partly to the survivors' differing levels of memory and attention to detail, but mostly to the sensitive emotional issue of gleaning information from people who have survived unspeakable atrocities. Many of them were initially reluctant to talk during interviews and responded in a highly emotional and erratic manner. Although eliciting specific responses to a schedule of questions might have produced a more journalistic product, such a process was found to distract the witnesses and ultimately to eclipse the powerful emotional coloring and sense of immediacy so essential to their stories. These were people who could not be asked for objective facts in any kind of systematic way, but who must be allowed to talk with the flow of their own memories and feelings and to emphasize what had been most important to them.

Because of the subjective nature of the testimonies, the information is not always complete; a few of them were originally given many years ago to Holocaust research institutes, making it difficult to trace the missing pieces. The chronology in some narratives is occasionally unclear, and sometimes people mentioned in the beginning of a story do not appear again. The Eibeshitzes have explained that any relative or close friend who "disappeared" from a story most likely did not survive the war, and that in the course of the testimony the witness found it too difficult to continue to speak about them. Extensive efforts were made to locate the survivors and to fill in these minor gaps, and the search was largely successful, but in a few cases the witnesses were no longer alive or could not be traced. The reader will excuse these occasional lapses of information, for the testimonies are not meant as historical documents but as documents of the soul, and as such they fulfill their purpose admirably.

IN THE GHETTOS
❖

A BRIEF SPRING

Sara Selver-Urbach
Lodz, Poland

Purim

A horrible massacre took place in Lodz in the beginning of 1940: the Germans shot and killed every Jew who had failed to evacuate the city proper by the deadline. The victims of this massacre were mostly old and sick people who had not been able to find refuge in the ghetto, as well as relatives who had refused to abandon them. My family reached the ghetto literally in the nick of time.

At first we moved into my grandparents' apartment, which consisted of one room and a kitchen. Our family alone numbered eight people, and though the main room was fairly large, it could barely accommodate the sixteen souls who now took shelter there. But we had to be thankful; so many others were less fortunate. In some cases, several families had to share a single apartment, and many who could find no roof at all were forced to crowd together in the old, deserted school building or in other public places. The Housing Allocation Office of the Judenrat had failed to provide apartments for all who needed one by the evacuation deadline. It was virtually impossible to squeeze over a quarter of a million Jews into the narrow confines of the Lodz ghetto.

There was scarcely room to move in the apartment because of the bags and sacks that were piled high in every corner. We slept on the floor, huddling together for warmth since no fuel was obtainable. In the mornings our parents had to scold us repeatedly to get us up, because we were warmer lying down than when we were up and about, even when fully dressed.

We stayed at my grandparents' home for a fortnight and celebrated Purim there. Despite the dismal conditions, we managed to lend the holiday a festive air. I have no idea how my grandmother, mother, and aunts contrived to prepare such a splendid array of sweets, but when the holiday arrived, the table was beautifully laid out and laden with cookies and cakes of all kinds.

In Lodz in 1940, public prayer was still officially permitted by the wartime government, even though the Germans arbitrarily forbade worship and directed many of their edicts toward the dissolution of religious practice. But we were not yet afraid of this, and that year on Purim we sat together around the table and sang *Shoshanas Yaakov* ("The Rose of Jacob") and *Arur Haman* ("Cursed Be Haman"). Every single word that we sang so ardently carried a double meaning, for here in our own time the Rose of Jacob was once again threatened by the curse of a modern Haman.

Father and Grandfather treated us to a veritable concert. Father carried the tune, and Grandfather provided the accompaniment in his deep bass voice. They sang *Ohr Panecha* ("The Light of Thy Countenance") with particular poignancy. Our apartment was on the ground floor, and people began to gather outside the windows to listen to the performance. Little did we know at the time that this joyful evening would become our last happy memory of our father, that this Purim was the last holiday we would celebrate with him.

Right after Purim Father found us an apartment at 38 Mlynarska Street. It consisted of one large room which had apparently been intended for a shop, since a huge plate-glass window took up the entire front wall facing the street. The window was new and as yet unpainted, and no floor had been installed; the owners had probably meant to lay tiles but had not had time to do so before the evacuation.

Father bought two large plywood boards and with the help of my grandfather and uncle turned them into a makeshift floor. The boards were too short for the room, and so the area near the entrance and the corner that was used for cooking were left bare. Our wardrobe was placed so that it divided the room in two, forming an enclosed kitchen as well as a space for washing and bathing.

Two big iron beds had been left in the apartment. We had a few folding beds of our own, and it took a great deal of ingenuity to devise a set-up and sleeping arrangements for eight people. When the preparations were completed, we gathered our possessions from my grandparents' apartment and installed ourselves in our new home.

Purim had come and gone, but the winter persisted in all its ferocity. The water froze in our buckets. Most of the ghetto houses did not have water pipes, and many people were forced to stand in line around the public well on our street. When the water froze in the well, we went to streets that were further away, where the water had not yet frozen.

High mounds of snow and heaps of dirty gray ice were piled up in front of every building and hut. The narrow streets of the ghetto were flooded with ankle-deep mud, and the snow turned into sludge under the feet of those who scurried around, trying to make a miserable living.

At that time the ghetto was not totally cut off. We still maintained some contact with the outside world as well as some vestiges of trade with the Poles in the city, although this was officially prohibited. My father, too, managed to sell all sorts of embroidery silks to the Poles, sometimes by sneaking out at dusk with a bundle hidden under his clothes. Once he was almost caught, and his face grew more and more haggard from day to day. My mother helped him as much as she could, for in those matters she was bolder than he. She was an extremely resourceful and ingenious woman and could improvise spontaneous escapes from almost any predicament.

My father continually encouraged us. "We must not despair!" he would say whenever the wind was particularly biting. "With the first signs of spring we will be warmer and things will get easier." When my grandmother wept over our doubtful ability to survive without money or property, he answered, "The soul is the essence! Our souls have been preserved, and so will everything else." He even made us laugh by poking fun at the absurdities of our new circumstances. But his bright, intensely blue eyes reflected his anxiety, and dread of the future tinged his complexion a parchment yellow.

Father

Two weeks after Purim, Father came down with influenza. He had seldom been ill until then, so we weren't especially concerned; after all, who doesn't catch cold once in a while? But a few days later his temperature rose, and he felt much worse. The doctor came and examined him and reported that the influenza had developed into pneumonia.

All of a sudden our household erupted into a fearful turmoil. No penicillin was available in the ghetto, and our doctors did their utmost with the limited means at their disposal. One of them sat with Father for hours, giving him injections and trying out various other treatments. A bottle of Carmel wine from Palestine was miraculously produced from somewhere in the hope that it would strengthen Father, but his ankles were already swollen, a symptom indicating that his heart had been affected.

The struggle continued for two days. Mother sat at Father's bedside and tried to cool his burning forehead with her delicate hand. Father fought for his life with all his waning strength and refused to die.

When things became unbearable, most of us children were sent over to my grandmother's house. Before leaving, we bent over Father to say good-bye . . . None of us really thought that we were parting from him forever, yet the agonizing fear was there. He was very feverish, and his beautiful, aristocratic hands, which we'd kissed so often and squeezed in joyful greeting, struggled restlessly with the blanket, clutching and releasing it spasmodically. His eyes looked at us unseeingly, so we only stroked his palms and caressed the bulging veins on the backs of his hands. Then we went over to Grandmother's house and recited Psalms for Father's recovery.

The following morning, our two younger brothers, who had remained at home, came to tell us that Father had passed away. Overwhelmed with shock and pain, we rushed home. I held my little sister Branulka in my arms and raced through the streets, shrieks of denial ringing in my brain, but as I neared home, I was gripped with a horrible fear. The sounds of mourning reached us when we were still in the street, and I was too paralyzed to go in. The door opened, and unfamiliar hands dragged us inside.

The scene in the house is imprinted in my memory, and I see it as though it had happened today. Father was laid out on the floor, the same floor he had installed only a few days ago, his body covered with his *yibbitzeh*—his black silk Sabbath coat. Mother was crouching over him, sobbing her heart out, dazed with grief and almost unrecognizable.

"Oh, how I am shamed! How I am shamed!" she wailed over and over again. This lament was meaningless to me at the time, and it was only much later that I understood how vulnerable and exposed to disgrace and mortification a woman can become when she is bereft of her husband.

The reality stared at us from the floor, but we were unable to grasp that this appalling thing had really happened to us, that our father would no longer talk to us, be with us, care for us, protect us, sing to us, encourage us.

Those were still the early days in the ghetto, but burial procedures had already become tangled and difficult. Father died on Sunday afternoon, but he was not buried until Tuesday evening. On the day of the funeral, the sun came out for the first time from behind the clouds. Father had longed so for the healing sun to shine and alleviate the plight of the needy, but it no longer shone for him. We followed his bier to the cemetery in a stupor, incapable of assimilating the knowledge that we were about to bury our father. As we walked, some Poles standing outside the ghetto fence treated us to a shower of stones and abuse, but it was not in their power to hurt us. Fate had already pierced our souls, dealing us the worst and most dreadful of blows.

In the cemetery the gravediggers had their hands full with death's harvest that day, and it was almost evening before Father's turn finally came. We were anxious, for we knew that the Germans often prowled around among the dead and did not hesitate to defile bodies where they could.

I saw him there, my father, and it seemed to me suddenly that he was still breathing, that his chest was heaving! I wanted to cry out, to shout a warning to prevent the diggers from laying him in the ground. But they were already placing him alongside his grave. And here was Grandfather, burying his only son, who had been his pride and joy; Grandfather, placing pieces of glass on Father's eyes in the ancient custom and folding his hands across his chest; Grandfather, bending over Father's body and reciting the *Tzidduk Hadin* prayer, the justification of Divine judgment. Grandfather remained bowed over for such a long time that it seemed he would never be able to straighten up again to his full height. And the tears streaming from his eyes trickled down his beard and into the open grave. In those short moments Grandfather's hair turned gray.

With our bare hands we scattered earth over Father's body until it was no longer visible, adding earth to earth, lump to lump, until we'd formed a small mound. The funeral was over. Father was gone, never to return, and he was only forty-four . . . his heart had stopped beating, his forces had deserted him. Grandfather said that the Germans had poisoned his blood. And my poor mother was left alone at the age of forty with her six children.

Night fell. We could not bear to leave the fresh grave, but the Germans hurried us out of the cemetery, and so we turned away and dragged ourselves to our empty home. Little did we know that in our family would be fulfilled the dire prophecy in *Eichah* (Lamentations) that the living would envy the dead. For Father had had the privilege of dying in his bed in his own home, surrounded by the people who loved him, and he had been buried with dignity and full Jewish rites. Oh, that my dear mother had been so privileged!

But at that time we were ignorant of the destiny that awaited us. Father's death was a severe blow that bowed us down and dissolved our yearning for better times into a meaningless fancy. Life seemed to lack significance, and the ache in our wounds did not diminish, but only grew worse with time.

We rose from the *Shivah* on the day before Passover Eve and celebrated the holiday without Father. On the Seder night we sat at the table orphaned, visualizing Father as though he were conducting the ceremony. We seemed to see him dipping the greens in salt water and handing each of us a portion, signaling wordlessly in his particular way

— for it was forbidden to talk at this point in the ritual — if one of us had erred and extended the left hand rather than the right. We saw him hiding the *Afikomen* under his pillow, heard him sing *Vayehi Bachatzos Halayla* ("And It Came to Pass at Midnight"), *Echad Mi Yodea* ("Who Knows One?"), *Chad Gadya* ("One Kid"), and other Seder hymns. His spirit was hovering over us, his memory still with us.

We grew numb, incapable of exerting the energy and vigilance required to handle the growing hardships in the ghetto. And my mother — I cannot begin to express the extent of her tragedy. All I can say is that when Father died, she died too. Her love for him was so strong that she never recovered from the loss. I remember how, during all our years in the ghetto, she used to sit near the huge front window, staring blindly into the distance. We knew what she was seeing in her mind's eye; we read it in the anguish on her face, in the look of distress that never left her eyes.

Throughout those long years of starvation, Mother was literally never hungry. Father's death had plunged her into a state of torpor which made her insensible to all physical needs.

When she was forced to fend for us, however, she did so wholeheartedly, undertaking any number of activities in the hope of putting a little more food into our stomachs. Nothing deterred her from this purpose, neither the exertion nor the inescapable humiliation. And yet it was evident that her thoughts and feelings were focused on one person — Father. Her life had ended with his. Afterward she merely existed, and this was solely for us.

The snows melted, and we hoped that the long-awaited spring would bring relief from the ordeals of the winter. A pale, unfriendly sun began to cast out its feeble rays, and the ghetto streets were soon riddled with mudholes and puddles of all sizes, dotted with stray bits of unmelted ice.

The ghetto had no sewer system. The outhouses in the courtyards of the buildings, which were used by all the residents, were grossly neglected. The unsanitary conditions grew even more abominable with the coming of the spring, for when the snow mounds which had accumulated in front of every building began to melt, they uncovered a great deal of frozen refuse and even excrement. As the weather grew warmer and the sun stronger, a horrible stench rose from the streets.

The ghetto was not completely sealed off yet, and packages still came in from the outside. One food parcel reached us from Mother's relatives who lived in Slupca. Later, when the ghetto became completely locked and barred, all contact with the outside world would cease, and no help would reach us anymore.

No concrete routine or system of operation existed at that stage in the ghetto. The Judenrat administration was poor and chaos reigned everywhere. This disorganization, in addition to the coarse food to which we were not accustomed and the foul odor that spread and poisoned the air — all of these began to take a toll on people's health.

With the advent of summer, a terrible epidemic broke out in full force: a bloody diarrhea called dysentery, which claimed countless victims. The days turned into an endless nightmare, for there was no escape from the continuous wailing and sobbing that rose from all the buildings in the ghetto as death struck over and over again. There was scarcely one household spared from the disease, one courtyard from which one or more dead were not removed each day. The black wagon which carried the dead to their lasting peace rumbled constantly past our plate-glass window. The death procession became a permanent spectacle.

There was a family by the name of Wirzberger who lived in our building. They had many children, and the epidemic hit them violently. I recall once going into their house to do some small service for them; most probably they needed someone to fetch a doctor, and it was impossible to refuse such a request, despite the danger of contagion. When I entered the front room, a horrible stench overwhelmed me. The family were all lying on filthy, stinking pallets, and there was not one among them who was strong enough to dispose of the sickening excrement. One of the sons tried to lift himself on an elbow in order to tell me something; his face was so gaunt that only his eyes were recognizable — huge, desperate eyes whose despair pursued me for a very long time afterward. They died one after another, without, as far as I can remember, a single survivor.

The Wirzbergers were not the only family to suffer this awful fate.

Branulka

A sudden change came over our Branulka. The child had always been somewhat sickly; she could not walk properly or talk, but in spite of this she had always been a merry little sprite — lively and vivacious, her small body in constant motion, her eyes radiating joy. Now this little one grew silent. A strange restlessness seized her, and her movements became jerky.

Branulka's malaise intensified on Sabbath evenings. She would stare at the door, and it became more and more difficult to hold her because of her violent twisting and turning. Finally she would begin to cry, and then there was no calming her. It was not difficult for us to discern the reason for her behavior; the child missed her father terribly. She waited for his return day after day, and on Friday nights her longing became pitiful. She had been so accustomed on the Sabbath to sitting in Father's lap and having him feed her and play with her, and now her yearning for him could not be stilled. Her unusually expressive face and eyes spoke to us, and we knew what they were saying.

We began to invent stories in which Father had taken a long trip and would return some day soon. Branulka listened eagerly, even hypnotically, to our tales, and each time we mentioned the word "father" her little face would grow radiant and she would jump about; but after a short while she would burst into long, disconsolate sobs. Even when we did manage to calm her down, her huge blue eyes would remain wet with tears and sadness.

Strange though it may sound, we saw and felt that the little one knew the truth and that she was expressing the pain in her aching heart as best she could. We pitied her so and made a special effort to pamper her, taking her in her stroller on outings to the end of Mlynarska Street, where one could see, beyond the ghetto boundary, a green horizon garlanded with the delicate buds of spring. But how could we make her happy when we ourselves were bereaved and confused?

And all around us, death marched on.

The first to fall ill was my older brother Raphael, whom we called Fulek. Mother nursed him day and night until he finally recovered, but he remained weak for a very long time. The next two to succumb were

Mother and Branulka. Branulka caught cold and started coughing; Mother's bloody discharges became so frequent that at the end of the first day she was already too weak to get out of bed. We children did our best to nurse her. When the doctor answered our summons and saw who was tending the patient, he wrote a note to the hospital to have Mother admitted right away.

The hospitals were full to capacity, and despite the doctor's urgent note it took Fulek one more day before he managed to arrange Mother's admittance. The night before was an extremely difficult one. None of us slept; Mother was gripped with nausea, and Branulka ran a very high temperature. Her coughing, too, grew hoarse and very painful.

The following afternoon two young orderlies came to take Mother to the hospital. When they laid her on the stretcher, a visceral fear seized us. The ambulance drove away, and we were left alone with our sick sister. We called in the doctor once again, and to our great consternation he diagnosed pneumonia! He gave Branulka an injection, doled out an unconvincing reassurance, and was gone.

I was exhausted; I had spent the previous night holding Branulka in my arms and tending to Mother whenever she needed me. When Branulka finally dozed off that evening, I decided to take a short nap too, but to my horror I slept right through to the following morning. My brothers did not wake me, and I shall never forgive myself for this awful catastrophe. Branulka's little face had undergone a terrible change overnight. Her lips were virtually scorched, her skin seemed transparent, and her charming, upturned nose looked pinched. Her breathing had grown labored, and when I took her in my arms I could feel through her clothes the murmur in her inflamed lungs.

I was horror-stricken. We called in Mrs. Goldman, one of our neighbors, for advice. Fulek fetched the doctor again, and he gave Branulka more injections. I held her in my arms, crying uncontrollably. I couldn't stop crying because I knew what was going to happen. Branulka's condition was getting worse by the minute. The other children, too, were greatly shaken.

Once again the struggle lasted for two whole days. For two days, poor Branulka was tortured by her labored breathing and rending cough. All this time I held her in my arms while my brothers recited Psalms. I wept and beseeched G-d to perform a miracle and preserve the little one's life.

On the second evening Branulka did seem somewhat better, and we clung to the hope that perhaps G-d would take pity on us after all. She had a peaceful night, and in the morning my brother Dovid tried to feed her some tea. Suddenly he cried out in fright, "Sara, she is not swallowing!" I snatched the child from him, hugging her close to me as if to infuse her with my own warmth and vitality . . . but to no avail. Her eyes were wide open but already glazed, and her little mouth was only a slit, through which a few drops of tea trickled onto her chin. But she was still warm!

We called the neighbors for help. They pried Branulka out of my arms by force and laid her on the bed. They lit a match and held the flame before her eyes to see if she blinked, then held a small mirror in front of her mouth and nose to see if her breath would cloud it.

Our miracle had not occurred.

I don't know who made all the arrangements. An old woman appeared in our house; she sewed shrouds, washed Branulka, dressed her, and tied a ribbon to the white cap on her head. Branulka's lovely light brown curls spilled out from under the cap. When she was stretched out to her full length on the floor, we suddenly realized that she had been tall for her age. We had never noticed this before because of her infirmity; she had never stood upright and always curled up when she went to sleep.

We were not allowed to go to the cemetery with Branulka. Fulek alone was entrusted with this task, since we were fatherless and our mother lay in the hospital. Fulek took Branulka in his arms and carried her to the black wagon. He never described her burial to us.

Two of my father's sisters came to look after us, but there was very little for them to do. We were unable to swallow even a mouthful of food. A peculiar humming ran through me all day long; I was numb with pain and so were the boys. Dovid's dark gray eyes seemed to bulge with an awful fright. He was, after all, barely fourteen, and his little sister had died in his arms. His resemblance to Father grew more marked from day to day, especially now that his face had turned yellowish from shock.

There are no words to describe the emotions of those days. Mother was sick in the hospital, and every day we feared the worst. The dysentery epidemic raged all around us; all day long the black wagon passed back and forth, back and forth in front of our window, a dismal sight which gave us no respite. We were not allowed to go and see Mother because of the danger of contagion, so Fulek alone would go each day to the hospital to inquire after her. When he came back to say that she was a bit better, we suspected that he was lying and did not dare believe him.

And there was this other, dreadful thing weighing on us -- how would we be able to look into Mother's eyes? How would we dare tell her about Branulka?

Mother's condition actually did improve, and finally my brother was allowed to stand outside her room and talk to her through the window. She asked how we all were and wanted very much to return home, but I — I, who rejoiced so at her truly miraculous recovery — wished secretly to postpone her homecoming a little longer. How would I be able to face her? My heart contracted in pain at the thought of that awful moment.

The day arrived, and Fulek went to the hospital. The rest of us cleaned the house and made Mother a fresh bed. We were so nervous that everything we picked up dropped out of our clumsy hands, and we froze at the sound of horses' hooves in the street.

The cart finally pulled up outside the house and Mother alighted, leaning heavily on my brother's arm. She was a diminutive, emaciated figure; her head had been shaven in the hospital and was covered with a scarf. My aunt Esther, with a wordless gesture, motioned to Mother to get into bed, and she was still so weak that she consented immediately. We approached her and kissed her but we avoided her eyes, and our voices threatened to betray us.

I lit the stove and made some soup, trying very hard to look busy, too busy to talk. Aunt Esther was an angel and kept up a steady conversation with Mother for a time; but at last came the dreaded question: "Where is Branulka?"

At that moment I was seized with an inspiration. "I'll go in a moment and fetch her from Grandmother's," I said. "Yankush took her there and I don't know why they haven't come back by now." Actually we had sent Yankush over to Grandmother's because we were certain that the little boy would not be able to control his tears.

In the late afternoon I left the house, ostensibly to fetch Branulka, leaving Mother with Aunt Esther and our dear neighbor, Mrs. Goldman, who had also come in to sit with her. When I reached my grandparents' apartment, I had a fit of some sort and began to cry and cry. I felt torn inside; how could I go home now? To make matters worse, my brothers Dovid and Eliezer soon showed up and within minutes were also in tears. They too had escaped from the house, explaining to Mother that they were wondering why I was so late coming home with the children and wanted to see what had happened. Only my poor older brother now remained behind with the two women who were keeping Mother company.

We were unable to return home. Grandmother told us to stay the night at her house, that someone was sure to tell Mother the terrible news or that she would guess herself. We agreed to stay, doubly burdened now at the thought of our poor mother who had returned home from the hospital weakened and spent, only to have her wicked children abandon her.

We went home the following morning: a group of young children prematurely aged, our steps dragging. We opened the door cautiously and entered the house. Mother was awake, and her eyes were red with crying. She knew everything. The two of us burst into fresh sobs and fell into each other's arms.

All of these things occurred within three months after Father's death. Mother's recovery lasted a long time, for she required a special diet of light, easily digested food in order to regain her strength, and this was, of course, unobtainable in the ghetto.

When the Germans began to starve us systematically, the hunger did not affect all of the ghetto inhabitants at the same rate. Food had been difficult to procure even from the beginning of the war, but there was one additional reason for our family's plight: we children were not aggressive and did not know how to force our way, a very necessary skill in those days. Somehow we always found ourselves at the tail end of the queue, and when the food supply was limited, we were among those who came away empty-handed. By great good fortune, my older brother Fulek was working in the post office, which enabled him to collect the few provisions we were allotted — a below-subsistence ration of three or four hundred calories a day — without having to stand in line for hours. He also received a large daily portion of soup at the post office, as well as some grits and potatoes, and he brought this food home to us.

Mother was quite different from us when it came to resourcefulness. She was quicker and smarter than we and knew how to get what was needed, not with brute force but with keen strategy. But at that stage she could do little to help us; she was still bedridden and could only get up for an hour a day to test her strength. She was given daily injections of calcium to fortify her system.

While she was still very weak, more bad news arrived. Her mother's entire household had been evacuated from Kalisz to the town of Wlodawa, near the River Bug, and her father had just died. He had been old and sickly before the war, yet he could have lived much longer if not for the present hardships. My poor mother gathered together whatever feeble reserves of strength she possessed and sat out the obligatory *Shivah* in silence, her face pale and drawn.

This news was the last we ever received of my mother's people. Two of her brothers and their families also lived in Kalisz, but I do not know to this day when and how all of them perished.

Reaching for Light

Summer was almost over. The yearning of the ghetto Jews for deliverance was so strong that G-d, so it seemed, could not but relent and give in to their entreaties.

The optimists claimed that the war would not last long, but in fact, the end of the war — even the faintest glimmer of its resolution — was invisible. For us the war had barely started. We were stricken and broken from the start, and we did not know that we were doomed to endure so many more years of starvation and torment. We could not imagine then how limitless was our capacity for suffering.

We groped about in our murky world between one vision of death and another, between one *Aktion* and the next, while our relatives and neighbors disappeared continually all around us. Many of them died, and others were either snatched, murdered, imprisoned, or deported, never to be seen again. A huge pit of despair yawned at our feet, and we longed for a beam of spiritual light to illuminate our pathway.

Each of us found his own individual way of groping through this darkness. A great hunger for learning seized all the ghetto youth, and when the schools closed down, all the youth movements launched a full spectrum of activities. Many wide-ranging political and cultural organizations flourished with a defiant strength during these anguished years. Lessons, lectures, discussion-and-interest groups, and gatherings to celebrate Sabbath evenings and holidays were held in a variety of frameworks in private apartments, attics, warehouses, vacant cellars, and any other feasible — and unfeasible — place. Indeed, in the midst of the monstrous reality which enveloped us, in the midst of our daily struggle for physical survival, such activities awarded us many blessed hours of pleasure and solace.

My brother Fulek found mental and emotional relief in the Zionist movement. Together with his friends, he organized activities and courses that centered around Zionism. One of the group's projects was the "publication" of a wall newspaper of very high quality. Fulek used to bring the pages of this paper home for me to read, and thus I was able to gather glimpses of a world that was so different from my own, a world of great beauty. I remember in particular one article entitled *"Akdamos, "* written by a girl named Etka Fried, who was a frequent visitor in our house. The article was about the Shavuos holiday, during which *Akdamos* is sung, and contained reminiscences of Etka's father. I also remember the writings of Mirka Taubus, a beautiful, dark-haired girl. Her poems were marked by harsh, dissonant rhythms and were saturated with longings for a better day.

Fulek's newspapers shone with a great love for the people of Israel and a strong craving for deliverance, and they were punctuated with numerous Zionist slogans. I had some misgivings about this movement because of the general attitude it took toward the land of Israel. I myself belonged to the Bnos Agudas Israel group, and I knew that Fulek's views did not reconcile well with the Orthodox outlook. This made me somewhat uncomfortable, but I did feel a certain closeness to Fulek's ideals, perhaps because he was my brother and perhaps because his movement had many positive facets and inspired such a strong love for the Holy Land.

In reality, each of our parties and organizations, ranging from the Orthodox Agudah movement all the way to the Communist Party on the extreme left, directed its gaze toward the same destination, and we disagreed only with regard to the means that would lead us there. Almost every political viewpoint was represented in my family, and very interesting meetings took place occasionally in our house.

Fulek was well-liked and respected in his group, and his involvement brought out his abilities to the fullest. His friends knew him better than we; at home he was usually silent and introverted, and it was not easy to penetrate his thoughts.

My brother Dovid was the only one of us who was apolitical. We claimed in jest that he was a member of the Anti-Parties Party. Dovid felt no need to defend his ideas with pathos, as some of us often did. He poked fun at our enthusiasm for ideals, but his lot must have been harder than ours because he was a loner. He not only refused to join a party but also avoided forming friendships. He actually did not have a single close friend, preferring to study by himself. He was very industrious, devoting entire days to the study of the Torah and the Talmud, and he did not neglect his secular studies either. When the schools in the ghetto closed down, Dovid brought home the appropriate textbooks and studied them on his own, and he and Fulek even made fair progress in English.

I loved Dovid as I had loved my father. A proud and sensitive person, he possessed the greatest self-restraint of us all and rarely raised his voice, bearing his burden without a murmur. He was a handsome boy, tall, slender, and fair, with large, expressive gray eyes which acquired a steely glint in moments of obstinacy and which darkened moistly in times of confusion or pain.

At home he sometimes acted haughtily and refused to do certain chores, as though they were beneath his dignity. We called him nicknames, such as "His Highness" or "obstinate mule." But in the end we always gave in to him — at the expense of our poor little scapegoat, Eliezer.

Leyzer, as he was nicknamed, was short and pudgy, with coal-black hair, a dark complexion, and a fiery temperament — but he also had a heart of gold. A single kind word would melt his heart and induce him to do any job or chore, no matter how unpleasant — and of these there was no lack: throwing out the garbage, dragging home a sack of rotten turnips from the market, asking a neighbor to return a loan. He belonged to the Mizrachi youth group, and his friends were always gathered around him. Among them was a particularly close buddy with whom he exchanged confidences and in whose ears he would bare his overflowing heart. We teased him about this and poked fun at his "best friend."

Even as a little boy Leyzer had possessed a great deal of charm and had always been a favorite of both his teachers and his fellow students. He was an impish child and often avoided getting a bad mark because of some timely answer or clever remark, which he held in great supply. And indeed, there was something remarkably bright in Leyzer's personality; much of our teasing resulted from envy, because none of us was as quick and sharp as he — not I, not Dovid, and certainly not little Yankush.

Leyzer too studied by himself when the ghetto schools closed down, though not with the thoroughness that characterized Dovid. Leyzer often dared to raise and discuss Talmudic topics whose deeper significance he had not yet grasped. This attitude irritated Dovid, who never drew definite conclusions and never defended a view before he had investigated the subject in depth and understood it perfectly. And yet Leyzer was much more successful despite his superficiality, often managing to extricate himself from a knotty point with the help of a *"pshetl"* — an improvised, last-minute argument of his own invention. For this last aptitude we labeled him *"Yiddel Dreyer"* (nimble-witted Jew).

It remains for me to describe our beloved Yankush (Jacob), the most sensitive among us. How shall I draw his sweet, tender personality?

His hair was black, and his blue eyes often looked imploringly at the dark world outside. Though he was the youngest, it was he who continuously attempted to tone down the stormy political debates in our house. We were often deeply stirred by the entreaty in his eyes, which begged so plainly for peace.

He envied us all because we were, according to him, "learned." He, poor child, had barely learned to read and write when the schools shut down, and he used to moan, "What will become of me? A *Tehillim yiddel?*" A *Tehillim yiddel*, or "Psalm Jew," was a term that denoted any illiterate Jew whose learning was restricted to reciting Psalms which he had memorized mechanically over the years. And Yankush did indeed recite a great many Psalms. He shared the destiny of his partners in prayer in another way as well, for he eventually became one of the numberless child victims of the Nazi machine.

As for me, I belonged to the Orthodox Bnos Agudas Israel, an affiliation which earned me constant ribbing and scorn at home, for Bnos was not an official political party but rather a group for learning and activities. I must admit that the barbed criticism hurt quite a bit and sometimes led me to question the soundness of my choice. However, I was greatly recompensed by an extraordinary privilege: I was given to bask in the warmth and light of my incomparable guide and mentor, Miss Fajga Zelicka.

Miss Zelicka

Before the war Miss Zelicka had been a teacher at the Sara Schenirer Women's Seminary in Krakow. She was young, in fact not much older than most of her eager listeners; but she opened whole new vistas before our eyes. I had never experienced this kind of teaching before the war, and never did afterward. Throughout every one of Miss Zelicka's lectures, I felt as though she were answering the very questions that bewildered me and gave me no respite, as though she were speaking solely to me — and I knew that each of her listeners felt this way. She formed a personal, intimate bond with her audience and with every person in it.

Miss Zelicka was not concerned with covering textual ground, but rather she *educated* us, using the texts to improve the quality of our lives. Her subject matter was the Bible, and we studied with her the Book of *Shemos,* the Book of *Devarim*, the prophecies of Isaiah, numerous psalms from *Tehillim,* chapters in *Pirkei Avos,* Samson Raphael Hirsch's *Horeb* (Essays on Israel's Duties in Exile), and portions of Rabbi Moshe Chaim Luzzatto's *Mesilas Yesharim* (The Path of the Just). We learned a tremendous amount, though not as much in terms of quantity as of quality. This study was an enlightenment that carved a clear path for us through the icy gloom in which we existed.

Miss Zelicka lived on Mianowskiego Street, at the far end of the ghetto, but we girls attended her lessons no matter how far we had to walk — in spite of the rain and frost, in spite of the mud and perpetual puddles along the interminable Dworska Road. Most of us wore wooden clogs, which made walking on ice an exhausting and dangerous exercise, but we helped each other along the way, lending and grabbing any available hand until we finally reached Miss Zelicka's house. And there, in that shabby, poorly furnished apartment, among the pans placed beneath the leaking roof, sitting two or more to a chair, wrapped in our coats against the freezing cold, we sat spellbound, not even moving our benumbed legs lest we miss a single word of those magical lectures.

Miss Zelicka infused us with a love of the Bible, uncovering its treasures for us and interpreting it as though it had been written especially for us. In particular she demonstrated to us the relevance of the Scriptures and their implications in our own days. Oh, the beauty of such Psalms as "How long wilt Thou forget me, O L-rd? Forever? How long wilt Thou hide Thy face from me?" or "My G-d, my G-d, why hast Thou forsaken me?" How well these verses expressed our own feelings! And the chapters in *Shemos* about the Exodus from Egypt — how wondrous this Exodus suddenly became, this state of conscious, alert anticipation of Deliverance that was so relevant to our own lives! Similarly, the verses in *Ha'azinu* in the Book of *Devarim*, beginning with "Give ear, O ye heavens," struck us with their immediacy.

Miss Zelicka forged a link between us and our past to help us better understand the present and to give us the capacity to believe in a future. She taught us the entire book of *Eichah* (Lamentations), never sparing our feelings as she described in great detail the destruction of the Holy Temple and the torments and suffering of past generations. She did this in open opposition to the prevailing attitude in the ghetto, which decried the practice of lamenting past destructions when our own tragedy was sufficient.

Miss Zelicka's lectures never turned into escapes from reality; on the contrary, she taught us to ache with the pain of reality. She believed that pain was a sign of life, both in the individual and in the nation as a whole. As long as we felt pain, she explained, there was hope for a recovery, for the greatest danger lay in apathy.

And so we would descend with her into the black chasm of our own days, into the tunnels of our distress, and try to shed light on the most torturing questions of our Jewish identity and our place in history. We would probe the sores of our humiliation and disgrace, and always emerged purified and stronger than before. The light that radiated from Miss Zelicka's personality projected into us, and her powerful influence was evident in our every step, for each meeting made our lot easier to endure. Thanks to her, it became less difficult even to bear the pangs of hunger and to control ourselves enough to set aside a portion of bread for the next day. Miss Zelicka was the greatest formative influence in my life.

In addition to helping us confront affliction, she also worked hard to emphasize the positive aspects of Judaism, to impart its spiritual tenets, its numerous ethical values and humane spirit. She instilled these ideals in us so profoundly that I still feel tied to them by indivisible bonds, despite the distance that separates me at present from those sources. My bond with my people and its spiritual heritage is deeply rooted and unwavering. And even though the Holocaust did ultimately break me and so many others like me, even though it succeeded in toppling our ideals and undermining our faith, I shall always return in spirit and mind to the unique philosophy inculcated in me by Miss Zelicka, remembering it as the sole support that was available to me when all the rest was ground to dust by the onslaught of the final horror.

Day to Day

At that time groats — *groypen* in Yiddish — were distributed as the major food ration. The groats were exceedingly coarse. We had never eaten such fare before the war, but now it was practically the only food that could be obtained, and so we had *groypen* and *groypen* until we couldn't look at them anymore. We had not yet reached the stage of starvation in which *groypen* would be considered an exquisite delicacy; those years were still to come.

The groats needed to be cooked at length before they were digestible, and fuel was very scarce. Many of the ghetto children would go to ruined houses and dig among the rubble to collect all kinds of rubbish and scraps of wood, anything that could be used for fuel. A few families had brought along some extra pieces of furniture when they came to the ghetto, and these were now used to stoke fires both for heating and for cooking. Only the most essential pieces were not burned. I knew families who burned their wooden bedframes and placed their mattresses on the floor; others used up all the shelves and partitions in their closets. The distress, of course, was greater in the winter, and there was not one single mild winter during those awful years in the ghetto.

I cannot recollect how my mother managed to open a small vegetable store, or where she obtained her wares. A "store" in the ghetto was very different from its modern counterpart; it may have had no more than a few barely-edible radishes and some beet leaves in it, but how important these were! Our huge window served as the counter; we placed scales on the window sill, and some of the passersby would occasionally stop and buy something. We were not particularly enthusiastic about the venture, feeling that it exposed our neediness to the public eye, and we hampered Mother by acting like little snobs. It never occurred to us that she was sacrificing her own dignity to provide for her ungrateful children.

Our vegetable store lasted two months. With the advent of winter, it became impossible to live with the window constantly open. Moreover, the business had become a losing proposition; in our inexperience, we always generously tipped the scales in our customers' favor and were left with very little profit.

Once the store closed, Mother began to look for other ways to earn some money, and she managed to make an arrangement with Miss Marila, one of our former neighbors from Piotrkowska Street in the city.

Miss Marila had a university education and came from a highly distinguished and wealthy family, of which she was the sole survivor. She was handicapped by a lame leg and could walk only with the aid of a heavy and cumbersome brace, and so she found it very difficult to take care of herself. She and Mother arranged a "partnership"; Mother would shop and cook for her, and she paid Mother generously out of her family's assets. In addition, we were given the leftover bones of the chickens that Miss Marila somehow obtained, with Mother's help, on the black market. Later on she came to live with us in our room. It still seems strange to me that such an assimilated lady could adapt herself to our way of life, since our home, however discordant politically, remained to the end a religious one. But oh, the strange alliances that were made in the ghetto!

I remember very vividly the night on which Mother brought home Miss Marila's leftover food for the first time. Chicken was a delicacy that was rarely seen in the ghetto, but nevertheless we felt completely disgraced. Mother's common sense told her that in times such as ours one must disregard one's feelings, and she encouraged us to eat. The younger boys, who were still growing, looked emaciated, and to Mother the means of survival was by now inconsequential. And so we ate the leftovers, trying hard to ignore our degradation. There were times when there was nothing left to lick but the bare bones, and lick we did — but we felt this loss in our self-esteem very acutely, as though the first drop of venom had already seeped into our souls.

It is well known that one of the Nazis' primary objectives was to break our spirits as well as our bodies, to degrade us in our own eyes until the last vestige of humanity was distorted in us. In effect, their entire strategy was directed toward that end, even the basic problem of cleanliness.

We had no hot water for our laundry, nor enough fuel to boil it. I was not very skilled at that chore, and all the things I washed seemed to come out as gray and soiled as before. In the winter it was too cold for us to wash our bodies properly, and to compound the problem we started to itch. To our chagrin, Mother discovered lice in the seams of our clothing. This caused enormous embarrassment, especially when a strong urge to scratch would seize us in the company of others. It was extremely difficult to curb that impulse, and we racked our brains trying to think of ways to rid ourselves of this shameful affliction.

My brother Dovid came up with a solution. He had always been mechanically inclined, and he now fabricated an electrical gadget that could give off heat and even boil water. The gadget, of course, was illegal, for we could never have afforded the electricity otherwise. For that matter, our whole electrical rigging was illegal; we had set it up during Father's illness without applying to the authorities, and neglected to report it afterward. Thanks to Dovid's ingenuity, Mother was now able to carry out a big cleaning operation — to our immense relief.

Scores of such problems, great and small, had to be tackled on a daily basis, and they required energetic initiative and constant vigilance. Particularly when a new disease erupted, relegating scores of people to their beds, tremendous effort was required to carry out the ordinary tasks of bathing, laundering, and changing linen. Many people simply were not equal to this moral struggle and remained in bed for days in their soiled sheets, languishing in helplessness or in total indifference. Staying in bed became a regular phenomenon in the ghetto, not only because people were sick but because they could not stay warm otherwise. In this way, the Germans found another mode of depleting our numbers — for many who did not die of direct illness succumbed to the more insidious fingers of filth and decay.

During that period Mother began to grasp the enormous importance of our lessons and political activities, realizing that they provided a sheer anchor against the inevitable degeneration that could result from staying in bed. She decided that I must have private lessons to continue my education, which had come to an abrupt halt after my graduation from elementary school. I therefore began taking lessons in Latin, German, history, and other subjects which were part of the general high school curriculum. I do not know how my mother managed to pay for these lessons, but in our strained circumstances this expenditure was certainly a very heavy burden.

Work

The threat of atrophy through inertia or resignation abated somewhat with the enforcement of compulsory labor in the second year of the war. Factories had been built in the ghetto expressly for that purpose, and all the ghetto inmates, young and old, were compelled to work. If you were not registered as working, by German statute you had no right to live and were liable to be deported at any time. Children under ten could not get a working card and were not eligible for food rations, so many of them were registered as older and were given jobs, even children as young as three or four years of age. Since the Germans did not come regularly to inspect the validity of each working card, this arrangement could buy some children a little more time.

Those people who had some pull were able to find slightly better jobs for themselves. My brother's position in the post office continued to benefit all of us, for in addition to temporary protection from deportation, he had access there to an extra ration of food. Not everyone was so fortunate.

The labor was a blessing in one sense since it forced people to remain active, but it also brought its own curse; for, having been systematically deprived of food, many people no longer had the strength to keep long, strenuous working hours, and thus the liquidation process progressed in its various forms. A new term gained popularity in the ghetto: *Wykonczalnia,* "the finishing department." Just as in the factories, where products traveled on a conveyor belt to the finishing department before being sent out, we too claimed in bitter self-derision that we had reached the final department, where our "finish" awaited us.

In the factories a potato soup was served twice a day. All day long our thoughts were focused on this soup, and eating developed into a hallowed ritual. Anyone who dared to disturb others while they were eating provoked outrage.

We depended greatly on the mercy of the woman who dealt out the soup. When she dipped the ladle deep into the pot and fished out five or six potato cubes for our bowls, our happiness knew no bounds, and when our portion of soup contained no more than one or two bits of potato, we were completely dejected. A jingle was composed and sung in honor of this very important woman:

Pani wydzielaczka, ich mine nisht kein gelechter
A bissele tifer un a bissele gedechter
Pani wydzielaczka, bist grob vi a balia
Der Prezes vet kumen
Un dich shiken tzu efecalia!

Madam Distributor, this is no laughing matter
Push your ladle in deeper, into the thicker soup.
Madam Distributor, you look like a washtub
The authorities will come
And send you to work at the *efecalia*!*

Our sense of humor had not yet deserted us at that time, and despite the bitter disappointment of a portion of watery soup with an isolated potato cube floating in its midst, we were still able to joke about our hunger.

The women who distributed the soup naturally favored their own relatives and friends, and so they became objects of envy and animosity. In addition to our "song of praise," various epithets and coarse remarks were frequently flung into these women's faces. In retrospect, their situation was a common and unenviable one; they were simply part of the Nazis' plan to turn the Jews against their own people. The Germans had given over most of the daily administrative tasks of the ghetto to the Judenrat, the Jewish administration, and nepotism was a rampant disease. Unfortunately, many more people could have survived if the food had been distributed more evenly, but it is impossible to make judgments after the fact about people whose actions, though perhaps reprehensible to the outside eye, were intended to protect their own loved ones.

That year my brothers and I all found employment. We received payment in scrip, but the amount was only sufficient to cover our food rations. Dovid worked in the Department for Electrical Appliances, and Leyzer and Yankush worked in the Carpet Department, where rugs were made from textile waste. Fulek left his post office job after a time and moved to the youth farm at Maryshin, an area inside the ghetto confines where groups of youngsters from all the political parties met to grow vegetables on miserable little plots which were allocated to them by the Judenrat. Their ration cards were transferred to the "farm," and for a time they led a genuine communal life, enjoying a little extra food and the precious gift of camaraderie. But after a while the border guards began

---

*The *efacalia* were the sewage workers who went around to all the buildings in the ghetto to empty the privies.

to complain about their singing, and the ghetto authorities feared that allowing too much group work might lead to "unhealthy" levels of organization; and so the farm was eventually dissolved and the young people were forced to find regular employment.

Fulek managed to get Mother a work permit for a job which did not necessitate leaving the house. She was registered in a shop which gave out handwork and thus was able to work at home. In order to make such an arrangement one needed *protektsye*,* and this was one instance when we were able to pull the right strings — a rare occurrence in our family.

That year I was employed in the office of the Glazer Clothes and Linen Department, where I worked in the storeroom alongside Mr. Warszawski, the chief accountant. My job was much easier than that of the factory laborers, who had to work for ten or twelve hours at a time on sewing machines or other equipment. Such employment would virtually suck the life out of them because they had to complete high, predetermined quotas no matter how hungry or tired they were. Night shifts were especially hard, but the worst lot fell to those people who were not capable of working at all. Without a work permit one became a nonperson, with no right to remain alive.

And so I considered myself extremely fortunate and sat gratefully next to Mr. Warszawski, filling out income and expenditure vouchers, compiling reports and . . . writing poems. Mr. Warszawski was an educated man of Chassidic background and a very easygoing person. Little by little we started to converse, until finally I mustered enough courage to show him my poems. He was not particularly enthusiastic but encouraged me to keep writing nonetheless. His consideration for me took various forms, the kindest of which was my Sabbath dispensation. He exempted me from coming to the factory on the Sabbath days and did my work for me. All of us who were Orthodox asked to be released from work on Saturday, but my own observance of the Sabbath gave me little satisfaction because I knew that I was causing another Jew to work in my place and to transgress the same commandment. It did not matter to me that Mr. Warszawski — with a sad, wise smile — had voluntarily agreed to this arrangement; on my day of rest I would always imagine him sitting

*Special advantage obtained through connections.

for hours on end in his dark corner in the storeroom, perpetrating "the sin," as he called it. On Sundays I tried hard to make it up to him by undertaking as much of his work as I could handle, but I never felt morally superior to Mr. Warszawski for having been lucky enough to exercise my priorities. On the contrary, I greatly respected him, as he so richly deserved.

The rest of the workers treated me with derision because of my orthodoxy, but with time I managed to gain their confidence. To this day I recall them so vividly: Spielberg, Kartowski, Ross, and Hirschmann, none of whom I saw again after the war. I remember them sitting around the "holy" soup, or carrying piles of garments to the storeroom; I remember their conversations. Behind masks of cynicism and scorn they concealed souls which yearned for redemption, as though a brutal hand had forced into hiding a gentleness and delicacy that refused to be extinguished.

Likewise, I never discovered Mr. Warszawski's fate. Once when he was sick, I went to visit him in the dilapidated apartment where he lived with his young children. The poverty and squalor I found there testified that Mr. Warszawski, too, belonged to those who did not know how to fend for themselves. I shall always remember him: a good Jew, a scholar whose bespectacled eyes reflected infinite love and tolerance for his fellow men.

Spring

And then it was spring once more, the spring of 1941.

An entire year had passed since Father's death. We went often to see his and Branulka's graves and to make sure they were marked, since most of the graves in the cemetery were indistinguishable. A small plate bearing Father's name and the date of his decease was nailed to a thin wooden stick at the head of his plot, and we would place stones around the plate to prop it up against the strong winds. We also placed a big rock at the upper end of the grave to serve us as a marker, since no tombstones were available. The earth on Father's grave was covered with grass and wild flowers, and as the light spring breeze brushed them, we would commune with Father's memory, our hearts full of a throbbing ache.

Mother was always unable to tear herself from the grave, and it took a great deal of coaxing before she would let us lead her away.

To this day it is an incomprehensible wonder to me that we were able to detect the fragrance of spring through the heavy fog of our existence. This first waft of warmth embroidered hope in our hearts, however frail it was. The ghetto streets were so narrow and densely populated, the houses so very decrepit and shapeless, and a blade of grass was nowhere to be seen; and yet, a thin strip of sky which grew daily bluer and brighter sufficed to awaken in us renewed longings. Those threads of wishful color that hung above us as we walked along the streets seemed anxious to prove that they were indestructible, and that at the right time they would burst open with the radiance of spring, in spite of everything.

We missed nature, yearning to throw ourselves into its lap and seek relief for our pain and outrage, and we treasured any trace of it. On Sabbath mornings my friends and I, accompanied occasionally by Miss Zelicka, would set out on a long walk to Maryshin, the sight of the youth farm, and there, under a solitary tree, on a narrow, balding patch of grass, we would take in great gulps of air and savor the glimmer of spring. I had never imagined that a mere shrub could tempt my creative fancy; but I found myself transforming this shrub in my mind into an entire grove of leafy trees surrounded by splendid meadows, creating a panorama of lush scenery in which each bud contained the promise of a new life, resplendent with light and brimming with pleasure.

My friends and I were eighteen then. Among this treasured group of people was Chaya Guterman, with whom I was especially intimate. When we first grew close, we happened luckily on a poem about companionship written by Jean Christophe which reflected our feelings perfectly: "I have a friend! Hurrah!" How wonderful it was to find a kindred spirit who sensed so promptly and so easily the vibrations of my own heartstrings and who served as a priceless vessel for the most pressing outpourings of my soul. Chaya penetrated the innermost confines of my nature, perhaps better than I did. She elucidated so many puzzling problems for me and gave me no end of encouragement.

I don't know if I returned her support in kind, because she was so much stronger than I and did not need as much help. But there was something special in our friendship, very reciprocal and so very precious — a blessing one is fortunate to experience once in a lifetime. Chaya would say again and again that our souls must have sprung together from the same source, issued from a single spark in *Otzar Haneshamos,* the mystical trove of souls in heaven; hence, this special intimacy of ours, this unique mutual understanding.

This, then, is how we sat in the spring of 1941, on a threadbare patch of grass, dreaming together.

Sometimes I was seized with shame because I felt happy. Happiness! How could it have entered my heart? From where came this tiny seed which longed to burst into ringing laughter, this urge in my soul and in my hands and in my arms to love, to embrace, to caress? We shared the same feelings, Chaya and I; we talked about love, about the great, wonderful, true love that might perhaps be ours in spite of all, the love that might still capture us and be our captive . . .

Today, when I think back to my long-lost youth in the Lodz ghetto, I must note that no matter how utterly illogical it seems, those were indeed the best and most beautiful years of my life. Neither before nor since have I been able to penetrate so deeply into the meaning of my existence, never again have I been capable of such profound and sincere faith, of such perfect unity with the universe; and this despite the daily deportations and relentless death that surrounded us.

In those years our arms embraced the whole world, our hearts and minds were alert and receptive to all the inner and outer phenomena in our lives. We attained the pinnacle of our mental development, of our ability to absorb and store infinite amounts of knowledge; we plumbed the deepest fathoms of our understanding. Following that climactic peak, there was an inevitable descent. The meaning of things and events began to glide away from us, and that invisible, magical gift of comprehension that had been lent to us for a short while began to shrink and blur rapidly. For it was not solely the fragrance of nature's spring that we were given to experience for that glorious interlude; it was also the spring of our own lives — a cruelly brief spring in which our souls flowered with such extreme intensity and such extraordinary splendor that even today, whenever I recall it, I am awed by its potency.

The "descent" that Sara Urbach refers to began with the Sperre, the embargo on all movement in the Lodz ghetto which took place from September 5-12, 1942. During this week all of the children, elderly, and sick people in the ghetto were deported to Chelmno, the first, primitive death camp. Most of them died, and those who survived perished later in Auschwitz.

Sara Urbach remained in the Lodz ghetto until 1944, when her entire family was deported to Auschwitz. She remained there for only one week and was then transported to a labor camp in Mittelsteine, where she was liberated. She alone survived of all her family. Today she is a grandmother and lives in the Yad Eliyahu section of Tel Aviv. She has written extensively on the Holocaust.

For an account of Mrs. Urbach's experience in Auschwitz, see "A Different Planet" in Volume Two of Women in the Holocaust.

BREAD

Chava Burstyn-Berenstein
Sister of Rabbi Aviezer Burstyn
Goworowa, Poland

This incident happened in our town of Goworowa, in the district of Bialystock, during the Days of Awe between Rosh Hashanah and Yom Kippur of 1940. The town was enveloped in a choking shadow of gloom; the greater part of it had already been burned down, the Jewish homes razed to the ground. Most of the Jewish population were now living in a few rooms in a flour mill owned by the brothers Rein, and there they clustered together like a flock of sheep surrounded by wolves. Those who could not crowd in had to rent rooms in the homes of gentiles who lived in the area.

It is hard to describe the kindness and self-sacrifice of the family Rein. Mr. Nuta Rein opened his door to anybody who knocked. He was especially generous to my father, the rabbi of the town; he prepared the nicest room of his spacious house for our family and shared his meager ration of bread with us. We felt very close to all the townspeople who huddled together under the Rein roof. We were like one big family, trying to help each other in whatever way we could, struggling to hold on until this hell would be over and we would be able to live a normal life.

Yom Kippur was approaching, and there was no food for the *Seudah Hamafsekes,* the obligatory final meal before the fast. The Germans had

51

confiscated the entire stock of flour from the Rein brothers' mill, which was the only one in the town. Everyone worried. My father feared that people might fail to fast properly because they had not eaten anything beforehand.

Suddenly an idea occurred to me: there was a Pole named Carolek in the neighboring town of Sochotchitz. He was a friend of the family and had always been favorably disposed toward Jews. Surely he would help us to get some bread.

When I related the idea to my father, he hesitated at first to allow his twelve-year-old daughter to travel such a long and dangerous road on foot. But after weighing the situation, he rose and said, "Go, my child! Go and bring bread for all the Jews of Goworowa."

Today one would question the sanity of a parent who sends his twelve-year-old daughter out by herself to a neighboring village when murderers are prowling the streets and abducting people at random for reasons beyond logic. But our logic, too, was different in those days; we did what was necessary for survival. At that time the question simply did not exist, for that same child who had been sent on a dangerous mission — and perhaps others in the family — could just as easily die of hunger. In our case, the ability of the entire Jewish population of Goworowa to maintain religious tradition was dependent on a supply of bread, and a young child was ironically in the "safest" position to provide it. Children had an advantage on dangerous errands because they could run and hide more easily than adults, and often they became providers for the entire family. Many were forced to work all day at very young ages in the ghetto, while others sold small items in the streets — radishes, cigarettes, candy — to provide a bit of food for their relatives. They knew no other life and were unaware that they had had no childhood.

Once my father consented to my plan, any fear I had felt dissolved, and I immediately set out for Sochotchitz. My friend Esther Lea Gamra joined me. We walked along side roads and overgrown paths to avoid the Nazis, who were swarming all over the highways, and we reached Carolek's house without event. When he and his wife opened the door, they looked at us in astonishment, as though we were ghosts from another planet, for they had heard that all the Jews in the area were killed out!

We told Carolek our story, and he immediately instructed his wife to bake a batch of bread as quickly as she could. In the meantime he sat us down at his table, offered us something to eat,* and inquired about his Jewish friends. By the time the bread was baked, it was already well into the afternoon. Carolek gave us several loaves for the people in the household, plus a special additional loaf for my father. As we were leaving, he asked that we not disclose his name if the Germans caught us. We gave him our promise and hurried home.

We arrived at Nuta Rein's house right before sundown, in just enough time to eat the *Seudah Hamafsekes*. The people in the house were waiting for us as anxiously as for the Messiah. My father's face especially was clouded with distress; perhaps he regretted having allowed me to go, but as soon as he saw us and realized how ecstatic his congregants were at the sight of our prize, his mood broke.

We were all overjoyed to have food, and the aroma of the fresh bread teased our appetites. Father divided the loaves of bread equally, and together we all sat down to the *Seudah Hamafsekes*. We were glad, and yet we were all absorbed with one thought. Just a few weeks ago we had each had a home, we had been respected residents of the town; now we were refugees without a roof over our heads, without a means of existence, without a future. We feared not only the murderous Germans but also our Polish neighbors, who had changed overnight into enemies. Fortunately Carolek had not betrayed us, but the feeling of mistrust was deep around us.

We were very concerned about Father. He had gone into hiding as soon as the Germans came, even before the move to the Rein brothers' home, for he was the rabbi of the town and rabbis were prime targets. We had heard many rumors: that the Germans were looking for him, that one of the local priests had informed them that Father was staying in the Rein household.

As if in answer to our thoughts, we suddenly heard the sound of military cars approaching the gates of the flour mill. Several Germans got

*Observant Jews in the ghettos maintained the practice of *kashrus* until it became life-threatening to do so. As less and less food became available and the only rations that could be obtained consisted of non-kosher food such as horse meat, or food that could only be smuggled in at risk from the Aryan side, many rabbis virtually ordered people to eat whatever was available in order to stay alive.

out of their vehicles, called Nuta Rein out, and demanded that he disclose my father's whereabouts.

In the confusion my father hid in the attic, but when he realized that the Nazis had not left the mill and that by prolonging their search he might endanger the welfare of Nuta Rein and the others in the house, he decided to give himself up. He left the attic and came down to confront the Germans, his back straight and his head up. They dealt him several brutal blows, plucked out pieces of his beard and *peyos*, and then ordered him to deliver several kilograms of gold to the German governor of Goworowa within three days. To make sure my father understood that they meant business, one of the Germans emptied a number of bullets into the air. Then they drove off.

An overwhelming panic engulfed the townspeople. Where on earth would they find several kilograms of gold when all their possessions had gone up in the flames of the Goworowa fire?

In the meantime the sun had set, and we had to begin the Yom Kippur *tefillos*. Some people were of the opinion that it would be better to pray individually in different rooms, for praying in quorum might arouse too much attention. My father did not agree and insisted on having a *minyan*. "If we merited to say *Kol Nidrei* at all," he told them, "then we ought to say it in a *minyan*." Thus, the entire congregation got to its feet in the spacious living room of Nuta Rein and with broken hearts began to pray. Heavy drapes were drawn across all the windows, and the Sefer Torah, which had been saved from the fires and which had thus far eluded the hands of the Germans, was placed on the table.

Because there was no cantor, my father recited *Kol Nidrei* himself. In a choking voice he started the prayer, his eyes moist, his face radiating an inner nobility. The women cried quietly, tears streaming down their faces. I stood together with the other young girls — Liba Kosowski, Miriam Rochel Herzog, the sisters Gamra, and a few others — on guard outside the house, prepared to signal in case of danger. So many of us were guards in those days; we had our own sophisticated code of signals and carried the burden of danger on our thin shoulders.

Suddenly, before we had a chance to react, a military vehicle pulled up in front of the house and a number of SS men jumped out. They had a movie camera, and amidst riotous shouting, they began filming the trembling Jews in the household, who had been caught in the act of praying. After they left, we had no more strength for tears, for we knew our time was limited.

This was the way we, the Jews of Goworowa, prayed the last *Kol Nidrei* in our town.

The Jews of Goworowa were later expelled, some to the ghetto in Bialystock and some to death. Rabbi Burstyn, Chava's father, was deported to Auschwitz and kept his beard until the very last minute. His son had urged him to cut it off to improve his chances of survival, and he replied, "I'm going to my death — and I should cut off my beard?" He was taken straight to the gas chambers.

His daughter Chava remained in Auschwitz until the end of the war. She now lives in Natanya with her husband, Rabbi Moshe Berenstein.

HUNTED

Mira Erster-Leslo
Skerniewice, Poland

In February of 1941, when I was almost fifteen years old, an announcement was made that our hometown of Skerniewice was to become *Judenrein*, "cleansed" of Jews. All Jews were ordered to leave the town within a span of two weeks. Many followed their first instinct and ran away immediately, leaving behind all the possessions they had accumulated over generations. Our Polish neighbors, with whom we had so pleasantly associated all our lives, soon demonstrated the extent of their "friendship" by looting the property of the fugitives.

Piziak, a gentile and the secretary of the town, was the one person we knew who was different from the rest. He risked his own security to provide us with forged Aryan papers and suggested strongly that we use them to assimilate among the Polish population. But we were six children, and my father was a Gerrer Chassid. He refused to entertain the notion of disguising himself as a gentile, even outwardly, and he certainly would not hear of cutting off his beard and *peyos*. He did not want to divorce himself from the common fate of the Jews, preferring to remain as he was and to share in their destiny.

We left Skerniewice for Mezricz, where the Jews were not yet crowded into a ghetto. We rented an apartment, and for a while our situation improved greatly. But after our bit of money was spent, the family decided that my sister Hinda and I should go back to Skerniewice, despite the danger of reappearing in a *Judenrein* town, and try to raise some cash by selling some of the merchandise we had left with Piziak.

When we arrived back in the city, we happened to run into a former classmate of my sister's, who disclosed her to the Gestapo. During the interrogation my sister was tortured to force her to reveal the name of the person who had provided her with the false certificate. Piziak, the town secretary, was the first suspect, and he was brought in to confront my sister. She maintained stoically that she was now seeing him for the first time in her life, and on the basis of her denial Piziak was released; but my sister was kept imprisoned for six long months before she was released.

In Mezricz life went on "normally" on the outside, though the conditions subtly worsened. The refugees in particular were sent to the worst work sites. We were assigned to drain the waters of Rogozienice, a swamp area, under the supervision of a German overseer whom we nicknamed "Der Shleger" (The Flogger). This barbarian frequently beat and killed people for enjoyment. I remember one incident in which he behaved most "politely": rather than pummeling a number of workers to death, he merely wounded them in the head, and since they had benefited from his fit of liberality, he later looted their homes.

In the meantime we began to hear reports of the Warsaw ghetto deportations and of the gas autos in Chelmno.* Two Jews of Zagurow, who had escaped from Chelmno, came to Mezricz with an eyewitness report of the first gas auto killings. The victims had been assured by the Germans that they were being transported to work in Besarabia, an area in Rumania, and they were even permitted to take along luggage. But after they boarded, the doors of the autos were hermetically sealed and they headed instead toward Chelmno. On the way the Germans released poisoned gas into the cars, and the people inside choked to death in the

*Chelmno, the first experimental death factory, was located in the woods about sixty kilometers from Lodz. It began functioning on December 8, 1941, with mobile vans which used engine exhaust gases. Several gases and methods for mass killing were developed here and exported to Majdanek and other death camps. Only four people got out of Chelmno alive, including the two men from Zagurow mentioned in this story, who escaped from the tightly guarded camp on a stormy night. Two other men remained in Chelmno until its liberation: Shimon Srebnik, who was kept as a tailor, and Michael Podchlebnik, who later testified at Eichmann's trial.

most brutal manner. They were dead by the time the trucks reached Chelmno. The two men from Zagurow worked the site where the victims were buried, and they described for us the tragic murder of these unwitting "passengers."

When we heard this story, we decided to escape to Hungary and from there to go to Palestine. My brother Yeshaya, who had what could pass for a Polish appearance, set out for Sanok, where he intended to contact a border smuggler. We were out of money, but a friend of ours who had a flour mill was ready to lend us enough to finance our trip.

Our plans were almost completed when the Germans encircled Mezricz on July 8, 1942, and with the help of their Ukrainian* accomplices, began deporting Jews. Those who tried to break through the encircling ring were shot on the spot; among them were my uncle Alter Lipshitz and his sons Raphael and Shlomo Leib. My father and my brothers and sisters were loaded onto the trains, and we did not know what happened to them.

In the animal madness that followed, safety became relative; there was no foolproof place to hide, and those who were not discovered owed their survival more to instinct and luck than to any conscious strategy.

My family scattered quickly to various hiding places. Most of us took cover in a cellar, but even though the entrance was well recamouflaged, our Polish neighbors disclosed us to the Gestapo. In one electrifying instant, the Germans burst into our hideout and dragged us amidst blows to a nearby street where many Jews were gathered. Before we reached the crowd, I found an opportune moment to slip away and ran back home.

In that short time that we were gone, the Polish neighbors who had given us away succeeded in robbing our house. They were still in the midst of carrying off their loot when I caught up to them, but they simply chased me away, screaming, "We don't want to suffer because of you!"

---

*During the summer of 1941, the *Einsatzgruppen*, the special-duty groups deployed by the security service of the SS to begin the implementation of the Final Solution, began to invade the Jewish settlements of Eastern Europe. They found willing accomplices in the Lithuanians, Balts, and Ukrainians, who were eager to vent both their anti-Semitic prejudices and their hatred of the Soviets. The Germans enlisted these vicious collaborators to assist them in door-to-door manhunts and in the roundup and murder of countless Jews in Vilna, Kovno, Lwow, and other cities in the Eastern territories. The Ukrainians were not officially admitted into the German army, but they were appointed as overseers in the camps and factories, and in some of the ghettos.

The Poles had been threatened with death if they did not divulge the whereabouts of Jews to the Nazi hunters.

I ran to the shed in the neighbor's yard where my mother was hiding and told her what I had seen. I urged her to hide herself well, for this neighbor might also disclose her, and I begged her to stay in hiding no matter what. Then I ran to our garden and hid beneath a pile of leaves.

From among the leaves I watched the Ukrainians hunting for Jews; they discovered one hiding in a shed not far from me. Several hours later, when the hunting and shooting had died down somewhat, I stuck my head out and noticed one of the Polish neighbors walking down the street with my sister's five-year-old daughter, Freidele. I dashed out without thinking, took my little niece from her, and led her to my hiding spot under the leaves. The girl understood the danger and did not cry or complain. She just looked at me with her big, bright, frightened eyes and did not move.

Toward evening the shooting stopped completely, and I went out to look for my mother. I found her huddled in the corner of the lean-to, brought her to my hole in the ground, and covered her with leaves. We were safer there than in the shed, which could easily be inspected if the Germans came around again. We decided that we would try to escape from the town and go to a labor camp that we had heard of. The rumors were that Jews in that camp were not being deported,* and we thought we might have better protection there than in the ghetto. We waited until it was dark and then came out of our hiding places. On our way out of town, we passed a Polish woman whom we knew and asked her for a piece of bread to still the hunger of my little niece. Luckily the woman gave it to us without any questions. Then the three of us left the town as fast as we could.

We ran for hours without stopping. We were so frightened that we did not even feel our exhaustion. When we came to a river, I took Freidele on my shoulders and we plunged in; fortunately the water was not too deep. After running for another stretch, we stumbled upon a haystack in a field, and we climbed into it and fell asleep.

* There were some labor camps that people paid to get into during the war. They felt it would be safer than running and hiding from hunts and deportations, and thought they had a better chance of survival if they were working for the Germans. Such strategies may have bought a few people some extra time, but in the long run there was no safe shelter.

We awoke at dawn and saw that we were very near the labor camp we were seeking. We spent five days in the camp, and during that time we heard that the slaughter in our town had stopped and that a ghetto had been established. In spite of the few horrific stories we had heard of incidents in the ghetto, we decided to run away from the camp and return to Mezricz, where we would be together with all the Jews.

When we reached Mezricz we did find a ghetto, but it could barely be called a place to live. The Jews had been crowded into a run-down conglomeration of rotting buildings, and even there they were not safe. On any given day they were in danger of being shot if they happened to be found outside. Many Jews took shelter in the fields, living in holes and in pits and returning to the ghetto from time to time to find food.

The first thing we learned upon our return was that my brothers and sisters had jumped from the death train after the deportation and had made their way back to Mezricz. We found them, but they were not the same people I had known before; they were broken physically and spiritually. We sat and cried together for a long time.

They told us everything that had happened to them. Father had said *Viduy* with them as they waited on the platform and then resigned the fate of his family to the hands of the Al-mighty. Toward evening, amidst bloodcurdling shouts and shots, they were pushed onto a death train. Six thousand Jews were shoved into this train, which could hardly accommodate three thousand. In the confusion the family was separated; Chana Hinda and Chava and her husband Itche Yoseph were pressed into one wagon, and the rest of the family into another. The children told us about the crowding in the wagons, about the people who had been shot because they dared to raise their heads from the floor. They decided that they would rather jump and die from a bullet than be choked to death in the gas chambers, and their jump was successful.

Now we all waited for my brother Yeshaya, who soon returned from Sanok. When he saw the destruction in the town, he turned back to try once more to get us papers so that we could smuggle ourselves out of this accursed country. He left that same evening but he never returned. After the war we learned that a Pole from Skerniewice had recognized him on the train and exposed him to the Germans, who shot him on the spot.

From then on we survived from day to day. We had no steady place to live, and our safety hung on a thread. The Germans would sometimes go on shooting sprees in the ghetto, and there was no way of predicting when this would happen. We envied every rat and worm in the world. They at least had some kind of freedom; we had none . . .

For some time we worked for the peasants in the area, who gave us a bit of food in return for our labor. Then the Polish winter arrived. We hid in all kinds of holes in the fields near the ghetto. The bitter cold and the hunger were unbearable, and the lice and worms ate us alive. One freezing night I could take it no longer; despite the danger, I decided to go to one of our former Polish neighbors in the city. When he and his wife saw me standing on the doorstep, they cried out, "You're still alive?!" The wife in particular was frightened to death, convinced that she was seeing an apparition from the other world, but in spite of their apprehension the couple did give me some bread and matches. I returned to our pit and burst into a convulsive sobbing.

Some time later, when the latest bout of killing in the ghetto had abated, we returned, preferring to endanger our lives in the town than to rot alive in a hole in the field. Even in the ghetto we had to remain in hiding, but at night I sometimes used to sneak out to the Aryan side and exchange some of the linen we had hidden for food.

Though I was a young girl, I was proud to bring home some food and keep my family from starving to death, and this feeling of usefulness stifled my anxiety for the time being. But my mother could not stand the fear and constant running and hiding, and she fell ill and passed away. People tried to comfort us; they said she was a virtuous woman because she had merited to be buried in a Jewish cemetery in Mezricz.

At Christmastime the German monsters burst into the ghetto again and murdered forty Jews, and another *Aktion* began. We ran to our pit in the field, but on the morning of the *Aktion* the Germans began to uncover the pits too. Finally we realized that we must leave the town altogether. We knew a Pole in a nearby village who had once promised to help us, and although this was a dangerous resort, it was our last one. There was no place else to go. Trembling with fear, we ran past the outskirts of the city and moved very cautiously in the direction of the village.

The Pole, to our amazement, kept his word and locked us up in his granary. I promised that I would reward him for his effort, although presently I had nothing to give him. For several days we stayed in that granary with no food or water, and it was obvious that we would starve to death if we did not take action. I thought of a young couple we knew who had hidden in our bunker in the ghetto. They still had a few possessions, and I thought that maybe if we could bring them to the granary and offer the Pole some assets, he might give us some food. My brother-in-law liked my plan, but the problem was that reaching the ghetto now was not a simple task. He and I actually crawled back there on our hands and knees.

In Mezricz we came upon a scene of utter desolation. During the last *Aktion* the Germans had gone from house to house in search of Jews in hiding, and they had laid waste to the last particles of the Jewish community. Most of the Jews, including many members of our family, had been sent away to the gas chambers in Majdanek. A handful of people remained in hiding, but they knew that their fate was sealed. In that devastated ghetto, a few four- and five-year-old orphans were walking around amongst the rubble crying and shivering with hunger, cold, and fright. Their time, too, was limited.

We heard that three men, Avigdor Speichler and the brothers Goldfarb, had put up a courageous resistance even though they knew they had no chance. They had obtained weapons, and while they waited for a safe time to join the partisans in the forest, they hid in a bunker. A Pole disclosed them, and soon a group of Gestapo men arrived at the bunker and ordered them to give up their arms. The Jews answered with fire and a fight ensued, during which a few of the Germans were killed. Finally, the murderers threw explosives into the bunker and blew up the bodies of the three men.

We also heard about Yitzchak Ber, the elderly butcher of our neighborhood. When the gendarmes came to take him, he had slapped one of them and was promptly shot.

There was no one left in our bunker; the couple we were seeking had disappeared. Only two mute witnesses remained — a couple of heavy knapsacks filled with goods which they had left behind. That moment was a grievous one, for we knew that we were now the beneficiaries of our friends' deaths. But we could not even mourn properly. Amidst spasmodic crying, we loaded the knapsacks onto our shoulders and hurried back to the granary as fast as we could.

Those two knapsacks saved our lives. Whenever we needed food, we took a small item from among the goods and gave it to the Pole in exchange for bread or potatoes; and whenever he brought us the food, he reminded us that the Germans were awarding great prizes for disclosing Jews. He did not succeed in convincing us of his saintliness, but at least he did not give us away.

In the meantime my brother-in-law learned that a railroad worker, for an exorbitant sum of money, was prepared to smuggle people onto a train bound for Przeworsk. Przeworsk was not far from Sanok, and we were ready to pay the price and take the chance. This was our last hope of escaping to Hungary.

Within a few days we sold most of the remaining goods from the knapsacks and came up with the necessary sum of money. Then, in the darkness of the night, we stole into the railroad station. There were seven of us: my sisters Chana and Chava, Chava's husband, a boy and his two sisters, and me. The time seemed endless, and our hearts stopped beating at each sound and rustle in the air. Finally we found ourselves huddled under a pile of boards on one of the train wagons.

Four days and nights we lay there, motionless, until the train began to move. We felt some kind of relief leaving this desolate town, which was drenched with Jewish blood; but it is impossible to describe accurately the feelings of a young girl who is leaving the place where she has lost her mother and most of her family. For such feelings there are no words.

The train sped through cities, towns, and villages. The sun rose; birds sang; and nowhere in the world was there a tear shed for an entire nation that was being slaughtered with the most vicious cruelty... We were able to follow the signs in the stations we passed, and after a while we realized that according to our map we were not going toward Sanok at all, but instead were headed in an entirely different direction! The railroad worker had deceived us, and we could do nothing about it. On the eighth day of our journey the train stopped. We were bitterly disappointed and had no idea what to do.

We began to walk. From one of the houses that we passed we were very surprised to hear voices speaking in Yiddish. The people in the house let us in, and we told them that we were gentiles who had just escaped from a transport on its way to a forced labor camp in Germany. They gave us food and drink, and after a while, when we thought it might be safe to do so, we confessed that we were Jews. They told us that we were in Strzemeszyce-Slaizja, near Sosnowiec, an isolated pocket where a few Jews still lived, but that the situation was very unstable. They advised us to notify the local Jewish police of our presence here, explaining that unregistered Jews were in danger of being deported. We took their advice and were promptly imprisoned. After several days the police transferred us to the Shrudola, the Jewish ghetto in Sosnowiec, from which there were frequent deportations.

We asked for a meeting with the chief of the Jewish police in the Shrudola and described to him the systematic slaughter of the Jews in the towns we had come from. We warned him not to believe the Germans' promises; we told him of the chief of the Mezricz Judenrat, who had conscientiously carried out all of the Nazis' orders and had been shot mercilessly anyway. But all of this was to no avail. The Jews here were just as trapped as in the other towns . . . there was no way out.

The disappointment we suffered was almost worse than any of the troubles we had been through. We could not make peace with the fact that after so many trials we had simply ended up in another ghetto, where the constant fear of deportation still hung over our heads.

We decided to try once again.

We contacted a smuggler who promised to get us into Rumania, but he procrastinated. The weeks dragged on, and new deportations took place. During one of them we tried to hide in an attic, but the Germans seized us and threw us into a train headed for Auschwitz.

Nothing remained but to jump. Many people considered this the better option: quick death by the bullet of a train guard rather than the flames of a death camp. Chava, her husband, and Chana jumped first. I followed them but my jump was very clumsy, and I must have lost consciousness. When I awoke I found myself on some strange porch. My head was as heavy as a stone, and my hair was glued together by clots of blood. I got to my feet, tore off the yellow patch that had been tagged to my sleeve in the Sosnowiec ghetto, and knocked on the door.

A young gendarme appeared. "What do you want?" he inquired.

"Could you show me the road to Sosnowiec?" I asked him.

He replied, "You'll be better off in the forest among the many Jews there."

I left his house, thankful that he had done me no harm, but my head wasn't clear yet. I walked and walked until I found myself back at the railroad tracks — but there I heard German voices. I turned around and found my way back to the house of the gendarme, climbed up into the attic by way of a ladder, and covered myself with straw. I fell into a deep slumber and must have slept there for a long time. When I awoke I was trembling, burning up with fever, and terribly thirsty. I wanted desperately to sneak out of the attic and go someplace where I could wash up a bit.

Through a crack in the wall I looked down into the yard and saw a few geese swimming in a tub filled with water. The sight drove me mad. I felt that I must have water at that instant or I would lose my mind. I ran down the attic stairs and out to the yard. The tenants in the house saw me almost immediately and notified the police.

When an official came around I was certain that he was going to shoot me on the spot, and I almost welcomed it, for then there would be an end to my suffering. But instead he behaved very mildly. As he leisurely wrote his report, he informed me that a girl called Chana, by the same family name, had just come through here, and he assured me that I would join her the very next day. I was so glad to hear that she was still alive! Later I found out that the entire transport had gone directly to the gas chambers in Auschwitz.

I was taken to the Mislowice Prison and assigned to a cell with fifty other Polish women, but I was never sent to rejoin my sister. For days I sat in the same place, too sick to move or talk to anyone. The guards had bandaged my head and my wounds slowly began to heal, but I did not receive anything to eat for a few days. I was achingly hungry and felt that my strength was leaving me.

I was kept in this prison for six months. Many of the other prisoners who passed through were Jewish girls who had been posing as Christians and living on Aryan papers. One woman, an authentic Christian and the wife of a professor, tried to convince me to convert to Christianity, explaining that the Jews were being murdered because of their sins. In spite of her own dreadful situation, her thoughts were still centered on snatching Jewish souls!

At the end of the six months I was sent on a transport to Auschwitz, at last to "rejoin" my sister, who was no longer alive when I got there. By this time I was too exhausted to struggle for my life anymore, and I did not try to jump from the train as I had done before.

Mira Erster was one of several Jewish girls assigned to the Union ammunition factory in Auschwitz. She took part in the courageous Auschwitz revolt, smuggling explosive materials out of the factory to members of the camp underground who attempted to blow up the crematoria. (For a more extensive description of this conspiracy, see "The Auschwitz Revolt," page 231.) She was the only member of her family to survive the war and now lives in Tel Aviv.

A BUNKER IN LODZ

Sarah Zeidof-Beker
Lodz, Poland

In the Lodz ghetto everyone had to work. I worked in a laundry *resort** under the direction of Zvi Hirsch Prashker, a young man of Chassidic background and the son-in-law of Aaron Cytryn, one of the most distinguished manufacturers in Lodz before the war. Prashker's relationship with all his employees was friendly, but to children in the plant he showed special consideration. I was thirteen years old, among the youngest of the child workers.

One winter day in 1944, I noticed Prashker looking at me with unusual attention. I became alarmed and feared that I might be a candidate for deportation. As I stood pondering what I had done to merit such scrutiny, Prashker approached me in a confidential manner.

"Can you keep a secret?" he whispered.

"Yes, of course," I said, without considering where my reply would lead me.

"I was thinking that you might be the right person for a special assignment," he said. "I was thinking that I could entrust you with a secret

*A *resort* was a workshop. There were no privately owned shops once the Germans occupied Poland. The laundry service that Sarah Beker refers to was established to clean the clothing of people who had been deported from the ghetto, which would then be recycled according to the Germans' needs. At first the laundry workers did not really understand the implications of their job, but gradually they began to recognize the clothing of people they had known.

mission which might involve great danger. I chose you because I know
your parents and your family." He looked straight into my eyes for quite
a while, as if debating with himself whether or not he had made a mistake.

After a prolonged silence he continued: "Not far from the Kripo there
is a broken-down shack which is barely noticeable. Behind that shack is
a pile of ruins, and in back of the ruins there is a concealed door. You'll
have to look hard for it. When you find it, knock three times and say:
'Hersh'l sent me.' A man will open the door. Give him this envelope."
Prashker handed me an envelope and added, "You've got to be very
careful. The lives of many people depend on the success of your mission.
Don't let them catch you—but if they do, remember that *you do not know
anything.*"

I was just a child, but I was aware of the danger and the responsibility
of such a mission. However, I did not withdraw from my decision.
Somehow, even though Prashker did not give me any details, I sensed
that this was an important undertaking, and I trusted him.

When I had finished my day's work at the laundry workshop, I went
straight to the "address" I had been given. I began searching in the heap
of wreckage, trying to appear as though I were searching for pieces of
wood for fuel, which was a very normal sight in the ghetto. When I finally
found the hidden door, I knocked three times, hissing: "Hersh'l sent me!
Hersh'l sent me!"

The door opened, and before me stood a young Chassidic man. His
looks shocked me. It wasn't that I hadn't seen emaciated boys with bony
faces before, but I had never seen such fierce eyes. I could not believe that
there were Jewish men to be found in the ghetto who still had their beards
and *peyos* (sidelocks). He looked to me like a man from another planet,
someone whom the war had not touched.

I handed him the envelope, and as my eyes adjusted to the darkness
in the room beyond him, my astonishment grew. I was standing at the
door of a large hall, a Beth Hamidrash. A long table stretched through the
middle of the hall, and around it sat about forty young Chassidim who
were studying the Talmud. It took a while for my mind to absorb this
sight; such a thing had not existed for years in the ghetto.

I repeated my mission several times, and each time Prashker warned me: "Watch out; be careful!" Later on I found out that the envelopes I had delivered contained money, financial support for these young men who were not registered in any workshop and therefore did not have ration cards. Zvi Hirsch Prashker himself had supported them all through the ghetto years to enable them to engage in their secret study of the Talmud. These boys never left their bunker and learned Torah all day under the very noses of their Nazi oppressors.

Whenever I think of those wonderful boys, my heart is filled with admiration for them, for the greatness of their spirit and their immense faith in G-d. They did not accept the yoke of the German regime and remained steadfast in their belief in the laws of the Al-mighty.

Sarah Zeidof-Beker was deported to Auschwitz and remained there until the liberation. She now lives in Kiryat Ata in Israel.

FOR MY MOTHER

Anna Landman-Eilenberg-Eibeshitz
Lodz, Poland

We Jews in the Lodz ghetto were hit with the reality of a new era, and none of us were in any way prepared for it. I was fifteen years old when the Nazis came, and I could hardly adjust to the idea of not going to high school, which I had dreamed of for a long time. The happy ordinariness of school days now belonged to another lifetime, and the dreary day-to-day struggle to stay alive took its place. I felt as though the world were closing in on me. Although I wasn't alone in this situation, I felt lost, and I sought refuge in a world of illusion — the realm of beauty and perfection found only in books.

I always carried a book with me if I was about to spend a long time in a line. I knew that I couldn't just stand there and think about our miserable plight; the fact that I had to wait in line just to get a piece of bread was awful enough. But I always felt uncomfortable. Other Jews would give me strong, unfriendly looks when they saw me reading, and it hurt me when they made remarks like, "Look at this stupid girl — she needs stories now!" In all honesty, it wasn't stories I needed, but something to lean on, something to cling to, and books gave me that indispensable crutch.

The real world around me was crumbling. Fear, death, and horror were part of our everyday lives. Every morning I asked myself two questions: How could I go on living, and why did we Jews deserve such punishment? Alongside these troubling questions was the fearful premonition that our present hardships would not be final, that worse times lay ahead of us. In the early days of the war, however, I could still think; I could still plan in my mind that I would fight, that I would not yield to circumstances, that I would not let myself be crushed. I would be strong and I would resist.

Books became the weapons in my struggle. Several of my most treasured volumes had been left to me by a cousin who had fled to Warsaw as the Germans were approaching. With these precious defenses, I tried as best I could to create my own safe world, but I did not succeed as well as I had hoped.

The onslaught of the Nazis was sudden and frightful. On Tuesday, September 5, 1939, in the early, sunless hours of the morning, the German oppressor took possession of our city of Lodz, only four days after the war had started. They came like a cloud of green locusts, a horde of brutes in human form; masses of flesh and steel, a stream of thunderous terror in dawn, heavy with foreboding. Even the smallest child among us could feel the abysmal evil and disaster that descended upon us. We were enveloped, as doomed to destruction as the sinful generation of the Flood.

The city went numb. Only the roaring noise of cannon fire could be heard. It seemed to have silenced all other life in the town. We listened in frozen stillness to the sounds of approaching shells and heavy vehicles; three days later, on September 8th, we listened to the distinct rapping of the marching troops and the rhythmic clack of horse's hooves. We listened to the sound of the Germans closing in on us.

Almost immediately after the occupation, placards went up all over town warning people not to be out of their homes at certain times and not to walk on certain streets. All the civil bureaus were taken over.

The first days of the war brought thousands of refugees to our city, seeking shelter in our midst. In the chilly pre-dawn darkness, parents and children clustered together in the obscurity of the cobblestoned courtyards. Some of these unfortunate people were wounded, others were in a state of shock; all were exhausted, dirty, and hungry. They told us of terrible experiences on their way to our town, of friends and relatives killed while fleeing, of others left to die on the road.

Despite their tales, which demonstrated so clearly the uselessness of trying to escape, many of our men decided to flee. There was a rumor going around that all the men of the city would be shot, and they decided to take their chances. They poured onto the roads without plan or destination, some to vanish forever, others to return soon afterward, telling of soldiers who were firing at the fugitives from low-flying airplanes. In fact, on the day after the invasion my father had taken my brother Benyamin and tried to run away, but they had come home that same evening. Benyamin told us that the planes were flying so low you could see people inside them, taking aim with their guns. In truth, there was no place to run.

A week later, on Friday morning, I was sitting in the house when I suddenly began to feel that the walls were leaning in and crushing me. Some inner force stronger than myself propelled me into the street. There I found myself swept along with a crowd of people who were watching a procession of marching soldiers. I ran after the marchers, and when I got to Piotrkowska Street, I stopped at an elevated spot to get a better view of our conquerors. To this day I cannot explain what I wanted to see. I just know that what happened next shattered some part of me forever.

As the soldiers marched, they began to sing: *"Whenn Judenblut von Messer spritzt / Dann geht's nochmal so gut!"* I knew enough German to understand the words: "When Jewish blood spurts from the knife / Then all goes doubly well!" Then I noticed our neighbor, Mr. Schultz. He was one of a few men among the spectators wearing a German militia uniform with a shiny black swastika on the arm band, and he was singing lustily along with the soldiers. A frightening tremor seized my whole body. For the first time in my life, I knew the meaning of utter despair.

Although Mr. Schultz was a Pole, my parents considered him our friend. He liked to spend time in my father's company and he enjoyed my mother's cooking, often joining us for lunch on Fridays. From the time my mother had started her weaving shop, he had regularly delivered rolls of fabric to her. Now, seeing him in his German uniform, I realized that he must have been our enemy all along. I pushed myself through the dense crowd and started for home. The main avenues were filled with marchers and spectators, so I took the side streets.

I had barely walked five minutes when I heard shots. Then I saw two German soldiers pull a man out of his house, throw him to the ground, and beat him savagely all over his head and body until he fell unconscious. Further along, a cluster of military men were walking down the street and shooting randomly into the windows of homes. I was terrified. My knees shook, but somehow I kept on walking, going faster and faster, until I was running. I stopped for a few minutes whenever I saw an open gateway and hid inside, trying to catch my breath and steady my legs, which were trembling violently. Finally I made up my mind not to give in to the terror or call attention to myself by running. I straightened up and resumed my journey with a firm step, not looking to the left or right. Exhausted and bewildered, I gratefully reached home.

On the following day, which was the Sabbath, the Jews experienced indescribable horror — mostly at the hands of the Poles. Their shops were looted, their homes were plundered, and many were killed in the streets. The Poles knew that they had to act quickly, because once order was restored their opportunity would be lost. It was also their chance to prove their loyalty to the Germans. During this feverish assault, the Nazis rounded up dozens of Jews, beat them mercilessly, hurled them into trucks, and drove them off to the outskirts of the city, where they were forced to clean stables with their bare hands. Others were ordered to scrub the city streets or to wash the Germans' own cars. Under the threat of bayonets and rifles, they worked day and night without rest or food. Some of these men died, others were maimed; all who came back were broken and sick. Panic spread through the town. Jews kept their doors tightly shut and did not venture outside.

My mother developed severe chest pains. She had never been strong physically, and the fear and tension of these events were too much for her. My father was aware of the danger of going into the street, but he also knew that my mother needed immediate medical attention, and he went to the nearest drugstore to call a doctor. I was afraid that something might happen to him and felt I should have gone along, but I could not leave my mother alone.

The Nazis usually stationed their trucks out of range of the area in which they were conducting a hunt. Most of the time when my father or brother had had to go out into the street, I would walk half a block in front of them to make sure there were no trucks and that they were not heading into a trap. The Nazis were looking for men at that early stage and did not pay much attention to young girls.

The drugstore my father had gone to was only a block away, in the far corner of our building, yet I was frightened. From the moment he left, I did not move away from the window. All I kept thinking was that I should have gone with him to protect him from the hunters.

I was still peering through the shuttered window when I heard shots in the courtyard. At the same moment I saw Mr. Schultz running through the entrance with a rifle pointed toward the staircase of our section of the building. In his haste he tripped on a long, thin piece of wood that stuck out from a pile of boards in front of the bakery, which was on the ground floor of the building. Mr. Schultz fell down, and blood gushed from his hands and face. I do not know who called for help, but people came immediately to take him away.

Dumbfounded, I was still trying to piece this sight together in my mind when my father came through the front door. He stumbled into the apartment and fell on the bed, trembling and speechless. Only after some minutes could he tell us what had just happened.

While waiting in the drugstore to make his call, he had seen storm troopers rounding up people in the street. When their truck was full and had driven off, he was immensely relieved and thanked G-d that he had been spared arrest. He quickly made his call and rushed out of the drugstore. Once in the street, however, he sensed that he was being followed. Not daring to look back, he quickened his pace, and so did the person behind him. Realizing that he would soon be overtaken, he started to run. He was only a couple of steps from our gateway when he heard his name called, and then shots rang out, narrowly missing him as he leapt into the courtyard. He dashed up the staircase, taking three and four steps at a time, until he reached the attic.

There were many storage areas behind doors in the sloping edges of the attic ceiling, and each tenant of the house had an assigned space where he kept his extra possessions. In one of these my father hid.

It was then that he knew beyond doubt who his pursuer was. He heard Mr. Schultz's voice calling him on each landing of the staircase, until finally he appeared in the attic doorway. As luck would have it, the attic at that particular time was completely empty of its usual maze of drying laundry, and the hanging lines were dangling slackly from the ceiling. Mr. Schultz had a clear view of the entire attic.

From his hiding place my father could hear Mr. Schultz opening the doors of the storage areas one by one, banging, ripping, shoving things aside. In his fury he knocked his head against the low ceiling, which further enraged him, and then he ran down the stairs into the yard. He was heading directly for our apartment when he stumbled over the piece of wood in the woodpile in front of the baker's shop and fell, bringing to a close his day of "bad luck."

By the time my father finished describing this scene, he was almost completely calm. He told my brother, my sister, and me to leave the apartment immediately. "Just take your overcoats and run! Run for your lives! Mr. Schultz will surely come back, seeking revenge for what happened to him."

We were panic-stricken, but we obeyed him. He instructed us to go to my grandfather's house, which was in a different section of the city, assuring us that he and my mother would join us later. He did not come along because he wanted to alert the others who lived in our building to the situation; Mr. Schultz would most probably vent his anger on them if he could not find us. When my parents finally left the apartment, they did not lock the door, so that it would appear as though they had just stepped out for a while. We did not return to the apartment for several days.

We children were shocked beyond comprehension — not just by the horror of the episode, but by the treachery of our supposed "friend," with whom we had shared so many hours. Mr. Schultz had been like a member of our family. We could not understand how a person could change so quickly to become the exact opposite of what he had always seemed.

But as time went on, we saw that Mr. Schultz's conduct was not unique. He did not really "change" overnight; he was only one of many Polish gentiles who finally had the opportunity to unleash the virulent strain of anti-Semitism which they had simply held in check all their lives — until now.

Many gentile friends of the Jews quickly showed their true colors and cooperated with the Nazis in carrying out the "Final Solution." These turncoats were very good at rounding up Jews for work, pointing out their hiding places, and giving out the names of the wealthy Jewish families — services for which they were well-rewarded by their German masters. Sometimes the Poles would agree to hide Jews in exchange for their possessions, and after they had extorted all they could, they would betray the Jews to the Gestapo anyway. In many instances Jewish parents paid large sums of money and valuables to the gentiles to hide their children, and as soon as the parents were killed, these Poles turned the children over to the Gestapo to be killed in turn.

The Nazis were very well aware of the Poles' deeply rooted hatred of the Jews, a factor which they carefully exploited in their systematic and methodical attempt at genocide. They needed the collaboration of the natives of the country in which they established their most treacherous death factories, and they found it easily among the Poles.

About a month after the war began, two SS soldiers burst into our apartment to make an "inspection" and then began grabbing things. They took our silver goblets, Sabbath candelabrum, and silver menorah, and one of them pulled my mother's wedding ring right off her finger while the other beat my father. My mother could take no more and fainted. After the SS men departed, leaving the house in disarray, my father called a doctor, who had her admitted to the hospital.

The doctor assigned to care for my mother was a German, and the hospital was at the far end of the city, where no Jews had lived even before the war. We were very much surprised to see that Dr. Milke treated my mother well, in light of the way she had just been treated by other Germans. Dr. Milke was also friendly to my father and to us children. Seeing that we were very frightened, he smiled and told us not to worry, that he would take care of my mother. When I asked him if I would be able to see her, he told me that I could even come to his house to find out her condition.

The Germans continued to close down on our city, tightening the screws with a harrowing bestiality. They trapped Jews in the streets and sent them off to slave labor camps or used them sadistically for their own amusement, beating them mercilessly, plucking or setting fire to their beards and *peyos*. Jews were vulnerable to assault and murder every hour of the day and night. Neither my father nor my brother would go out into the street, since both wore beards and *peyos*. My younger sister was too small and fragile to take care of things outside the house, and so it fell upon me to become my family's sole provider and its link to the outside world.

I was the only one able to visit my mother in the hospital, and when I was not with her, I worried constantly about her welfare. Jewish life was rapidly losing its value. Although I knew my mother couldn't stay home, I feared that something terrible might happen to her in the hospital; she was the only Jewish woman there. Who knew? Poison, G-d forbid, could be put in her food, or she could be given a lethal injection, and it would then be reported that she had died of "natural causes." I had terrible dreams about her at night, and I was always desperately impatient for the sun to rise so that I could run to the hospital and convince myself that she was still alive and that no evil hand had touched her.

The hospital was Christian, and we knew that my mother would not eat most of the foods there. Early the first morning, my younger sister cooked a light soup for her. I packed the pot in a basket, summoned all my courage, and ventured out.

The streets were almost deserted. Here and there I could see a woman or child walking with hurried and furtive steps, anxious to reach shelter unseen. A few peasant women were about, carrying loaves of bread wrapped in white cloths under their arms or in baskets. These women frequently came in from their villages and brought bread from the Aryan side of the city to sell to Jews. They knew their merchandise was more valuable than gold; bread had vanished immediately at the beginning of the war, when all industry was confiscated by the Germans, and the Jews would literally exchange their gold for one of these women's loaves.

I smelled the fresh aroma of the loaves, and it made me feel hungry; it was almost a month since I had eaten a piece of bread. My mother had begun substituting potatoes and some kind of grain she had acquired at the start of the war, and we ate what she cooked rather than stand in line all night in the hope of buying some bread. But now, when the peasant woman passed me with her loaf, my mouth started to water, and I felt an overpowering desire to sink my teeth into that fresh, crusty dough. I was quickly ashamed of my thoughts and tried to subdue this lust. I had more important things to think of, I had to reach the hospital as soon as possible. Maybe my mother was hungry and waiting for me to come.

I still had a long distance to go, and I quickened my steps. The streets I now passed through were completely desolate. The big apartment houses gave way here to small, one-family homes; none were Jewish. Some dogs heard my footsteps and began to bark, and I saw that people were staring at me from behind closed shades. I walked with an outwardly secure step, but inside I was terrified. The emptiness and silence of the streets frightened me.

My heart was palpitating wildly, as if it wanted to free itself from my imprisoning chest. More ghastly thoughts raced through my mind; I imagined the worst. I began to run, and I ran and ran until I was out of breath. I lifted my eyes and saw in front of me a three-story building. I fished around in my basket for the scrap of paper on which I had scribbled the address of the hospital, and sighed with relief. I had come to the right place. I touched the towel which covered the little pot of soup and was glad to find that it was still warm. With a heavy heart I entered the building.

My mother was very weak, but unafraid. She told me that the nurse in the ward had compassion and that the other patients were indifferent to her, too preoccupied with their own illnesses to show her any hostility. Seeing how calm she was and knowing that she was well treated, I allowed myself to relax a little.

When I left her, I went straight to Dr. Milke's house. He was just as kind to me as he had been the first time. He told me that my mother had had a slight heart attack and that her heart was enlarged, and he advised that she stay in the hospital for at least another week, regardless of the unpredictable situation in the city. He must have read my thoughts, for he reassured me again that he himself would take good care of her. With a lighter heart and a more confident step, I started for home.

The week my mother stayed in the hospital was the longest of my life, for on every single day new decrees were published by the Germans, singling out Jews as undesirable citizens. Even though the hospital itself had seemed reliable, my mother was now the only "undesirable" patient there, alone amongst enemies. My fears for her well-being increased as the terror in the city worsened with each passing day. I would not take an easy breath until I was able to bring her home.

One of the first decrees to come forth that week was the requirement for all Jews to wear a yellow arm band. Disobedience was punishable by death. The intention was clear: any Jew who could easily be distinguished would be an easier target for the Germans. This decree was followed by another which declared that Jews were not to show their faces in non-Jewish sections of the city, and yet a third forbade Jews to walk on Piotrkowska Street, the busiest, most popular, and most luxurious street in Lodz — and also the most Jewish. Jews who were prepared to pay for the privilege, however, could buy permits to walk on this street; if caught without one, they could be sent away and never heard from again. To make their intentions clear, the Nazis burst into the most elegant cafe on Piotrkowska Street one evening when the place was full of diners, arrested half the guests, and shot the other half on the spot.

After the yellow bands came the yellow star. We were ordered to wear the star on the front and back of each of our garments when we went outside. Then, after having restricted us from walking on most Jewish streets, the Germans listed the hours we could walk on permitted streets — between 8:00 a.m. and 5:00 p.m. Those who violated these edicts were sent away or summarily shot.

These were the conditions under which we lived for about three or four months — beyond the protection of the law, apart from society, separated from a normal economy and from any possibility of existing as a normal people.

In the beginning of December 1939, the rumor began to circulate that Lodz was to become *Judenrein*, free of Jews. At night these rumors occupied my mind and did not let me fall asleep. I thought: Free of Jews? Then we would have to move. But where to? I had no way of knowing that moving would not be the worst of it, that we would have to endure the impossible.

I looked around the house and thought: Will we be able to take our furniture with us? Will I be allowed to take my books? And even more — will I be allowed to read them?

The Jews of Lodz became very alarmed. Those with money fled to other towns, especially to Warsaw, but those of meager means had to stay put. My family was in this category, for we had no money and nothing of value to exchange. An escape could only be carried out with the help of Poles or Germans, who exacted enormous fees for their services. They certainly were not interested in saving Jews, only in feathering their own nests. But even those who managed to get out of Lodz discovered quickly that the Nazis' arms were long. There was no eluding their clutch; it reached all over Poland. Only those who escaped across the border to Russia were safe for the time being.

The rumor materialized. On December 15, 1939, the Nazis decreed that all Jews would soon have to clear out of Lodz, and at the beginning of February 1940, they announced that a ghetto would be created for them in the Baluty section, the poorest neighborhood of the city.

Never in my life will I forget our move to the ghetto. It stands out in my mind as vividly as if it had happened only yesterday: mothers with crying children at their sides, some holding nursing babies in their arms, some pushing upended tables piled high with all of the family's possessions; old people carrying their belongings tied to their backs, white-bearded elders clutching bundles of books tied with string under one arm and bags with prayer shawls and phylacteries under the other.

The procession to the ghetto lasted many days, a haunting sight, portending the doom of our people. Nature, too, seemed to have conspired with our enemy, for the frost bit our faces and froze our breath, and the violent wind tugged at our shabby clothing and head coverings. I remember that it was 25 degrees below zero. The old people said that they could not recall such a brutal winter.

I felt degraded and horrified at the thought of what awaited us in the future. The sense of helplessness was a morass which threatened to drown me. I wanted to run, but I felt caged; I wanted to die of the cold, but I had obligations to my family; I wanted to rid myself of life — but then there would be no one to take care of my mother.

I stood on the street, watching other families drift about in a haphazard, tangled procession, and I tried to figure out in my head how we might move all of our belongings to the ghetto. This was actually less of a problem than how to transport my mother. She had come home safely from the hospital but had hardly recuperated from her heart attack. The situation seemed hopeless; the distance was too far for her to walk, and the frost was too cruel. I was in a dilemma. My father and brother could not help, for if they left the house to make arrangements, their beards would give them away and they would be caught immediately. To whom could I turn? Everyone else was in the same position. Crying children, the old, the lame, and the sick were all marching, breathing into their cupped palms, knocking foot against foot, hitting the hardened snow with the soles of their shoes to keep their toes from freezing. Everyone needed help.

A thought flickered through my mind: I would try the *Linas HaCholim*! The *Linas HaCholim* was a health agency partially supported by the Kehillah, the organized Jewish community. We had sought their assistance often, since my mother's health had always been fragile. I would go there and insist that they provide transportation for her.

The office was humming with people, so many that I had a hard time squeezing myself through the door. Once inside, I made up my mind that I would not move until my request was granted. Finally I got a chance to present my case to one of the officials, but he hardly seemed to listen. All he would say was that in view of the tragedy that had befallen all the Jews of the city, he could not take care of my problem.

For a moment I was taken aback. Perhaps I was being too egotistical and selfish. There were so many old and sick people, so many in dire need of help; of what importance was my one small request amongst these? But my instinct told me that I could not give in so easily. I was not asking anything for myself, I was asking help for my sick mother! I wiped away my tears of shame and straightened my back, my resolution once more firm.

The officials were running back and forth, in and out, and the commotion was so great that one could hardly hear himself speak. For a while I didn't approach anyone; I just sat and studied the faces of the *Linas HaCholim* employees, closely observing the manner in which they dealt with people.

One of these workers was a young man who was sitting behind a small window, and I noticed that he spent more time with people than the others did. A long line had formed outside his door, and I got into it. The line moved very slowly; each time it came to a halt, the people near me started to grumble. But each person who finished his conference with the young man behind the window seemed to undergo a complete change of mood.

I knew that I was in the right place if I wanted to get help for my mother, but the clock was ticking away, and the young man could not sit in his place forever. Then, just as I reached the window, he stuck his head out and announced that he was finished for the day. If he had hit me with a brick he could not have hurt me more. I felt abandoned. My only hope was gone. The people in line behind me started to shout and scream, but the man apologized and left. One by one the other officials left too, and the people began to drift into the street, disappointed and bitter. I did not leave. I told myself that it would be better to sleep in the street than to go home without getting help for my mother.

When the hall had emptied completely, I began trying the doors. They were all unlocked, but the rooms behind them were empty. I had opened about eight doors when, in a far corner, in what looked like an exit, I found yet one more door and opened it. There I saw a young woman in her thirties sitting at a table, in a room the size of a closet. She looked at me in surprise but asked me to come in, and then she pulled out a chair from behind her desk and told me to sit down.

I was not prepared for kindness at that moment, and all the sobs that were locked in my throat welled up and escaped. The woman let me cry, and when I had finished, she listened to my problem without interruption. She asked me to wait and returned after about ten minutes, accompanied by an elderly man. When she repeated my story to him, he looked at me briefly, gave her instructions to make a telephone call, and left the room. She made the call and then informed me that a *dorozhka*, a horse-drawn carriage, would be waiting for me outside in the street. I wanted to say something to thank her, but the words stuck in my throat and I could not force them out. The woman looked at me with her big black eyes and said that she understood. I later found out that she was the fiancee of the elderly man, Chaim Rumkowski, the head of the Lodz ghetto Judenrat— "the king," as he was known to the ghetto Jews.

There was no happier person in the world than I when I saw the carriage roll up to the entrance of the building; and when I rode into our courtyard, my parents could hardly believe their eyes. There was still an hour to sundown, but we had to rush because of the curfew. Hastily, I grabbed our down quilts, laying one on the seat of the carriage and wrapping my mother in the other one. I tucked some of her essential things into the carriage, as well as some linen and bedding.

Before we left, a strong urge took possession of me. I ran back upstairs to our apartment, climbed up on a table, and tore the electric wires from the ceiling. Then I went around and ripped all the wires out of the walls wherever I could find them. If a German had seen me, the consequences would surely have been severe, but my anger was greater than my prudence. Somehow I knew that German people would come and live in *our* house and use *our* electricity, and I didn't want to leave it for them.

I went downstairs, climbed onto the carriage step, and gave the driver my uncle's address in the section of the city where the ghetto had been created. The rest of my family came on foot.

Whenever I recall my trip to the ghetto, a great anger wells up in me. I can still feel the degrading pain that bit into me when I joined that procession. Thousands of Jews were walking toward their fate along the one street they had been permitted to use for their relocation. They were carrying some of their possessions in their hands and others on their backs, and sliding still others along the frozen street; rich and poor alike were leaving the homes where they had lived all their lives. Very few of them had a place to go to. They were simply running away from death, which would eventually catch up with them.

The Jews going to the ghetto were not allowed to use the sidewalks, and so they had to move aside to make space whenever a vehicle passed by. As I stood on the step of our slow-moving carriage and watched people shuffle brokenly to the side, I felt dreadfully embarrassed, for no one else had a carriage. There was such an anger inside me that I wanted to destroy everything in sight. I was piercingly aware of my own powerlessness and that of all the people around me. I wondered if they felt as I did. Was there really nothing left for us but to follow orders blindly? By the time we finally reached my Uncle Fishel's house, my blood was boiling.

Uncle Fishel was my father's youngest brother. He had seven children; the oldest, Mordechai, was fourteen, and the youngest was an infant girl born just a few months earlier, in November 1939. They were the only relatives we had in the section now proclaimed the ghetto. At the end of December, in the darkness of the night, the Gestapo had unexpectedly entered the neighborhood where my uncle lived, dragged many Jews from their beds, and deported them. None of the deportees ever returned. Among them were Uncle Fishel and five of his seven children.

My Aunt Gittel had been bedridden at that time with a blood clot in her leg which had resulted from the delivery of her latest child. When the Gestapo took away my uncle and cousins, they sealed the apartment door from the outside. For five days Aunt Gittel and the two remaining children — Mordechai, the eldest, and the baby girl — were locked in. On the sixth day Mordechai managed to break the door, and he came running to tell us what had happened. All we could do then was give him food; and now we were coming to my uncle's house again, this time seeking help for ourselves.

When we arrived it was already evening. We found that many of our relatives had sought the same refuge, and there were a total of twenty-seven people in that small space. The apartment consisted of an average-sized bedroom and kitchen, and a walk-in closet with a small window, which served as a children's room. We were welcomed, and we began the task of making sleeping arrangements.

Most of us slept on the floor. The relatives were all greatly concerned for my mother's health, and she was given the table to sleep on, the best place in these circumstances. My sister and I slept under the table. The room was airless, and the contours of the apartment made the stuffiness almost unbearable. The ceiling in the bedroom sloped on one side, and the slope in the children's room was so steep that a person five feet tall could not stand upright. Only a small child could be comfortable there.

My mother's restlessness woke me in the middle of the night. She was short of breath. Not knowing what else to do, I forced open the window to let in air, but as I did so, a sheet of snow swept in from the roof across the alley, and a cold wind engulfed the room. The wind was so strong that I couldn't close the window, and I started to freeze.

My mother was right in front of the open window, and I was afraid that she would catch pneumonia. What could I do? I looked for things to cover her with, pulling out whatever garments or linen came to hand and laying them on her, not caring to whom they belonged. She started to cough, softly at first, then spasmodically. I prayed to G-d for the night to end, though I didn't know what I would do in the morning. I just knew that this night was frightening me.

I was not worried for myself or my family; our discomfort was unimportant. I knew that there were families who didn't even have a crowded apartment to stay in and no money to pay for a place to sleep. Many of these unfortunates slept on staircases and in the gateways of houses. If not for my mother's health, I would have considered myself lucky, but I was in anguish about her. Where would I get a doctor for her? After this night she would need medical help again.

Early the next morning I woke up my brother, Benyamin. I told him to wrap his face in a shawl so that his beard and *peyos* would not show. It was so cold outside that a covered face would arouse no suspicion. I said we must go out together to look for an apartment, that one more night like this would cause Mother to have another heart attack. My father gave us some money and we went from house to house, asking if there was an apartment available. There was none. My brother reasoned that we had no chance of finding a decent place in the heart of the ghetto, but that if we ventured closer to the Aryan side we might do better, since few Jews wanted to risk living in close proximity to the border guards. In our case we had to take that risk in order to do what was good for my mother. Benyamin had a totally logical mind. His judgment had always been good, and he was right this time too.

The sun slowly slanted upward from the horizon and the snow stopped falling, but the wind was unrelenting. With hasty steps we walked toward the outskirts of the town. When we were out of the Jewish section, I became a little uneasy. My brother noticed and asked me what was wrong.

"Can't you see what's happening to us, Benyamin? The Nazis hunt us down like animals. Our lives and our future are turning to dust and ashes in front of our very eyes. It seems that we are doomed! Are we just supposed to accept our fate and thank G-d for it?" I demanded in anger.

"Did you ever read any Jewish history books?" he asked me. "Do you know that our ghetto happens not to be the first one? There were ghettos before. For centuries the Jews have suffered persecutions, a long chain of suffering. The only difference is that now we ourselves happen to be a link in that chain.

"As long as you, my dear sister, only had to read about what happened to our nation, you could tolerate the pain others suffer; however, when you are the one facing adversity, you're ready to lose yourself, to lose your sense of obligation as one of our people. Are you ready to doubt your faith because you suffer? I think that now is the time to learn to be strong, to know how to act in the face of suffering — and to understand the meaning of it."

I did not interrupt him. He had made me realize that our enemies had always wanted to crush us and that this time was no different. The Nazis' aim, he had pointed out, was to destroy our faith, and we must do everything to make sure they did not succeed. I felt ashamed, and my boiling blood cooled. He was right . . . I sensed that I was not as strong as he, and I envied him.

Immersed in our discussion, we did not realize that we had reached a sparsely populated area. We were still inside the ghetto confines, but here small houses with modest lawns and tall trees dotted the landscape. We arrived at a fenced-in garden, adorned with a wooden bench and shaded by a broad-branched tree. A bench under a tree in a garden full of flowers is exactly what Mother needs now, I thought, and my brother echoed my thought aloud as he pulled the wire bell at the low wooden gate. A gentile woman came out and asked what we wanted. She could see immediately that we were Jews. We knew that she would soon leave her house for a much finer one which had just been vacated by a Jew on his way to the ghetto.

We asked her if we could rent part of her house, and she said we could, but that she wanted two hundred *zlotys*. It was a cruel trick, I thought to myself. Why should she ask us for so much money when she knew as well as we did that she would soon get a luxurious Jewish apartment in the city for no money at all? I opened my mouth to say something, but my brother stopped me. He turned to the woman and asked: "Would you move out today if we gave you the money?"

"Yes," she replied. When she saw my brother reaching into his pocket for the money, she added, "If you pay me the full amount I'll go now, and I'll leave you two iron beds besides."

Benyamin gave her the money, and she led us into the house. We came to a room, ten by fourteen feet, with two windows looking down into the garden. The room was completely empty except for the two iron beds which stood against the long wall. The woman showed us that the mattresses had fresh straw. The fact that the room had no other furniture led me to think that she had already moved out before we came and was only waiting around a while longer for an opportunity to press some money from Jews.

She put our bills in her pocket and gave us the key. I looked at my brother, telling him with my eyes that I thought the woman had taken advantage of us. Why had he been so quick to give her the money? Why hadn't he bargained with her? Ignoring me, he put the key in his pocket and wished her all the best.

On the way home I reproached him for being too hasty.

"It doesn't matter if this woman took advantage of us or not," he answered. "What counts is that we got exactly what we needed for Mother. To wait another night would have been too dangerous . . . But the more important thing to remember is that we are approaching a new phase in our lives, and we have to learn how to act, even with a gentile woman. She is also being resettled. Sometimes the grandest apartment cannot take the place of a poor home when the home is taken away by force. If we will not stand guard and see the importance of even the smallest things that happen to others, we will be crushed — morally — very fast."

My brother was four years older than I. Until his bar mitzvah we had always played together, taken walks together, and shared experiences. But then he began to change and became very serious in his studies of the Talmud. He had little time to "waste" on me and my sister, and I, in turn, became busy with school and friends. Now I felt again a real closeness to him, the kind of closeness which gives meaning to life. I felt that his spiritual strength would be my support in time of need. What I learned that day was that Benyamin was more prepared than I was to cope with the rigors of our new life. At a time when I felt angry with the whole world, he showed balance and wisdom; while I had only agitating questions, he had answers.

The purpose of the ghetto was to crush the Jews spiritually, and so our inner survival was as important — if not more important — than our physical survival. My brother had awakened in me the spiritual resources I would need for the ordeal that lay ahead.

Anna Landman spent almost five years in the Lodz ghetto before being deported to Auschwitz. She spent six weeks there and was then moved to Halbstadt, a town in the Sudeten in Czechoslovakia, where she worked in a spinning factory for nine more months, until the end of the war. She is now married to Jehoshua Eibeshitz and lives in Bayit Vegan in Jerusalem.

Her brother Benyamin contracted tuberculosis and passed away in the ghetto at the age of twenty-one.

ON THE ARYAN SIDE

❖

LEAVING THE GHETTO

Sarah Erlichman
Lublin, Poland

I arrived with my family in the Warsaw ghetto on July 22, 1942. We were wrong in assuming that our living conditions would be any better here than they had been in Lublin, and we soon realized that there was no escape. The same persecution we had experienced in our hometown was awaiting us in Warsaw, with one exception: in Warsaw the *Aktions* and deportations were announced beforehand and took place during the day, with Jewish police participating in the roundups.

The very same day that we arrived, the Warsaw Judenelteste,* the engineer Adam Czerniakow, committed suicide. Czerniakow sacrificed his own life rather than supply the Germans with a list of ghetto inmates for deportation. He did not want to have a hand in exterminating his own people.

Though his death was noble, it did not deter the Germans from their strategy. The deportations in Warsaw operated on the same principle as they had in Lublin: elimination of the non-working element. Only the working segment of the Jewish population retained the right to exist and to live in the ghetto. As a result, new working certificates were issued daily to save as many Jews as possible from death.

*Head of the Judenrat.

As refugees from Lublin, we knew that after each of Himmler's* visits a deportation took place. We also knew that deportations were fatal, and we tried to escape them at all cost. We did not realistically nurture any hope that hiding would enable us ultimately to save our possessions and our lives; yet by the same token, we couldn't believe in our hearts that all the deportees were really being exterminated. It wasn't that we trusted the German promises and assurances; we were convinced that these were all lies and deceptions. But we simply could not assimilate in our minds the idea that they would actually exterminate tens of thousands of able-bodied people at a time when they needed a work force for their war machine. We were naive and wrong, for the Germans perceived us not as workers but as roaches. Our naivete was one of the reasons we did not attempt self-defense.

We also permitted ourselves to deny the possibility of total destruction because of the new workshops which began to multiply like mushrooms after a rain. These workshops were producing all kinds of goods for civilians and for the German army. The management and workers in these shops were strictly Jewish, but the owners were the German Wehrmacht.

In Warsaw, as in Lublin, workshops were called *platzuwkas*, and the people who worked in them were a little better off than others. The security of protection from deportation was only a temporary illusion, but at least these workers were able to come in contact with non-Jews from the city and to exchange personal items for food. Each of the political and social organizations in the ghetto quickly conformed to the requirements and turned its institution into a "workshop" in order to employ its own members. If it did not succeed in gaining status as a workshop, the organization sent its members to the existing ones.

Generally, the workshops were set up so that there were one thousand non-skilled employees to every two hundred to four hundred skilled workers. All workers were furnished with working certificates, which

*Heinrich Himmler was appointed in January 1929 as the head of the SS, with the official title *Reichsfuhrer-SS*. This made him, in effect, second in command to Hitler, with free reign to carry out the mass terrorization, deportation, and murder of the Jews. Himmler built the SS into a massive and deadly police surveillance system, and he also orchestrated the set-up of the death camps in Germany. Himmler was the technical author of the Final Solution.

protected them—so they thought—from deportation. This arrangement led us to believe that our work was essential, and we were tempted to accept the rumors that even those who were deported would be working in factories in a different area. We never received any information of their whereabouts, but we attributed this to the fact that we were cut off from the outside world and that no mail was being delivered to the ghetto.

Because working papers were a life-and-death commodity, an "industry" producing working certificates and Aryan papers came into being. These false papers helped many Jews to escape the city for Czestochowa, Bendzin, and even the forests. The escapes could be undertaken only by those who had a "good" Aryan look.

I had been trained as a nurse before the war, and at that time I was about to leave my job in the hospital. Many people did not believe that the hospitals would be subject to deportations, but I did not share their trust. My patients did not suspect that I was about to leave. Whenever I came to the hospital, they asked: "Nurse Erlichman, how was it in Lublin? What did they do to the patients and the hospitals?" I told them of the tragedy we had suffered in Lublin, and on one occasion I became so immersed in these events that I did not realize how intently the small children in the ward were listening until I saw their frightened faces.

And now the same thing was happening here. Here too the Jews were trying desperately to save their lives, but to no avail.

The first thing I did was to get a work certificate for my mother. I registered her as the wife of her own brother-in-law, but when the *Aktion* started we hid her anyway because we didn't feel secure about her papers. We also had to hide the younger children. Our struggle for such a wretched existence was so hopeless and so tiring that often I just wanted to give up and die.

Each time we saw a man running in the street, we thought that an *Aktion* had started. We hid, each one in a different place. And when we heard shouting — *"Alle Juden herunter!** — we did not heed the command and remained in our apartment; but we were ready with knapsacks on our backs if they should come for us. Whenever we heard the sound of their heavy steps in the corridor, or rapping on the doors, or

*"All Jews come down!"

the throwing of furniture, we trembled with fear. And when we heard them approach our door, our hearts would thump and we would hold our breath. Then, when it became quiet, we would let out a sigh and ask ourselves: "How long can we go on living like this?"

One day during this time my mother and I went to visit my father's workshop in a nearby building. As soon as we entered the courtyard, we were arrested by an SS man. He herded us to a corner of the street where a number of other women were waiting and ordered each woman to "supply," within five minutes, one man from the building. To prove his seriousness, he grabbed hold of an obese woman in the group and threatened to kill her if we did not deliver the quota.

I knew that my father's shop was in that building, and that my brother was working there with him. What if a woman would choose either of them as her candidate? I approached the SS man and told him that I was not a resident of this house. As a reply he kicked me in the back, and I had no choice but to join the others and climb the stairs in search of a man. I thought: Shall I deliver a man for deportation and death, or shall I let that poor woman die at the hand of the German?

In the meantime the murderer was downstairs counting: "Four minutes! Three minutes! . . ."

As the clock ticked away, I became more nervous and more desperate. "Why didn't he take me as a hostage?" I thought to myself. "It would have been so much easier . . . But this poor woman? No doubt a mother of children . . ." She was probably not past forty, but looked much older. The war had aged countless people.

As I raced from door to door, telling the men to hide, I heard another shout from downstairs: "Two minutes! One minute!" These barks were followed by screams and blows. I ran downstairs, not thinking of the potential danger of appearing without my "quarry."

The daughter of the hostage woman was at the feet of the murderer, kissing his boots and begging mercy for her mother. "You must have a mother too," she pleaded in tears. In answer the German kicked her, shouting, "You swine! How dare you mention my mother!" and he kept on kicking her with all his strength until the young woman lost consciousness. He had come on a hunt, and now that he thought he had killed this young girl, he left the courtyard, his blood lust temporarily satisfied.

The hunts were relentless. We were hunted in the streets and we were hunted in our hideouts. The problem was that there weren't enough places to hide in the ghetto. People were relying on miracles, hoping that wherever they were they would not be caught. But I couldn't take the stress anymore and decided to color my hair light blond and get out of the ghetto altogether.

Before I had a chance to leave, another *Aktion* was announced. This time I hid my mother and our younger children in a bunker, while my older brother Yisroel and my sister Chanka hid on the roof. I hid behind a chimney, a few steps away from them. I heard the sound of approaching steps and froze; I was afraid to move my head, because my tinted hair might betray not only me but the others as well.

In a moment, shots and shouts rose from the street, and a series of bullets splattered on the roof. I feared the bullets were directed toward Yisroel and Chanka. "The murderers must have discovered them" flashed through my mind, and each minute seemed to last an eternity. Suddenly I felt that someone was staring at me. I remained riveted to my post, expecting a bullet, but a second went by and I was surprised to find that I was still alive.

It was an innocent Jew who had scared me so much. He too was looking for a hiding place on the roof.

After this terrifying episode I felt I had no strength left to keep hiding, and I resolved firmly to flee the ghetto at any price. Our lives were hanging on a very thin thread, with no prospect of survival. But my decision did not materialize as quickly as I had hoped. I could see no way out of our dreadful situation, and I fell into a deep resignation.

In the meantime the price of food on the black market continued to skyrocket. A kilogram of bread reached the price of a hundred *zlotys*, and we had no way of earning any money. There were workshops which paid a bit of money, but getting into them was very difficult.

My brother Yisroel tried to get a job in a workshop, not for food, but because he wanted to get in touch with the Polish underground, hoping to acquire weapons from them and organize a string of partisan groups.

At the same time, my sisters and I, who could pass for Aryans, decided to return to the familiar grounds of Lublin. We were hoping that we might even be able to reach some village and find work on one of the farms there. We planned extensively and held on tightly to our hopes because we were drowning and had to grasp at straws . . .

Our plan began to seem real when I colored Rochelka's and Justinka's hair blond. Rochelka's looks, however, remained a problem, for in spite of the blond hair her beauty and charm remained visibly Jewish. We had to come up with another alternative for her.

At last we decided to separate. Yisroel, Chanka, and Rochelka remained in the ghetto with my father and baby sister Leah'ke. Yisroel stayed on at his job in the workshop, Chanka resumed her job in the Jewish Community Council, and Rochelka took over my nursing position, using my papers. (It mattered little that she was not a trained nurse. In that time of perpetual emergency, anybody could become anything overnight.) My mother and I were ready to leave the ghetto, along with my eleven-year-old sister Justinka.

I was in charge of preparing knapsacks for the three of us, and in each one I put some of our valuables and a nurse's uniform. All of the hospitals eventually were emptied into the Umschlagplatz, the deportation center, but I knew that nurses were often kept behind to clean up or to help out with administrative tasks. If we were caught, G-d forbid, we could put on the nurses' uniforms, mingle with the staff, and escape at an opportune moment. I was not very worried, for I planned to contact some acquaintances from Lublin who would surely provide me with some money.

September 15, the day of our escape, arrived. Chanka and Rochelka escorted us to the ghetto gate at Gensia Street. To our great disappointment, we had to part without a proper leave-taking. Some Polish women smugglers arrived at the gate, ready to "buy" goods from Jews who were being deported, and in order not to arouse suspicion my two sisters quickly left.

That night we couldn't jump the gate because the *Wach* — the sentry's post — was rigorously kept. We had planned to bribe the guards as a last resort in any case, but escape at night was doubly dangerous because of the curfew. We had no choice but to spend the night in a neglected, broken-down shack, in the company of professional Polish smugglers. Pretending to be one of them, I asked if they had succeeded in buying any special "bargains" from the ghetto Jews, and to show off my cleverness I revealed to them that I was wearing several dresses, a suit, and a coat. (I was very skinny.) I showed them how to pull off this caper, and thus, by assisting them, I was able to convince them that I belonged to their ranks.

All that time Justinka kept quiet, pretending to be asleep, and Mother stayed in the other room. In the darkness, no one saw her.

Soon enough the Polish girls began to talk about what they had seen in the ghetto. One of them said, "The Jews in that ghetto suffer terribly. But what can we do? We've got to make a living." Another spoke of a Jewish woman she had seen on the Aryan side the previous day: "Can you imagine? The woman was wrapped in a sweater and wore a big cross; she surely must have been Jewish. But I didn't want to make a fuss. She'll fall into the hands of the *shmaltzowniks** anyway." A third girl remarked, "If I would have seen a Jewess, I swear, I would have disclosed her to the Germans with no qualms. Why should we be concerned with their fate?"

I feigned avid interest in their conversation, and all the while my heart was bleeding. But I had no choice. If I wanted to live, I had to pretend that I was one of them.

Finally the night came to an end. In the morning each of us paid a "head tax" to the extortionists, the middlemen who had to bribe three sets of border guards and police — Polish, German, and Jewish — to allow us to pass the gate. Even with the bribes our entire venture was a gamble, for we had no idea what would happen to us in the city.

I had faint memories of the Aryan side of Warsaw, but it looked different than I remembered it. The ghetto fence had greatly altered the appearance of the streets. Justinka, Mother, and I proceeded with firm steps, though our hearts pounded wildly. Mother's predicament was much harder than ours. She had changed enormously since we had come to Warsaw. She had always been a strong, healthy woman, full of energy and self-confidence, but now her feet could hardly carry her emaciated

---

*Shmaltzowniks were Polish blackmailers who extorted money from Jews who were disguised as Poles.

body. Her eyes, overcast with heavy fear, drifted around aimlessly, a pattern so characteristic of all the ghetto inmates.

We could not afford to draw attention to the fact that we were a group, for Justinka's looks were more markedly Jewish than mine. Mother crossed the street and began to wander on alone while we kept an eye on her from the opposite side. Suddenly we noticed a band of *shmaltzowniks* approaching her, and we heard them say, "Jewess! Pay now or . . ."

I couldn't leave her alone to deal with those ruthless robbers. I crossed over quickly and tried to make a deal with them, offering them our golden rings, but they would not let us go until I had given them fifty *zlotys* per head. The negotiation had to be carried out swiftly and quietly so that no passersby would notice; according to the German law, a Jew found on the Aryan side was to be killed instantly. But we were lucky. Nothing happened, and we continued to walk without stopping for a moment, more frightened than ever.

Our destination was the train depot, but it was too dangerous to arrive there before dark. In broad daylight someone was bound to recognize us. We walked undisturbed until we reached the center of the town. Then, out of nowhere, two well-dressed Polish "gentlemen" stopped us and demanded our papers. I asked to see their credentials, proof of their right to stop people on the street.

"Of course, dear lady, you are right," they answered, presenting their Gestapo identifications. I showed them my "certificate" with my picture, which proved that my name was Ziutkowska, but they were not satisfied: "Excuse us, lady, but this isn't sufficient. Nowadays everyone has to have working papers and a *kenkarte.** Dear lady, we took special courses in identifying Jews. It is our profession now."

"Oh! It's a very admirable profession," I responded ingratiatingly.

"It's a profession like any other — it brings in income and it's prestigious. Now, let's not hold up the traffic or stir up any attention."

We had been walking all this time, one of the men next to me and the other alongside Mother and Justinka. They requested a "fee" of 1500 *zlotys.* "It isn't much, is it?" my companion asked me.

The amount of money they were demanding was almost all we had

*A general I.D. card required for both Jews and gentiles.

taken with us from the ghetto. The extortionists at the gate and the first band of Poles had already taken a large portion of that sum, and we were only at the beginning of our venture!

Our two polite "gentlemen" expressed their astonishment: "How could you undertake such a journey with so little money and without thinking of all the eventualities?" They finally agreed to take half of their price in cash and half in valuables. I took off the English suit I was wearing and added a few small items, and the gentlemen were satisfied. They excused themselves for the "inconvenience" they had caused, wished us a successful journey, and advised us: "Wait until sundown. We had a hard time recognizing you as Jewish, but your little sister has a very Jewish face. And if no one pays attention to her because she is just a little girl, they will surely pay attention to your mother. Her fear and lack of self-confidence are clearly visible in her eyes." Our two gentlemen bowed politely and departed.

All the time the man was talking I wondered how it was possible that one could remain composed and show confidence, how one could carry on as though nothing were happening. How is it that I had not collapsed in terror at the feet of those two evil men? And yet, this was just the beginning; who knew what lay ahead of us? . . .

After this close call we were exhausted, and we decided to find a small grocery and buy some food. We had almost forgotten how real food tasted. Now, under the clear and open sky, we ate fresh bread with butter and tomatoes. The sun was shining, and for a short moment we forgot the misery of our existence and the danger abiding in every corner. "How is it possible," I thought, "that so much brutality is hiding under such a beautiful sun?" Suddenly, Chanka and Rochelka flashed into my head. I wondered what had happened to them, in what bunker they were hiding now, what had befallen Father and my baby sister Leah'ke. Were they still alive? . . .

I watched the Poles all around me. They were free, running and rushing about their business. They didn't have to hide, they weren't hunted, they could talk loudly, and they could laugh. How strange; I had already forgotten that people can laugh! And thinking about laughter, my brother Yisroel came to mind. How he loved to laugh, and how he had always made us merry! Would I ever hear him laugh again? Would I ever see his shining white teeth and his smiling jet-black eyes?

As if awakening from a beautiful dream, I was suddenly drawn back into the present. I had to decide quickly what to do and where we could go until nightfall. We had time left, and we couldn't stay in a place where so many people were walking around. As we wandered on, we came to a cluster of wrecked houses, and there, in a heap of ruins, we spent the balance of the day.

As we sat there, absorbed in our thoughts, an old Polish woman emerged from a nearby house. She noticed us and came over to offer us a drink of water. It must have been obvious to her that we were Jews, and we were very suspicious of her kindness. A few minutes later she was joined by her neighbor, a young woman, and the two of them shared their problems with us: the Germans had imprisoned the young woman's husband and taken into captivity the old woman's two sons. Both women cursed the Germans, the occupation, and the war.

We sat and listened to them talk as darkness closed in, trying to decide in our minds how we should proceed. We couldn't walk to the railroad station together. I couldn't go alone and leave Mother and Justinka by themselves, because the train schedules now were very haphazard and it might take several hours until the next one arrived. I thought the best plan would be to ask the young woman to go and buy the tickets for us so that we could come to the station only minutes before the train departed, thus minimizing the danger of being discovered. I offered to pay her generously for her effort, hoping that she might understand and help us since she herself had suffered at the hands of the Germans. I gave her the money and she left.

She did return — but not alone. She had brought a Polish policeman! "Not much," he told us. "Only 1500 *zlotys*." I tried to explain our position, begging him to understand, but he remained unmoved. We were out of cash; we had no leverage and could not resist his threats. It seemed our game was up.

He brought us to the police station. Here everything was "legal" and no bribe would help us. We were handed over to an old Polish policeman who was sitting behind a desk. He was annoyed with the young officer who had brought us in; presumably his dinner had been disturbed, and he did not want to be bothered with a lot of lowly Jews. The young man apologized, saying that he had just wanted to make some money, and then quickly withdrew.

That night is deeply engraved in my memory. It was a dreadful night. I remember my dear mother falling at the feet of the old policeman and begging him to spare our lives. I felt a shattering inner shame at that sight. I knew that my mother loved life, but why did she have to humiliate herself to such an extent? And for what? For a miserable existence — for the life of a dog? I couldn't understand her!

"Sir," she pleaded, "have pity on us. For years we have lived together, side by side, and it was good. The Germans are our common enemy, don't you see? . . ."

Of course he did not see — for we found out quickly that he was a Volksdeutsche! He pushed my mother away with his shining boot. Why had she humbled herself before him? Her behavior was beyond my comprehension, but I controlled myself. I was ready to go to my death.

All that time I kept quiet. If I were to die, I wanted to die in complete apathy; I did not want to give this boor the satisfaction of an emotional display. I did not react, but my eleven-year-old sister had different ideas. She approached my mother and in a quiet and even voice said: "Mother, do not cry and do not beg. Keep calm. We have committed a terrible sin for which there is no forgiveness — we were born Jews! For this sin we have to pay with our lives. Let's pay the price quietly and in peace."

A sudden hush engulfed the office. The other policemen turned around, and some even had tears in their eyes. One of them offered Justinka his own supper, but she refused. When he insisted, she took a few bites, but she choked them down amidst her tears.

All this sympathy availed us nothing, for a short time later the three of us were imprisoned, locked up together with several other "professional" criminals.

I became hungry, for we had had nothing to eat since noon. I took off one of the dresses I was still wearing and offered it to a woman smuggler in exchange for bread and a cucumber. We ate in silence, certain that this was the last meal we would ever have.

Somehow the night passed, and in the morning they transferred us to the ghetto prison at Gensia Street. Six policemen, Polish and German, led us through the ghetto. When we passed Novolipia Street, one of my co-workers from our old shop was standing outside, and I saw the shocked expression on his face. I managed to hand him 250 *zlotys* to give to my sister Chanka. I knew we would not need it anymore . . .

Sarah Erlichman managed to make contact with the Gordonia Zionist organization, to which she had belonged in the ghetto. They secured her release from the Gensia Street prison and smuggled her over to the Aryan side once more, charging her with the mission of carrying information to a prominent underground activist in Sosnowiec. However, she was caught again, and on the basis of her papers and non-Jewish appearance was sent to a Catholic nunnery in Katowitz. She refused to take the vows and registered instead to work in an ammunition factory, where she also served as a nurse. She stayed in this factory until the war ended and then spent a short time in France before coming to Israel in 1946. She married and now lives in Afula. Her experiences during the Holocaust are recorded in her book In the Hands of the Defiled.

PROVIDENCE

Helena Gavrielowicz
Krakow, Poland

I began writing down my memories of the war ten years after it ended, and although my recollections were blurred by then, I continued mainly for the sake of my oldest daughter. She was born in the ghetto and suffered with me all the anguish of that era. In addition to being a testimony to Jewish suffering during the Nazi regime, I hope that my memoir will serve as an explanation — and a justification — for why I could not devote as much attention to her as I did to my other children who were born after the war.

The Lines

One deportation had already taken place in Krakow when the Germans encircled the ghetto in June of 1942. No one could enter or leave the ghetto that entire week. Anyone who dared to leave his house took his life in his hands; it was known that any German might shoot a Jew just for the fun of it.

We were ordered to bring all of the sick and elderly to the hospital on Juzefinska Street. My old grandmother had been paralyzed on one side, and I had to take her there on a stretcher.

The hospital was terribly crowded. Simply to reach the front gates,

I had to step over people who were lying on the ground. There were very few "lucky" ones who had come early enough to find a bed. Miraculously, I managed to secure a mattress from someone and very gently settled my grandmother on it. I left her a bit of food and promised to return. She asked for nothing and did not manifest any sort of shock or anxiety; she accepted her fate with the simple statement: "It's a punishment from Heaven!"

I visited her several times a day, each time bringing her something to eat. She begged me repeatedly to stay at home: "Do not run around! They shoot!" And yet each time she saw me, her face lit up with happiness. She behaved as though she were simply a guest in a hotel or convalescent home and I was her visitor, and she felt sorry for the other patients, who had no company. She was alert, constantly concerned for others, and quite insensitive to the dirt, heat, and crowding. Here she was forced to remain for several days.

One day the Germans commanded all the Jews of Krakow to appear on Juzefinska Street to have their documents revalidated. Most people did not consider this order of special importance. On the contrary, they were relieved that the summons entailed no worse inconvenience than the possibility of having to stand in line all day long, as had happened before. My husband decided to avoid the line by going to Juzefinska Street very early in the morning.

The next day happened to be extremely hot, but everyone came and the line was endless. At eight in the morning I went out to bring breakfast to my husband. The crowd was so dense that I did not notice at first that the line had been encircled by Gestapo men. I was trying to make my way to my husband when a man suddenly pulled me aside and whispered in my ear, "Where are you pushing yourself? Don't you see that this line is being deported? Do you want to join them?" The food dropped from my hands. My knees began to tremble uncontrollably and I leaned against the nearest wall.

After a while I went to the Optima, a factory in which had been confiscated by the Germans and was now being used as a deportation center. All the deportees were gathered there, and my husband was very relieved and glad to see me. The first thing he asked was that I prepare a knapsack for him. He then asked what I thought I would do without a certificate, because he had given in both of our working certificates for the Germans to sign, and the papers hadn't been returned. I couldn't think so quickly on the spot and told him that I would rather go home first and see what had happened to my parents. But actually I had already formulated a decision: if the Germans had taken my father's certificate, then we would all go to the deportation together. This seemed the most logical course of action, for I could not just leave my parents to their fate.

The problem, however, was that I was in my seventh month of pregnancy, and there were rumors that the sick, the feeble, and the pregnant would not be deported. The hospital had given me a certificate stating that in my condition I was unable to travel, and I decided to try and use this to our advantage. The first thing I did was to return home and pack a knapsack for each of us, just in case my plan fell through. Then, armed with my hospital document, I summoned all my courage and went to the Optima. I approached the officer on duty, a fat German with the sly, boorish face of a thief. Without even looking up, he flung out his long, fat arm and chased me away. I tried to talk to another German, and then another and another, begging them to release my husband because I could not travel with him.

One of the Jewish policemen saw me running around from officer to officer and warned me that if I did not stop, he would throw me out. I left the office in a daze and began to walk aimlessly in the streets, running back to the Optima from time to time to see if my father was there. In between these trips, I visited my grandmother in the hospital.

The sun was scorchingly hot that day. Tired and sweating, dressed in several layers of clothes, with knapsacks on their backs, the people stood in endless lines and waited . . . and waited.

While I was ambling anxiously in the streets, I saw Heshek Bauminger, a neighbor of ours, sitting on the steps of a house near the Optima. He told me that his parents had been taken away and that the German who had worked for him could do nothing about it. I sat with him until noontime and then continued to wander.

Suddenly someone caught my arm and began screaming: "Where were you all this time? I've been looking for you for an hour! Listen, your husband is in the O.D.*—"Before he had a chance to finish his sentence, I was on my way, running in the direction of the Jewish police station.

I spent a long time in the station because they could not find my identification card, which put me in an extremely vulnerable position; if I was caught without it, I could be deported at any time. The paperwork required by the Germans and the endless registrations and validations did not seem to have a rationale, for the rules changed frequently; on any given day the SS might announce that all those over sixty would be deported, or all those with long noses, or all those whose last name began with "B," or all those with swollen feet, or all those with blue cards or red or yellow cards — or *no* card. To second-guess this absurd strategy was virtually impossible, but most people worked desperately to obtain whatever card was currently valid and hang onto it, for it was believed safest to have one.

While the search was going on, my husband came out and told me that he had been rescued, strangely enough, by the German who was in charge of the deportation. This man had arrived at the Optima and determined quickly that the Jewish police had rounded up more people than the quota required. He gave an order to free the young, able-bodied men who would be useful workers in the German war machine. The next day the deportees left the town, and the *Aktion* ended.

We returned home, consumed with relief and joy at finding all our dear ones together, even though conditions continued to worsen. During this time the Germans reduced the area of the ghetto, forcing more people to share less space. We were now living with two other families in one room and a kitchen on Limanowska Street. Little by little people returned to work and tried to adjust to the increasingly harsh limitations. My baby was born during this precarious time.

A rumor began to circulate that someone had seen the deportees with his own eyes, working and living peacefully in the area of Lublin. People latched onto this rumor with a zealous grasp, for no one was quite ready yet to believe the horrifying truth. Looking back now, I realize that the human will to survive is so great that a man will believe until the very last minute of his life that a miracle will happen precisely to him.

Ordnungsdienst, the Jewish police force, appointed by the Nazis to keep order in the ghetto.

Unfortunately there was plenty of eyewitness evidence to belie these hopeful rumors. Through a concealed window that he carved in the wall of the carpentry shop where he worked, my husband himself witnessed several killings in Plaszow, an area right outside the ghetto confines which housed a factory and labor camp. He told us that once he had seen a transport full of Poles arrive at the camp. They were ordered to strip and put away their clothes in perfect order. Then they were shot in groups of ten. While waiting for the next call, a boy walked over to his bundle of clothes, took out a piece of bread and ate it, and then rejoined his group of ten, who were the next to be killed.

My husband also witnessed the shooting of a little Jewish boy who had been caught with Aryan papers — false non-Jewish identification papers — while he was cutting flowers, totally unaware of his imminent fate.

In the meantime the young people in the ghetto began to organize an underground resistance. Our neighbor Heshek Bauminger arranged a secret meeting in our carpentry shop and tried to persuade me to join the movement. He even promised to arrange a hiding place on the Aryan side of the city for my two-month-old baby Halinka, and maybe even for my mother, but I refused. I could not abandon my family. I had been instrumental in furnishing working papers for all of them, and they depended heavily on my assistance. In addition, I had a better chance of finding support for them through unofficial channels, since my looks were not distinctly Jewish.

In October 1942 the Germans staged another deportation. I hid my little baby in the attic of my husband's carpentry shop, and my mother hid in the cellar. Only my grandmother remained in the apartment. The Gestapo men burst into our shop, screaming and cursing wildly. Without thinking, I instinctively stationed myself at the steps leading toward the attic, where my baby was hidden. This caught the attention of one of the men, and with his weapon in hand he went up the stairs.

By the greatest good fortune, Halinka lay quietly in the attic during the entire search, and because of the darkness the German did not find her. My mother too remained safe in the cellar and was not discovered. The *Aktion* lasted for hours, and all this time we stood and waited.

I was forced to watch helplessly as my father was led to the deportation, clutching his *tallis* and *tefillin* under his arm. Then it came our turn to be taken, but a second time we were the beneficiaries of a miracle; the German manager of the carpentry shop intervened on our behalf, convincing the Gestapo that we were "indispensable workers," and so they allowed us to stay.

The Germans once more decreased the ghetto boundaries and restricted our access to the city. We were only permitted to go out to work in groups, and if one had to enter the city for some other essential errand, he would have to attach himself to a group. On one such excursion I had a frightful experience.

Walking along in the street, I felt suddenly that I was being followed. I froze in fear and for a few moments lost control of my senses. Thousands of feverish thoughts attacked me, and my mind could not work through the chaos. I kept thinking: "What will I do now?"

I stopped in front of a show window. Instinctively, I took a hard apple from my coat pocket and stabbed it with my teeth. The physical exertion of puncturing that apple roused me from my emotional impasse. I had no doubt that I was being followed, but I could now think clearly. I finished the apple, then moved in a deliberately unhurried manner away from the window and slipped nimbly into the shelter of the first courtyard that I passed. I exited on the opposite side and jumped onto the first trolley that came by. This was one of many occurrences which brought me face to face with death, and I credited my survival to a chain of strange coincidences, plus a bit of cunning . . . and providence.

March 13

The Germans proclaimed March 13, 1943, as the date for Krakow to become *Judenrein*, cleansed of Jews. All the Jews were to be expelled by that date. Many dreadful memories of that expulsion still cling to my consciousness.

On March 12, one day before, we smuggled my mother and my baby to hiding places on the Aryan side of the ghetto wall. I had not wanted to do this before, but now there seemed no other choice. For this dangerous venture one had to find a gentile who would be willing to hide a person for a sum of money, and it was also necessary to obtain false Aryan papers to be used as a last resort in the event of discovery. Those who had papers tried to keep low profiles in any case so that they would not be recognized by anyone who had known them when they lived in the city.

Transferring the baby was a perilous undertaking. First we gave her phenobarbital and put her in a traveling bag, but the plan failed; she woke up before we reached the passage gate, and we had to turn back. Next we tried to bribe a Polish policeman, who succeeded in smuggling the baby through a hole in the wall that separated the ghetto from the city.

On the morning of the deadline, my husband was taken to the labor camp in Plaszow. He had escaped deportation twice before, but his luck could not hold out forever. Alone of all the family now, my grandmother and I remained in our apartment, but I found myself in a tremendous quandary; for I too was to be deported, and I did not know how I could leave my grandmother.

I went to visit our neighbors. I watched them packing their belongings, packing and repacking, trying to choose those items that weighed the least and which would be most useful and important for the "trip." Did they know where they were going? . . .

Many workers left that day for the Plaszow camp. People from the Ghetto B, the smaller ghetto into which the non-workers — the "useless element" — had been herded, watched us through the wire fence as we prepared to leave our homes. They were confused and bewildered and feared for their lives; they lingered wretchedly at the fence, despondent and forlorn.

In the Ghetto B I had a cousin, a lonely man whose entire family had been taken in the deportation of last October. Right now he lay in bed with a broken leg, indifferent to his fate, desiring only to die in peace. He knew that the Germans would shoot those who were bedridden, and he did not care — but I was very concerned. Not knowing what else to do, I took an axe, summoned all my strength, and broke the cast on his leg. I forced him to dress, pinned my mother's working number on his coat, and helped him to get into a line. Instead of being sent to the crematoria, he was chosen to go to a labor camp, and at the time this seemed like a victory;

but later on I wondered in anguish if I had acted appropriately, for it seemed that my intervention had only prolonged his suffering. With his broken leg he was assigned to a back-breaking job in the quarry of Zakopane, a mountainous area in the south of Poland, and eventually he perished in the ovens of Auschwitz.

On that morning of the deportation, I remember walking from our now-empty apartment to the marketplace, which was humming with a confused mass of frenzied people. I was torn between my desire to join my husband and the decision I had to make regarding my grandmother. I could do nothing for her, and she knew it. She had accepted her fate some time ago and now lay in bed quietly, dressed of her own volition in her burial shrouds. I wanted to talk to her, but I didn't know what to say. How could I explain to her that I had no choice but to leave her here, which meant certain death? How could I tell her this?

In the end I said nothing, but she understood. She asked no questions and did not reproach anyone; rather, in her quietly dignified manner, she continued to make tactful suggestions to the neighbors about which items they should take along on their "journey." And all the time she kept begging me: "*Nu*, go! Go already, you might be late . . ." We cried and clung to each other, unable to separate.

Finally I left. There was no time to absorb or express our despair.

In the line right next to me stood a woman. One of the Germans discovered her little boy in her skirt and killed him in front of her eyes. I remember, too, another woman who had hidden her baby in a basket, and I remember how the German grabbed that basket and tossed it onto a wagon piled high with scraps.

The calamities visited upon the Jewish people were beyond belief, taking so many varied forms that we could not anticipate them. My own suffering was great, but there were many whose agony was more terrifying than mine. All of the *Aktions* were conducted at such a mad tempo that it robbed us of our ability to think, and this too was a method calculated to destroy the Jewish masses, to wrest from them the last trace of independent thought.

I still remember the overwhelming apathy of this stream of people going to their deaths. The succession of spiraling losses and atrocities turned their minds blank and froze their reasoning processes. Many of them simply lost their feelings and were unable to move — not from fear, but from paralysis. They were benumbed, like mice in a box with no way out.

Anyone who has not experienced this kind of entrapment would never be able to comprehend why so few people put up resistance.

Plaszow

When I came into the Plaszow camp, along with four hundred other women, I saw my husband but was unable to go to him, for as soon as he approached me a Jewish policeman gave him a powerful slap. The women were herded into a gigantic hut, a feeble wooden structure lined with three-level bunks. In the middle of the hut stood three large ovens. Some of the older women tried to get a place near the ovens, where it was warmer, but the younger and stronger ones pushed them aside. It stunned me to see that even here reigned the law of the fist and not that of Jewish compassion and justice.

My unfortunate grandmother came to mind, and I tried to console myself with the thought that perhaps she did not suffer anymore. The next day I learned that the Germans had gathered the elderly who remained in the ghetto and shot them point-blank.

From the minute I stepped onto the ground of Plaszow, I decided that I must try to escape, but my opportunity did not come for two more weeks. Fortunately the camp was still in the initial stages of organization, and the conditions were haphazard. I took advantage of this unsettlement by not responding to any order or registering in any group, something I surely would not have gotten away with at a later time.

One day the Germans ordered an *Aktion* within the camp. The hut was sealed shut, and no one could enter or leave. Pails were brought in for our bodily needs.

Suddenly an uproar rippled through the hut: "They are going to poison us! They are going to shoot us!" Some women fainted, others vomited, and still others screamed in fear. The pails quickly filled up, and the stench became unbearable. In the midst of this hysteria an SS officer walked in and demanded that we relinquish all of our valuables, threatening to shoot anyone who did not obey. To drive home his threat, he fired several random shots which came very near hitting some of the women. In fright, we quickly gave up whatever we had.

Some of the women had entrusted their valuables to Poles who lived in the city, and they were now reassured that this had been a very smart thing to do. Unfortunately, in most instances the Poles who had been given valuables for safekeeping never returned them, and some were even vicious enough to expose the owners to the German authorities, thus assuring that these Jews would be killed and they could then keep all their assets. However, there were also honest Poles who did return most or all of the goods that had been entrusted to them. I personally received all of my jewelry back after the war, an astonishing piece of good fortune.

Many people believed that money and assets would be the answer to everything; and there were others, like my husband, who believed that in such turbulent times assets were of no value and that it did not pay to endanger one's life for them. This was not a practical outlook, for it was virtually impossible to get out of the ghetto and hide on the Aryan side without money — a reality which I was soon to discover.

After I had been in Plaszow about two weeks, an opportunity for escape presented itself. Along with the Jewish inmates there was a small group of non-Jews, mostly Polish intelligentsia, who were also imprisoned in the camp. One day I saw them being marched out of the grounds in a column. I gathered my wits in a flash, removed my arm band, and slid into the line. The Polish prisoners marched all the way into the Aryan side of Krakow, and no one noticed that I was among them. As soon as we were inside the city limits, I dropped out of the line and slipped behind the wall of a building. I was free . . . so to speak.

Thus began a new phase in my life, one in which every step I took was fraught with danger.

Outside

As soon as I set foot on the cobblestones of the city, several Poles with whom I had been acquainted in the "old days" literally attacked me and tried to extort money from me. I was shocked, partly because I had lost most of the little bit of money I still possessed, and partly because of terrible disappointment in the character of the Poles, which I had not anticipated. I refused to accept the help of these blackmailers, realizing at the same time that I had to keep away from them as though from fire. It was fortunate for me that no German was around at the time, and that if these extortionists did report me to the police, they were not able to find me afterward.

I quickly located my mother and baby, and the day after my escape the three of us found ourselves on the street, for I did not have enough money to keep paying for the hideout. My mother became frantic and was on the brink of an emotional breakdown. There happened to be a terrible snowstorm that day, and I had no idea where to turn. We walked in the streets for a very long time. Finally, when we were on the verge of freezing, I thought of Romek, one of our former employees, and we went to his house.

Romek welcomed us with open arms, a surprise which brought home to me the irony of fate. All the time that I was planning my escape from Plaszow and trying to think of people who could help me on the other side, I had never even considered Romek as a safe refuge. It wasn't that I had no trust in him, but he was not very intelligent, and I felt it would have been too dangerous to sign our lives into his hands. However, it turned out quite the contrary; Romek followed my orders blindly, never refusing a request, and more than once he endangered his own life for our sake.

We stayed in his house for two weeks and then moved in with his sister, Zosia, who was equally helpful. We remained in her home until the end of the war. This was a remarkable demonstration of loyalty, for there were very few Poles during the war who kept people without compensation, in light of their own risk.

My greatest concern now was to equip myself with working papers. Otherwise I would become suspicious in the eyes of the gatekeeper of our apartment house. Every resident of a building had to be registered, and if one had no papers, he could not stay longer than twenty-four hours. All the excuses I had made to the gatekeeper had been exhausted already, and I had no alternative but to turn to the German employment office and ask for work. The problem was that there were two clerks there who knew me, but I took the chance.

At the entrance to the employment office I asked the guard if the two clerks were in. He apologized and said that they were both absent today; one was on vacation, and the other happened to be sick. He added that there was a substitute who would take care of me—a substitute, I thought with elation, who would not know me from Adam! I ran up the steps and with one sprightly jump found myself in the new clerk's office. I introduced myself under an assumed Polish identity, and she arranged my papers while I waited. In my wildest dreams I could never have imagined such providence.

The clerk wanted to give me a job in the Madritz company, where many Jews from the Plaszow camp worked during the day. Perhaps the company's objective was to gradually replace the Jewish workers with Polish employees, but in any case my main concern was that none of the Jews there should recognize me and destroy my cover. I managed to convince the clerk to send me to a different company, where I worked as a saleslady until the end of the war.

With my "legal" working papers safe in hand, I next went to the Statistics Office. There I registered as an unmarried woman with an illegitimate child, putting down both my own name as it appeared on my false document and my daughter's name. My rationale was that the authorities would not bother to trace the father of an illegitimate child, and my assumption proved correct. We were now legal "gentiles."

Soon after I began to work, Romek helped me contact my husband, who was sent in to the city every day from Plaszow to work in the Optima factory. Romek's nondescript appearance proved to be a valuable asset. He would stand near the gate of the Optima, casually leaning on an umbrella, and since his appearance did not arouse any suspicion, he was able to visit my husband twice a week and deliver messages. I tried to convince my husband through these messages to leave the Optima and run away from Krakow, but the plans were made too late. On the day he was to leave, Plaszow was completely sealed off, and an escape became impossible.

Nearly a year passed. One day on my way to work I came across a Polish woman whom I recognized. She had formerly owned a store in the city, where I had often shopped when I wore my arm band with the Star of David on it. My first instinct was to run, for if anyone recognized me I would have to flee the neighborhood and look for a new apartment. But such sudden action would surely have seemed suspicious, and so I did the opposite; I walked close by her, relying on the premise that she would never suspect a Jewish girl from Krakow of the audacity of taking her life in her hands by walking around freely on the Aryan side of the city. Even I was amazed at the boldness of my own ploy, for since leaving the ghetto I had not changed my hairdo, my clothes, or my coat, and I had not colored my hair. The woman had plenty of evidence to jog her memory, but she did not respond to my presence, and I took this as a sign that she had not recognized me.

One Sunday we met again. The benches on the avenue were ordinarily occupied on a Sunday afternoon, but I had found an empty one and was sitting quietly when I saw the woman walking toward me with a little girl by her side. They happened to sit down right next to me on the bench, and we began to converse. Suddenly she cocked her head at me with an oddly scrutinizing look and asked, "Didn't you once come to shop in my store?"

I was prepared for this and answered calmly, "Possibly. I'm here only a short time, but when I was looking for an apartment, I stopped at several places in the city."

She remarked, "You resemble a teacher, a good friend of mine from Lwow."

With a broad smile I thanked her for the compliment and motioned to my mother to come over and make a new acquaintance. From then on, she and my mother became good friends. They kept each other's place in line to get milk for the girls, who were the same age, and I kept a place for her on the bench every Sunday.

The Underground

During this period, one of my friends who was also in hiding on the Aryan side helped me to contact a Jewish smuggler who went by the name Wladek. At that time it was still possible to smuggle people out of the country, and many Jews were saved this way. Wladek smuggled people across the Polish border into Hungary. His height and blond coloring made it difficult to identify him as a Jew, so for a while he was able to carry out his operations undetected.

When I sought out Wladek, my heart and mind were focused constantly on one person only — my husband. I prayed against hope that somehow I would find a way to get him out of the Plaszow camp where he was held, even though it was now completely sealed off. My wish could not be realized in the meantime, but I found that if I could not help my husband right now, I could be of service to others. I had another relative who was imprisoned, and Wladek and I made a deal: he would smuggle my brother-in-law out of Skarzysko, a closed labor camp near Radom, and across the border to Hungary; I would pay part of his fee immediately and the balance when he returned.

On the day that I was to meet Wladek in his apartment, I made sure that my mother and daughter were sitting on a bench near the building, at some distance but close enough to keep an eye on me in case of any dangerous development. I was not worried about my mother because a middle-aged woman of Aryan appearance with a little girl at her side would not arouse any suspicion. I entered Wladek's building most carefully, but again I had the hauntingly familiar feeling that someone was following me.

Wladek's apartment was located all the way in the back, near the exit of the house. I walked through the hallway nonchalantly, looking at the numbers on each door to give the impression that I did not know exactly where my party lived. I did not want my visit to look prearranged. When I reached Wladek's door, I put my hand on the knob and was about to turn it when I happened to glance through the peephole. I saw many people in the front room, and it seemed to me that one of them fleetingly signaled to me with his hand. To this very day I do not know if this really happened or if it was just an illusion, but I instinctively withdrew. I stepped back slowly as though I had made a stupid mistake and walked down the steps and out of the house.

My mother told me afterward that when she saw me she didn't

recognize me. I was white as a sheet and could not utter a sound. Only after a few moments, when I had recovered myself, was I able to tell her what had happened. There is no doubt in my mind that it was my deep intuition that saved me from death — a precious asset which served me more than once.

I later learned that the Gestapo had been on Wladek's heels for some time. At the time of my visit, detectives had already surrounded the house, and anyone who walked into his apartment was arrested. The next day all the people I had seen in his living room, with the exception of a few foreign citizens, were shot in Plaszow, including Wladek himself. I had escaped death by a hair's breadth — but my best friend Leika was not so lucky.

Leika too had escaped the Germans' grasp and was living in the city disguised as an Aryan. One day her former maid recognized her in the street and disclosed her identity to the Gestapo. I used all my resources to secure her release, but I did not succeed. She was shot on the hill in Plaszow. Her murder was a terrible shock to me, and immediately afterward I began to involve myself actively in the *Armia Ludowa*, the leftist Polish underground. I hoped that through underground contacts I might still find some way to help my husband escape. While I waited for this fragile hope to materialize, I made contact with a Hungarian boy who became my smuggling liaison. I did not trust him as I had trusted Wladek, but with his aid I did succeed in helping a number of other people to safety.

The man who headed the *Armia Ludowa* in Krakow was named Orlosh. I learned of him from Mr. Morgenbesser, a Jewish refugee who, on my recommendation, stayed in Romck's house for several days before escaping to Hungary. Mr. Orlosh and I met several times and explored many different strategies for rescuing people, most of whom were not Jewish. He furnished me with several sets of false Aryan documents, with which I succeeded in getting apartments for a number of escapees. Mr. Orlosh knew nothing about me, not even my address; if I needed him, I contacted him by telephone. I never had any evidence that he suspected my Jewish identity.

Once during a phone call he seemed quite agitated and demanded that I meet him immediately. At the rendezvous he informed me that he had taken into his home a Jewish professor from Czechoslovakia. The professor had a broken leg and was riddled with lesions and lice. To make matters worse, he had no documents and neither spoke nor understood Polish. The neighbors had begun to take an interest in him, and it was of the utmost importance to move him to another place before he was investigated.

I knew of several apartments that were used as temporary resting places by fugitives on their way to Hungary, and I took Mr. Orlosh to one that had just become vacant. We arranged everything in a hurry, including the finances, and only one obstacle remained: how to transport the Czech professor to the new apartment without attracting attention. Quickly I thought of a plan.

It was Christmastime, and there were many drunkards roaming the streets. Without wasting a moment I called Romek, and together we carried the professor into a horse-drawn carriage, informing him that for the duration of the ride he would assume the role of a hopelessly inebriated man. We laughed heartily and told silly jokes as we rode in a "drunken stupor" through the entire city, including the Gestapo quarter. Finally we reached the apartment, safe and sound — but here a new problem arose.

The professor refused to leave the carriage. He broke down, screaming at us to let go of him and crying that he was tired and did not want to live anymore. I summoned all of my physical and emotional energy to calm him down, and then, with some sort of hidden strength that I did not even know I possessed, I carried him in my own arms to the apartment. Orlosh gave me money every month to deliver to the professor, and later on he took the money there himself. The professor, for the meantime, was safe.

One day when I phoned Orlosh, a woman answered and told me that he wasn't home. I called again, and again I received the same answer. I understood that something must have happened to Orlosh, and I went to his apartment.

His wife invited me in. She told me that he had been arrested and that the Gestapo interrogators had tortured him into giving out many names and addresses, including the hiding place of the professor. Providence had intervened for me once again; Orlosh had not disclosed my address because I had never given it to him — but he did inform them of my "Polish" first name, Marysia. This revelation made my blood freeze, and I left without asking the woman any further questions, for something about her seemed suspicious. From there I went directly to the professor's apartment building.

The landlady's daughter told me that the professor had been arrested. She had been sitting on the window sill of her front room when she noticed a car pulling up outside the house. Petrified, the girl immediately climbed out the first-floor window and hid in the bushes, afraid that they were looking for her or her mother; no one knew when the Nazis might come to take people away, even on the most irrational of charges. From her hiding place in the bushes, the girl saw a few Gestapo men get out of the car and knock at the door of the professor's apartment. When no one answered, they broke down the door and burst in, and a few minutes later they emerged with the professor, who was white as chalk and could hardly drag his feet. The Gestapo sealed the apartment, and the girl's mother fled the city.

Although Orlosh had given the Gestapo my Polish name, no one came after me and there were no further consequences of that incident. I continued to work diligently at my job and to lead an outwardly normal life — whatever normal meant in that perverted context.

Ironically, my diligence worked against me, for my boss decided to promote me to manager of one of the branch shops, which happened to be located in what had formerly been the Jewish section of the city. He took me in a carriage to the shop and introduced me to the managerial staff, and all the time I was quaking. I had frequented this neighborhood in the days before the war and had even worked there, and I feared desperately on two counts: one, that someone would recognize me and expose me as a Jew, and two, that anyone who did recognize me would suspect me of collaboration with the Germans. But I had no logical reason to turn down the position.

My sojourn in the company was one of the most nerve-wracking periods of my life. Every time a door opened, every time I heard the slightest scratching sound, my heart would leap into my throat and cut off my breath; all I could think of was that perhaps they were coming to arrest me now.

I went to consult a close and trustworthy friend of mine to ask him how I could get out of this predicament, but once more the hand of providence intervened. Only a short time later, the Gestapo made a surprise inspection in the shop, causing a fearful commotion and leaving the workers paralyzed until their search was complete. When they finally left, I realized I had the perfect excuse. I went to the chief administrator and told him that I could not cope with the pressure of managerial responsibility under such trying conditions and that I preferred to return to my former job as a clerk. Thankfully, he consented.

In 1944, on a pleasant summer day, I met Romek on my way home from work. When I approached him, he said quietly, "Come to my house. A man is waiting there for you. He escaped from the Plaszow camp and has regards from your husband. He hopes that you'll see your husband soon."

At first I was stunned and didn't know what to do. Maybe it was a trap. Then I rationalized that if the man had found his way to Romek, he could surely find his way to me if he wanted to, so I had nothing to lose. I followed Romek to his house.

The man's name was Sheidlinger. He was still carrying the sign of his imprisonment, a cross which had been shaved onto the back of his head, and Romek urged him to cut his hair as soon as possible to erase it. Sheidlinger told me that he believed my husband would soon find a way to escape, explaining that at this point escapees were not being killed on the spot but were only given a beating. His assurances gave me the wildly fragile hope that I would soon be reunited with my child's father.

In the meantime the war was drawing to an end. Soviet troops had finally begun to close in, and I heard from connections in Plaszow that the Germans were making desperate attempts to erase the atrocities they had committed by burning graves and deporting the prisoners.

On the crest of this promising turn of events came the most devastating news: I learned that on October 15, 1944, my husband had been deported from the Plaszow camp to Germany.

When I heard this, my hopes crashed to the ground. I lost all my desire to live. I could not make peace with the thought that after I had endangered my life by staying in Krakow all these years for the express purpose of maintaining contact with my husband, I had lost him. All these years I had continued to encourage him to look for a way to escape; all these years I had nourished the hope that one day he would find the courage and the opportunity to run away. I had put my life in utter peril to help so many other people, constantly running, exerting myself, arranging apartments and hideouts for total strangers — and for the person closest to me I could do nothing!

I became indifferent and lost interest in everything. For a while I trudged to and from my responsibilities in a fog of despondency, unable to summon the strength to perform daily tasks or to concentrate on my work. When I was on the brink of complete emotional exhaustion, I was shocked back into reality one day by a neighbor of mine, who approached me out of the blue and said: "There are rumors going around in our building that your child has a Jewish father."

I was dumbfounded. To all outward appearances, and according to all my documents, I was considered an unmarried woman with an illegitimate child! Suddenly a flood of rage suffused me, and all my survival instincts came rushing back to the surface. I nearly struck the woman. I began to scream at the top of my voice, using the one method of psychological intimidation that was most likely to have an effect: "Tell me immediately who told you that lie! If you do not tell me this instant, I'll turn to the police and file a claim of slander against you. I'll tell them *everything I know about you and your friends!*"

I knew that almost all the Poles at that time were involved in some sort of illegal business or other — the black market, foreign currency, and the like — and I took the chance that this woman too had something to hide. Apparently my tirade was the last thing she expected, for she looked at me open-mouthed and gave me the name of the man who had ostensibly told her the "lie." Then she quickly turned on her heel and hastened away.

I told my mother about the incident, and together we tried to decide how best to meet the crisis. If my true identity had really become known, the safest thing would be to stop working, move to another apartment, and go into hiding, but this was not feasible. I had to work in order to pay for food and rent, and there was no telling how long the war would go on, so we could not stay in hiding indefinitely. At this point I did not even have a vacant apartment which we could use as a hideout. What an irony — I had been able to supply so many refugees with hideouts, and when I needed an apartment for myself, there was none!

I was left with only one option: to intimidate the person who had spread the rumor about my child's "Jewish father."

I looked up the name that the woman had given me and ran down to the man's apartment. He turned out to be a middle-aged man, and it was not difficult to tell that he was entirely dependent on his wife and daughter. I barged into his front room in a white rage and laid all my cards out on the table: "I hear that you are spreading lies about me and my child. Do you know what such rumors mean today? Do you think that you can talk with contempt about my daughter because she doesn't have a father? Do you think I'll tolerate it? *I will not!* I will take whatever action is necessary to stop these vicious lies!"

Turning toward the door, I added, "I've got nothing more to say to you now — *but you'll hear from me yet!*" As I pulled the door open, he caught my hand, but I broke loose and dashed out of the building, weak and breathless.

Later on he came up to our apartment in a state of extreme agitation. He kissed my mother's hand and said apologetically, "It's a terrible mistake. I did not say a word to anyone. Now my wife and daughter want to chase me out of the house . . ."

"It's none of my business," I snapped. "And if you want to live in peace, then take back all you've said!"

He apologized and assured me that it would never happen again.

That was the last encounter that seriously endangered my survival on the Aryan side. In fact, when my neighbors heard of the manner in which I had defended my family's "reputation," I gained even greater respect from them, and I was able to live quietly in the city without further suspicion from then on. This in itself was miraculous, for there were very few Jews who managed to sustain an Aryan cover for the entire duration of the war.

Shortly after this incident Krakow was liberated, and we were free.

Helena Gavrielowicz, along with her mother and young daughter, survived the war together. Helena was reunited with her husband, and the entire family moved to Israel. They presently reside in Jerusalem.

THE LIAISON AGENT

Chavka Raban-Folman
Warsaw, Poland

The Hechalutz Center

My parents were always enormously proud of me as a young girl. I was their only daughter, and they frequently showed me off, asking me to recite poems and to perform for any visitors who came to our house in Warsaw. I used to enjoy playing a lion, imitating its roar with all my strength and powers of mimicry. My brothers would always taunt me: *"Nu,* make a lion!" But their remarks did not deter me; on the contrary, I felt spurred to improve my performance. I looked upon my brothers as being too superficial and shallow to understand the importance of acting. Their attitude toward me changed greatly later on during the war, when I began working in the underground — the most challenging and dangerous "role" I would ever play.

As a youngster I attended a Polish public elementary school, and then a Zionist high school for girls called the Judeah School. It was a respected institution, with a respected staff; one of our teachers was Emanuel Ringelblum, the famous historian who would soon become the keeper of the underground archives of the Holocaust. My classmates were mostly from well-to-do families, daughters of Zionist leaders. Many of these

124

friends emigrated to Palestine after their graduation.

This was the first time that I had formally studied Hebrew. The school was very expensive, but even though we didn't have much money, the importance of a Jewish education was paramount to my father, and he was insistent that we learn Hebrew.

During my senior year a group of youngsters organized a learning circle called *Dror* (meaning "freedom"), under the leadership of Antek (Yitzchak) Zukerman, one of the members of our group. Antek was eight years older than I, a young man of strong conviction and social conscience. He convinced many of us to join the learning circle, where we studied various subjects as well as Zionist philosophy. We also spent many hours discussing the threatening drift of events in the world; but the reality of our own blackening situation did not strike me until one afternoon when a group of young anti-Semites accosted us in the park. Instead of fighting back, my friends and I tried to engage them in an ideological discussion. We invited them to sit down and asked them: "Why do you hate Jews?" We thought we might succeed in showing them that their ideas were wrong. How naive we were! Their vicious, irrational responses, the poisonous look on their faces, opened my eyes for the first time to the scope of the danger that surrounded us.

That summer I attended a camp in Kazimierz run by the school, and I returned home one day before the war broke out.

In October 1939 the Germans invaded Poland and took over Warsaw, and a chapter of the highest degree of Jew-hatred in history began to unfold in front of our eyes. One of the first decrees issued by the Nazis was to close all Jewish schools. We children understood the importance of education and immediately set to work to organize our studies in private homes. When we began to understand that the Nazi regime was not just a temporary aberration but a long-term threat, Antek Zukerman decided to set up a *gymnasium*, or high school, under the supervision of the Dror movement which he had started. My brother Marek took over the directorship of the school, and I became one of its first students. The gymnasium began to operate in 1940, before the ghetto was closed.

The Dror school was not just a course of study. It meant active participation in the organization and its ideals, an identification which became supremely important in those days of escalating danger. I belonged to the children's group in our organization; most of the members were ten years older than I, but my dedication was no less fierce. My first act of membership was to move into the dormitory of the Hechalutz Center at 34 Dzielna Street, a building which housed many organized group activities. Although the Center was right across the street from my home, it was like moving to a different world. Here I came under the influence of our excellent teachers, including the great poet Yitzchak Katzenelson. Our studies were on a very high and intensive level. Katzenelson instructed us in the Prophets, and his teachings in particular left a permanent imprint on my entire life.

There was an ongoing and fiery debate in all the ghettos at that time about the relative virtues of organizing an active resistance — a resistance which would be doomed to failure in any case. I remember being impressed by the fact that Katzenelson, a great thinker, identified himself with the resistance movement. He tried to make us feel that we were part of the suffering Jewish nation and that regardless of our tragic situation we were never to lose faith in a better tomorrow. However, our better tomorrow tarried infuriatingly, and conditions in Warsaw worsened from day to day.

To camouflage our true activities on Dzielna Street, we labeled our building as a center for refugees, and indeed, seventy people who were refugees from Lodz and other towns lived there. The building had several single rooms for lodging and a large dining room for the refugees, but the major activities that took place there were those of Dror.

In the Hechalutz Center we lived a *kibbutz*-style life. Everyone had to work. We cleaned the entire house at night, and during the day we studied. Hundreds of people visited our Center, and the activities expanded even as the danger grew. Here our friend Tovia Borzykowski issued his first publications. Once when the Germans made an inspection, he ran to the attic to hide, taking his typewriter with him. We also had a sewing machine sitting out in one of the front rooms, and whenever the Germans came we would quickly abandon our activities and show them that we were simply doing manual work.

As we worked together, the ghetto closed down and the hunger grew. Once the Center sent me out to do housekeeping chores in my parents' house as part of my duties. My mother begged me to eat some food that she had prepared, but I adamantly refused. I did not want to eat when others in the Center were starving. I remember that even when I was sick I continued to work. My mother again begged me to eat, but again I refused. She then went to Tzyvia Lubetkin, one of my friends in the *kibbutz*, to ask her to intervene. Tzyvia came and insisted that I was allowed to eat because it was *pikuach nefesh*, an emergency measure necessary for survival, and so I conceded and ate.

Some people in our group did not fare well under the increasing hardships. I remember in particular a girl named Chancia. Chancia was born to enjoy life. When the sun was out, she could often be found lying down and warming herself in its glowing rays . . . She was always immaculately dressed — a difficult accomplishment in the ghetto in those days — and the whiteness of her sweater sparkled. Although she was so clean and always wore gloves, she contracted scabies just like everyone else in the *kibbutz*. I too eventually fell prey to this horrible condition.

My close friends, most of whom were older than I, were very active in the movement, especially Antek, Tzyvia, Tovia, and Frumka Plotnicka. Antek and Tzyvia were the ones who influenced me most. They molded my character and left their signatures on my thoughts and actions during the war and all through my life. They were also very close to my family; in fact, Antek and my brother Marek, who were the same age, were best friends, and it was thanks to the two of them that the ghetto gymnasium had opened.

My friendship with Antek and Tzyvia was something I never experienced before or after the war . . . We lived together and we starved together. I was at Antek's side when he received the news of the destruction of the Jews of Vilna, his beloved hometown. His entire family perished in that catastrophe. Everyone in our group admired Antek greatly, and his frame of mind affected us powerfully. I remember how strongly moved I was by his great loss.

The Polish Shiksa*

The ghetto closed, the hunger grew, and the cold of that winter of 1940-41 was unbearable. Hundreds of people died daily in the streets, and the sight of corpses on the sidewalk was a familiar one. That winter, when I was fifteen years old, the underground endowed me with a special mission: I became a liaison agent. I was entrusted with the sensitive tasks of making contact with others in the movement, bringing reports, and delivering publications to various cities annexed to the Reich. The Germans had officially prohibited Jews from congregating and had also forbidden travel, with the result that contact between organizational groups in different cities could be maintained only with extreme difficulty. With forged documents I was able to rent a room on the Aryan side, and I lived part time in the city under an assumed Polish name, part of the time in the ghetto, and most of the time on the road. My studies had to be abandoned.

The underground had begun to prepare special documents for the Jews and to falsify identification cards, and my first assignment was to go to Krakow and deliver material to produce such documents. Needless to say, these trips were extremely dangerous, but their value could not be overestimated. A report that our organization in Warsaw continued to function, that we planned an uprising, that people were not dispirited, were all of critical importance to the Jews in Krakow and in other more secluded places. I remember that I once traveled by horse-drawn wagon, under my assumed identity, to an isolated town. The people were elated at my visit and begged me to come once more, and I promised that I would; but before I had a chance to return, the town was liquidated.

My underground activities made a great impression on my brothers. I was no longer their "little sister," but an equal. In every situation and in every place to which the war dragged me, the thought that my brothers were alive motivated me to continue to struggle. They were young, courageous, and daring; and if I had known that they had perished, I wouldn't have fought so hard for my own life.

My oldest brother, Vovek, was ten years my senior. He was strong and fearless and had a great deal of common sense. Industrious and

*Gentile woman.

unafraid of challenges, Vovek joined the P.P.R., the *Polska Partia Robotnicza*, the Polish leftist underground national army, and his official assignment was to falsify documents. Later on he joined the partisans under the Polish cover name Watzlav Marchiniak.

Vovek was an architect by profession. Before the war he had been an assistant to a Jewish architect, and together they had undertaken an ambitious project, a plan for a modern settlement for working-class people. The nature of his work brought Vovek into contact with members of leftist and Communist circles. These people provided him with Aryan documents, which he used to smuggle his own family and several of his wife's relatives to the Aryan side. He found places for his wife and child in Zhilibizh, a suburb of Warsaw; for three of his wife's brothers, one of whom he placed in a gentile home; and for my mother, who had a "good" Aryan face. The only person he could not help was my father. Father had a very Jewish face, and Vovek spent much time trying to prepare hiding both for him and for Yitzchak Katzenelson. He was tough; he did not wait for things to happen but moved them on his own.

My other brother, Mordechai Yitzik — or Marek, as we called him — was more delicate, but during the war he hardened. He fought in the forest and was an active member of the underground *kibbutz* movement in Bendzin, which gave aid to refugees. Though I loved both my brothers, I felt closer to Marek, perhaps because he was very sensitive and closer in nature to me.

My brothers and I saw each other sporadically once we became involved in the underground. For a while I worked together with Vovek, trying to smuggle groups of young *chalutzim** out of the ghetto to join the underground forces on the Aryan side. We also began to search for arms supplies. Any brief contact between the three of us was treasured beyond description, moments that we snatched from the compelling prison of our activities and the danger they entailed.

Because of my Polish looks I was soon able to penetrate as well to the Polish underground, the *Armia Ludowa*. I told them that I wanted to help them, and they allowed me to choose my own cover name. I decided to call myself Eva Marchiniak, choosing the same family name my brother

*Literally, pioneers; young people who aspired to immigrate to Palestine and build up the country.

had used. This was convenient, for we looked very much alike, and at meetings I could identify myself as his sister and communicate freely with him. The *Armia Ludowa* furnished me with excellent papers which made my travels much easier, and I was able to pass along much of the information I gathered to the Jewish underground.

On April 17, 1942, the Germans came to the Warsaw ghetto with a list of all the Jewish intelligentsia, prepared to arrest any whom they could find. They came to 34 Dzielna Street, looking in particular for my friends Antek Zukerman and Tzyvia Lubetkin, leaders of the underground. Antek and Tzyvia were not in the building when the Germans came — but a number of other people were there, including me.

When we heard the signal, some of us ran to hide in the attic. Several remained where they were and introduced themselves as refugees. When the Germans could not find Antek and Tzyvia, they arrested a neighbor and his son and killed them instead. The next morning I went to Tzyvia and Antek in their hiding place to report what had happened. On the way I saw many dead bodies, and I recognized among them several Jewish leaders I had known.

The youth of the ghetto began to organize and to prepare themselves for an uprising. I too learned to handle weapons; the suitcase under my bed on the Aryan side contained the first stockpile of weapons reserved for the organized fighting division in the ghetto. I was now living mostly on the Aryan side, but after each journey that I made I always returned to the ghetto, which was home to me; there I had my friends, warmth, everything I needed to keep me going, but unfortunately I could never stay as long as I wished. I had to continue my work on the Aryan side and to keep traveling on assignments.

I learned to sleep in any place I found myself, whether it was on the floor or on a bench in the railroad station. I was often sent to places where no Jew should be found, and I got away with this only because I was blond, with the face of an eighteen-year-old *shiksa*, and my Polish accent was perfect. I always carried a Polish translation of a book by Marcel Proust to give myself an "intellectual" air, and I would frequently strike up friendly conversations with other passengers on the trains. Whenever the talk turned to Jews, I had to join in — and if I wanted to avoid suspicion I could not use mild language. For a very long time, no one suspected that I was Jewish.

Many times I felt instinctively that I was being followed, and I was always afraid, even though I had learned to behave with robust self-confidence. Once, when I was traveling with a packet of false documents secured to my belt, the Germans made an inspection on the train. I was sitting next to a man with whom I had been having a friendly chat. When one of the German officers approached me, this man put in a word for "a nice, innocent girl," and the German left without investigating me. Was it fate? Was it a miracle? . . .

Chrobieszow

Most often I traveled to Chrobieszow, one of the strongest pockets of the underground, where I was always welcomed warmly. I knew all the buildings of that branch and all the members, who eagerly awaited my reports of the activities of our organization. We met mostly at the homes of Aaron Frumer or Bracha Kamm, and though the road from Warsaw to Chrobieszow was long and dangerous, I looked forward to those trips.

Frumka Plotnicka and I made this journey together on one occasion. We bribed the Jewish guard at the ghetto gate, hastily removed our arm bands, and jumped onto the first trolley car that came along. Our mission this time was to meet with our friends in Chrobieszow and prepare them for the possibility that our contact with them might be severed. At that time, during the spring of 1942, the first detailed reports of the gruesome slaughter of the Jews in Vilna and the surrounding areas had just come to light, but life in the Warsaw ghetto continued as usual. No one spoke of mass killings or gas chambers; the resistance movement was thought of as a reaction to repression, but the idea of mass extermination had not reached the surface of Jewish consciousness, and no one wanted to admit its possibility. Frumka and I were not quite prepared for what we saw on this trip. We really did not know how serious the danger was.

As the train trundled along, I looked at Frumka. What a tranquil face she had! She did not look very gentile, but she was dressed elegantly and her lips were painted red to improve the masquerade, a suggestion to which she had agreed with reluctance. Frumka was always the first one to volunteer to travel and was never concerned that her looks might betray her. I thought that her self-confidence and composure lent an Aryan expression to her demeanor.

The rail line from Warsaw to Chrobieszow was the most dangerous one. At stops in intersections there was often an eight- to ten-hour wait, during which travelers' documents were meticulously scrutinized. We had to present our forged papers with ease and assurance and do our utmost to quell the hammering of our hearts. If the gendarme lingered over the inspection of the signatures on these homemade documents, my nerves would tighten so much that I felt my heart might explode at any moment.

This time as we approached the Chrobieszow station, we saw an unusual concentration of people on the platform and a great deal of movement. Unaware of what was happening, we stepped down from the train, only to find that we were the only travelers who had disembarked at that station. We realized that these masses of people were Jews. Men, women, and children stood pressed against each other, trying to hold on to their bedding and bundles. Screams and crying mingled with the barks of the Germans. Then we noticed four fat, red-faced Germans on horseback, galloping along the platform, swinging their whips on all sides and treading upon people and their packages, aiming purposely at mothers with little children. All this took place under the rays of a golden sun, shining in the clear sky.

I looked at Frumka. She was terribly pale. Without words we grasped the gravity of the situation, yet we couldn't leave the place. Flight would attract attention, and in any case we were intent on making contact with our underground friends. We entered the waiting room, which was void of passengers. Even the Poles had refrained from leaving their homes that day; perhaps they were under curfew.

I begged Frumka to sit down, hoping to shield her from the sights on the platform. She perched on a bench, her gaze turned blindly at a random point in the distance. I stayed at the window and looked outside.

I saw a German officer leading four very bewildered-looking young men wearing traditional black *kapotas* (long coats). They were given spades and ordered to dig a pit. The murderer lashed them with a horse whip, ordering them to work faster. Minutes later their bodies were sprayed with bullets, and they fell into the pit they had dug.

The German forced another group of Jews to cover the grave with dirt, and he then returned to the square to continue whipping and killing. A woman's scream was heard, then a shot. The woman fell to the ground, dropping a baby from her arms, and in another moment horse hooves trampled its tiny body. At once the mass of thousands fell silent. A wave of dizziness spun my head, and I had to catch the window sill to keep from falling to the floor. My first thought was that Frumka should not see this horrifying sight.

Someone entered the waiting room, and I knew we had to disappear quickly. I forced out a smile, took Frumka by the hand, and led her from the station.

We walked in the direction of the town. The road was filled with wagons carrying sick and elderly Jews. Our hearts were crying that sunny day, and yet we had to wear our smiles of disguise, our Polish tickets to safety. We had to pretend that it was a beautiful day and a perfectly ordinary world . . .

We passed the alleys and side streets we knew so well; we passed the place where Aaron Frumer lived. No human being could be seen there now. I told Frumka to remain downstairs while I climbed to the second floor. The apartment was desolate; each corner, so familiar to me, was screaming with emptiness now. The doors were wide open, and all kinds of things were spread out on the floor, even the bedding.

Frumka looked at me. We needed no words. She asked, "Where do we go from here?"

As we stood undecided under the awning of the building, we saw a group of young Poles marching through the center of the town with two Germans following close behind. The Poles were pointing out the hideouts of the Jews. They carried hatchets which they would use to knock down doors and to break open the hiding places where the Jews had stored their valuables.

We went out into the street and began to walk through the half-vacant city. After a short time we realized that people in the street were beginning to pay attention to us, and we had to walk with confidence, as though we knew our destination. We proceeded toward the church, and at the gates we bought violet wreaths. Frumka stayed in the church yard while I went out to do some investigating in the town. Moving about was not as dangerous for me as it was for Frumka, since my appearance was less suspicious.

I approached several familiar houses. All were deserted, the doors flung wide open. In a "casual" conversation with a storekeeper I learned that the Jewish youth had been concentrated on the outskirts of the town and would be led away separately, apart from the other Jews, because they were young and useful for work. "The others, dear lady, are going to be wasted . . ." the woman said with a smile of satisfaction, and I had to answer back with a smile.

"How can I reach the young people?" I asked, as if out of evil curiosity.

"It's impossible to reach them. They are guarded by the Ukrainians," she explained with the smug air of someone who holds important knowledge.

"And yet, I would like to see them . . . it might be an interesting sight," I replied in a low and composed voice.

"This is impossible, lady. You can't go there — not today. Maybe tomorrow."

I returned to Frumka at the church and shared the news with her. We decided to stay until the next day because we were very anxious to make contact with our friends. We knew it was not a wise choice to stay overnight in a local hotel, where we might attract attention, but if we wanted to meet our friends we had no choice.

As we registered our names on the hotel roster, the owner babbled defensively in a confidential tone of voice: "Nowadays — and especially today — I've got to be careful with all formalities. You do know, dear ladies, that they look for Jews even in our place. But this, of course, wouldn't concern you — would it?"

Her little ploy yielded no result. I burst into loud, almost hysterical laughter, and replied: "Dear lady! What a wild idea!"

She gave us a key, and we went up to our room. Finally we were alone. Night fell and dragged on forever; we couldn't fall asleep. Frumka caressed my head without uttering a sound. It was a great relief not to have to wear our metallic smiles when our hearts were bleeding.

Finally the blessed dawn broke through, and we thought we might finally fall asleep now, at least for a short time, but suddenly a staccato knock at the door jarred the stillness. "It's only an inspection," came a voice from the hallway. Apprehensive about Frumka's semi-Jewish looks, I pulled the blankets over her head and opened the door. Two people in civilian dress came in and began hurling questions at us: "Show your certificates! Why did you come here?"

I handed them my papers and instantly fabricated a story: "We came to see an aunt who lives in the village, but we found no transportation and we were delayed . . . I've got only my birth certificate and a confirmation on top of the picture. My transit papers weren't ready yet."

They listened doubtfully, and their reply was short and cutting: "We'll check."

As they riffled through the papers, I kept on chattering in a complaining tone. "Right . . . nowadays extreme caution is required. So many Jews wander around and slip away . . ." I threw them a friendly, coquettish smile. Yes — I had even learned how to do that.

They ordered us to appear that same morning in the police department and then left. We decided that we must get out at once. There was a train leaving at eight a.m., and we hurried through alleys and back streets to the train station. We hoped that if we left unnoticed now, we might still be able to return at some point and meet with our people.

When we reached the station, an extremely long freight train was standing on the tracks. We heard rumors that all the Jews of the town would be transported to Belzec in that train. The platform was strewn with heaps of items: pillows, baby carriages, pots, books, clothing. At a short distance stood a group of Polish boys, waiting for the train to depart so that they could attack the pile of possessions the Jews would be forced to leave behind.

We knew that Belzec was an extermination camp, and we were certain that this was a transport of Jews going to their death. We were witnessing for the first time the destruction of the entire Jewish population of one town, and our eyes were opened to the reality of the German scheme. Now, with proof in our hands, we returned to Warsaw to warn the Jews there of the oncoming catastrophe.

We were the first eyewitnesses who brought reliable and irrefutable information to Warsaw about the mass murder of the Jews of Europe. But I remember how shocked I was when I realized that *people did not want to believe our reports.*

I went to my parents. That was the first and last time during the war years that I could not hold back my tears; I felt I would burst from all the sensitive information I had been forced to keep in confidence for so many months. I broke into an uncontrollable sobbing and told my parents what I had learned on this trip. I remember the way my father looked at me; I remember his wide-open, disbelieving eyes. He plainly refused to accept that I was telling the truth.

"It's impossible . . . it's impossible!" he kept on repeating. Maybe he did not want to doubt me, and yet he could not accept the possibility of such brutality. It is painful to remember how my father tried to deny the information I gave him. For him it was a double blow; not only was this news so devastating, but it had been brought by his little girl. When had this little girl grown up? . . .

My father worked on the Aryan side as an electrician. The last time I saw him was at his place of work in the vicinity of Praga, on the other side of the Vistula River. He gave me the silverware he had succeeded in smuggling out of our apartment in the ghetto and instructed me to give it to my mother so that she would be able to live off the assets on the Aryan side. We planned more meetings, but he was captured during an *Aktion* and brought to the Umschlagplatz, a deportation center from which people were taken away and never seen again.

The Jewish police could often be bribed to exempt people from deportations, and many people were indeed saved that way, but not my father. He was taken in a transport and perished together with the others. He was the first member of our family to die at the hands of the Nazis.

After I had witnessed the tragic evacuation of the Jews of Chrobieszow, I went back to that town twice to try and find the young members of our movement. Some of them had been transferred from the local concentration camp to Varevkowica to work in a sawmill. We went to Varevkowica and were able to smuggle some of our friends out of the labor camp to the forest, where they could join the partisans.

When I came to Chrobieszow the second time, the town was *Judenrein*, completely cleansed of Jews. I met secretly with the head of the Judenrat, which was still nominally in existence, and he told me that his father had committed suicide.

After this trip I was sent out from Warsaw again, to verify the rumors that people were being cremated in Treblinka. I did not have to seek very hard for the answer; at the station right before Treblinka, I heard Poles on the platform talking about the smell of burnt flesh and bones, which had come to them all the way from the next town. I was then sent to Treblinka itself to find out more precise details of its operations. The leaders of the resistance felt it was of the utmost importance to find out how serious the danger really was and to make the situation known, because the suspicion was now strong that all the European Jews were headed toward their deaths.

Missions to Czestochowa, Radomsk, and other cities followed, and my tasks were many and varied: I gathered information, gave warning, trained young people to handle weapons, smuggled more people out of the ghettos to join the resistance in the forest. Once I had to arrange transport in a covered carriage for a man who had a Jewish nose so that no one would see him, and that was not the only time I transferred someone whose Jewishness had to be concealed. These missions became more and more risky, but my gentile appearance and accent continued to protect me for a long time. I was fully committed to my work. I had no hesitation about what I was doing; it was self-explanatory, natural, and unquestionable, and no doubts crept into my mind as to the importance of my missions.

Until . . . I was captured and arrested.

I saw both of my brothers and my mother for the last time on December 22, 1942, the day that I was to leave on a mission to Krakow. At that time Tusia Altman and Tema Shneiderman, two of my underground friends, were sharing my apartment on the Aryan side. My brother Marek came in from Bendzin, where he was involved in an organized center for youth activities, and before he smuggled himself into the ghetto he came to my apartment. I was still asleep when I heard the knock, and at first I panicked, thinking that it might be the Gestapo — under my bed there was a suitcase containing grenades and pistols! Then I heard Marek's voice in the front room, and my panic turned to joy. I jumped out of bed and ran to embrace him with all my strength. Sadly, he couldn't stay long, and after a quick exchange he left and slipped into the ghetto.

That evening I had dinner in Vovek's apartment on the Aryan side. Vovek had married Rina in 1940, and their son Rafi was born when they still lived in our old house in the ghetto. My mother was with us too, and I remember that she served us borscht. I had a chance to see all my family for the last time on that memorable day; soon afterward I was arrested.

The Action in Krakow

After I left Vovek's house that day, I waited for Antek Zukerman on the corner of Zielona and Lesna Streets, in an unpopulated area. It was Christmastime, and we were scheduled to leave for Krakow that same evening. Laban Lebowicz and Dolek Liebeskind, two of our friends, were planning to hold a meeting with the commander of the Jewish underground in Krakow, and we were hoping to attend.

When Antek finally arrived, I couldn't help but laugh. He was sporting a long, curly moustache, a short coat, and high boots, all of which contrived to give him the perfect appearance of a Polish aristocrat.

Traveling at that time was a bold enterprise. The trains were crowded with smugglers peddling cigarettes, butter, potatoes, and lard — all valuable wartime commodities. From time to time there were inspections and arrests, but the danger was not as great for the smugglers as for those who were found with false documents or weapons. Anyone who looked intelligent was searched more thoroughly, and it was always important to keep a cool exterior. Because of our impeccable Aryan appearance and my perfect command of Polish, Antek and I had reached Krakow several times before without incident.

We had the address of an underground member on the Aryan side of Krakow who was to provide us with false permits needed to pass from the ghetto to the city. We were scheduled to meet him at 4:00 p.m., but before that we had another appointment with our two friends, Laban and Dolek. Since we had arrived very early, we took a walk and then lingered for a while on a park bench.

At the appointed time we moved on to the designated meeting place, with which I was familiar from my previous visits to Krakow. We saw Laban coming toward us alone; he was tall and wore a German officer's green leather coat. He led us to a closed carriage and drove us through the dark streets of the city while we talked.

From the very start we noticed that Laban was agitated.

"Why did you come today?" he asked. "You've got to leave this evening! . . . There's an action against the Germans scheduled for 7:00 p.m. tonight. The Jewish fighting organization and the P.P.R. have planned this together. Everything is prepared: some of our boys, armed with hand grenades, are to enter the yard of the Cafe Cyganeria, and at exactly the same time another group of boys will go into the yards of the smaller cafe houses. Simultaneously, all of them will ignite the German garages. While the boys are busy with this mission, the girls will place anti-Fascist posters on poles and on the walls of buildings. The action will cause chaos, and hopefully there will be enough confusion to give fifteen of our boys a chance to escape from the ghetto and join the Polish underground fighting party on the Aryan side . . ."

We were aware of the danger involved in the "action," but we also knew that our moral responsibility was to stay with our friends, regardless of the consequences. We weren't assigned any special function, but we were convinced that in an emergency we might be needed. We pressed our stand while the carriage wound through the dark and silent streets, and finally Laban acceded to our request.

The carriage stopped at Skavinska Street in front of the hospital, which was now unoccupied. Through a back door we entered a corridor which took us to a dark room. All the members who were to take part in the action were assembled there, sitting quietly on the floor. The room was narrow, in total darkness; its windows faced the SS barracks next door, and the slightest rustle could betray us.

I recognized some of the people in the room from my previous visits to Krakow. The Warsaw underground movement had sent them to organize a resistance party here. They were all young, eighteen or nineteen years old at most. We spoke in whispers and checked our weapons and supplies: hand grenades, pistols, posters, food and water for several days. We expected massive persecution after the action and did not foresee a means of escape from our hideout.

Antek, Laban, and Dolek went to their headquarters in an apartment in one of the houses occupied by Volksdeutschen. Here the three friends had a hidden radio. They were posing as Poles and had been able to carry out their underground work securely until now because the apartment was right under the noses of the enemy; no one would suspect a Jew of having the audacity to rent an apartment in the same building with the Volksdeutschen.

Antek had advised me to come along with them, but I preferred to stay in the hospital with the other members of the action. In the meantime the general curfew hour imposed by the Germans was closing in. In most cities during the war, people did not walk around at night.

The first to leave for the field of action was Menachem Beigelman, a member of the Warsaw Dror organization. He was assigned to the Cafe Cyganeria. He parted from us with a smile, and we wished him success. Others followed silently.

At 8:00 p.m. the members of the action began to return from their mission. They reported that they had been successful; the grenades were thrown with great precision, the posters were glued to the walls, all were unharmed! Our joy knew no bounds.

At 9:00 p.m. every single member was back except Menachem. We began to rationalize that he was fighting his way through streets filled with Germans and that he would surely return soon.

At 10:00 p.m. Menachem still had not come back. Our fear deepened. We sat pressed against each other on the floor of the narrow room, heavy with worry. It was hard to sit and do nothing, so one of the girls began to busy herself preparing a meal for us: a slice of bread for each person, with a sliver of salami. We were all tired but none of us could sleep.

Finally we decided that we ought to find out what had happened to Menachem.

Before we had a chance to make a move, rifle butts were banging on the door, threatening to break it down. One of the boys leaped up to get grenades from behind the furnace, but it was too late. The door burst open and we were surrounded on all sides by the Gestapo, their rifles drawn. How satisfied they were! They had known of our existence for a very long time but hadn't been able to find us.

"Hands over your heads!" they ordered sharply and pushed us into the corridor, commanding us to stretch out face down on the floor, boys and girls separately. Guards were stationed at the doors. A moment later we heard shouts of triumph from the room where we had stored our hand grenades, pistols, and bullets. They packed all of our ammunition in sacks and then began to interrogate us.

There was no doubt now that we were Jewish, and we knew that our false documents would not help us anymore. The Germans walked in their heavy boots on the boys' backs, all the while shooting out questions: name, address, birthplace. The boys gave their Polish names. The Germans beat them over the heads with rifle butts and whips; blood was flowing, and we could not raise our heads. They kicked us all over our bodies and then led us to a truck waiting at the gate of the hospital.

In one corner of the van, illuminated by the bright rays of the moon, lay Menachem's body, in a puddle of blood.

A terrible depression seized our hearts. Each of us wondered if he had betrayed us—but we were wrong. We learned later from other members of our group that Menachem had carried out his mission accurately and loyally. He had thrown a few hand grenades into the Cafe Cyganeria, killing a number of Germans and wounding ten SS men. Nevertheless, we knew that someone had disclosed us.

That night was a beautiful night. Not a single soul could be seen on the streets. The truck halted in front of a familiar house, where one of our boys boarded with a Polish gatekeeper. In a second the family of the gatekeeper was dragged out of the house and forced in among us. The truck halted several more times. Already over twenty people had been pushed into it.

We were brought to the Gestapo headquarters on Pomorska Street. I was aware that I would be killed soon, yet I was calm and content, for our group had successfully accomplished its mission and caused damage to the Germans. For many months I had known that we would one day fall into their hands, and now, after all this, I felt only a sense of relief because Antek, Laban, and Dolek weren't among us. And how good it was that my mother and brothers and my friends in Warsaw were alive and did not know what had happened to me! What a strange but serene feeling! I was happy that we alone had been discovered and that others would continue our work.

The Germans were nervous. They were talking among themselves, and I caught the words "*banditim,*"* "Cyganeria," and "dead." In a few minutes we would be taken to our own deaths, but that was unimportant; the important thing was that the "banditim" had shown that they too could take action.

The death that I waited for that first night in jail did not come. Instead there were interrogations, beatings, and blood. They tried to wring out of us the names of friends and members of the underground, but they did not succeed. They searched for suspects in and out of the city; they surrounded neighborhoods, staged arrests, moved the curfew hour back from 11:00 p.m. to 6:00 p.m. The events of that evening of December 22 dominated the news in the city.

It was in prison that we found out about the two informers who had been planted in our party in Krakow. They were the ones who had informed the Germans of the action and were responsible for our arrests. We felt guilty for even having suspected one of our own . . .

The Gestapo did manage to apprehend many members of the Krakow underground during their massive alert, and every day new captives were brought to the prison. From them I learned that Laban too had been captured and imprisoned the morning after we were found, and they told me the manner of his arrest.

Laban and Antek, who had stayed at their headquarters in the Volksdeutsche building all during the action, were worried because they had not heard from any of us, not even from our contact person, who had also been arrested. Unaware that the entire area was surrounded, they

*Murderers.

went to the hospital to inquire what had happened to us. The Germans were lying in wait for them inside the gates. As they entered the garden and proceeded toward the back doors, all was quiet—and then in the next instant, Antek was hit by a bullet. He ran and hid in the bushes. The Germans combed the grounds but could not find him. When they entered the hospital to search, he crawled out from beneath the bush, strode toward the gate with an assured step, and leisurely lit a cigarette. Then he strolled down the road.

Antek had been hit in the leg and his boot quickly filled with blood, but he tried not to limp. He knocked at a few random doors, but no one let him in. For several days he wandered in the streets of Krakow until an old woman, a gatekeeper, had pity on him and took him in. She gave him water to drink and washed and dressed his wound. He then got on a train and returned to Warsaw. Tzyvia Lubetkin, his old partner, and my brother Marek were waiting for him. When he saw them, he said, "Everything is lost," and fainted. Marek treated his wound and took care of him.

In the meantime the Gestapo continued to interrogate the members of our movement, and I insisted repeatedly that I was Polish. Once they lined up several of us with our faces to the wall, and finally the boys confessed that they were Jewish.

The next day I was taken to a different cell, where I met a girl who also knew Laban Lebowicz. We decided that we would give the Germans similar stories. We would say that we had been traveling to make money "on the side," and for that purpose we had bought falsified identification cards. I would claim that I had fallen in with this group of "terrorists" unknowingly, my one interest being to make some money through unofficial channels. Many people were engaged in smuggling now, and I calculated to myself that such an admission would yield far less severe consequences than admitting to being Jewish. But the Gestapo officers who questioned me continued to call me "Jewish Eva" nonetheless, and when I was returned to my cell after the next interrogation I mumbled audibly that the Germans were idiots for confusing me with the Jewesses.

The questioning continued, but I stuck to my story. At one point they put a mask to my face to obstruct my breathing, but I repeated the answer I had given so many times already: "I am Polish! This is the name that was given to me at birth!" One of the Germans was writing the protocol, and I heard him tell the others that I gave the impression of being an honest person.

When the protocol was ready, they made me sign it. It stated that I was not Jewish but that I had helped the Jewish *"banditim."* I was now certified non-Jewish, but I could sense somehow that this status would not buy my ticket to freedom.

I remained in prison for another month. Later I found out that my brother Vovek had come to Krakow during that time to try to get me out of jail with bribery, but he had failed.

One day a woman guard came in and began calling out the names of the prisoners. She said that we were leaving but that we did not need to take anything along, for we were going to Auschwitz.

On my way out, I saw Laban Lebowicz through the keyhole of one of the cells.

Auschwitz

We arrived in Auschwitz at night. Several months ago I had been sent on a mission to Birkenau, and I had stood on these same tracks. The memory came flooding back to me now.

*"Heraus! Heraus!"** the guards yelled. They flashed searchlights into our faces, beat us with truncheons, and set gigantic dogs loose among us as we got down from the transports. Once we were inside, our heads were immediately shaven and numbers were imprinted on our arms. My number was — and still is — 32291.

I entered Auschwitz officially registered as a Polc, and so I was given the uniform of the Polish political prisoners: a striped dress with a red triangle painted on it, and a pair of wooden shoes. The Jewish women were in a separate line and wore old civilian clothing. For a very long time I feared that the Germans might single me out and take me for a special investigation because my record said that I had helped Jews; perhaps they might even discover that I was Jewish. But they did not come. They were

*"Get out!"

too busy with the transports that were arriving continuously and the crematoria that were working twenty-four hours a day.

It was January, and the cold was fierce. I had no covering for my head nor any underwear to keep me warm, until one day when one of the Polish Blockowas took pity on me and found me a kerchief and some makeshift undergarments.

My assignments were changed several times during my stay in Auschwitz. My first job was in an outside kommando. Our task was to carry stones; we picked up stones and put them in a pile, and then we picked up the same stones and returned them to their original place. We walked several kilometers each day doing this purposeless work, wearing our wooden shoes and holding on to each other to keep from flying off the ice. The stones reminded me of the parable of the prisoner who was set to work for twenty years turning a wheel in a mill, only to find out that the wheel was not attached to anything. Our work, too, was futile; its sole purpose was to exhaust us and to make us suffer the cold.

The only time I was permitted to work in a closed barracks was during my "sojourn" in the Ephinger Kommando, one of several sorting units in Auschwitz. Here I was assigned to sort and classify the clothing and possessions of people who had been sent to the gas chambers. There were piles and piles of documents: identification cards, passports, birth certificates, bachelor's, master's, and doctoral degrees from the Sorbonne and other universities, and pictures — mountains of pictures!

Once a photograph caught my eye. The people in it looked so familiar. On closer scrutiny I recognized one face: Antek's! I couldn't believe it; my whole being felt chilled. I cut his head out of the photo and kept it with me for almost three years. That tiny photo was my only reminder of the world outside — and I wanted to believe that Antek was still alive.

One of my tasks was to search for any hidden valuables amongst the clothing and objects I sorted and to turn them over to the Germans. When I did find gold pieces or dollars, however, I took them and threw them into the excrement pit in the latrine. This was my way of doing sabotage.

Our overseer was Ephinger, for whom the kommando was named. He was a twenty-two-year-old deranged sadist. He designed special punishments for us, making us jump in and out of pits in rapid succession and forcing us to learn songs and sing while we walked. He also had his own room where girls, including Jewish girls, entertained him.

The regimen was designed to reduce us to some lower life form, but in this area I was determined not to succumb. When my beautiful blond hair began to grow back, I tried to take especial care of my looks. I took in my dress and made myself a belt from the extra pieces of cloth. Whenever I was able to find a bit of water I washed myself, hoping to feel, at least for a short time, like a human being.

But the real reason for my survival was Zosia. Zosia was a Polish girl who worked as a supervisor in the Ephinger Kommando. Ironically we first met by getting into a fight. I don't remember exactly what the argument was about, but I knew that she was wrong, and I was so furious that I lashed out at her. We were angry at each other for some time, and then we became best friends.

Zosia was a plain salesgirl from Warsaw, but her "organizational" abilities — which in Auschwitz meant the ability to procure anything necessary for survival — served both of us well. Once we became friends, she helped me in many ways. Perhaps she respected me because I was educated, perhaps she sensed that I stood on a higher moral level; but whatever the reason, there is no doubt that she saved my life many times.

Once, Zosia and I were chosen to work on a farm called Harmenza, not far from Birkenau. Domestic animals were raised on the farm — chickens, rabbits, geese, and ducks. Some of the animals were used to feed the German personnel in Auschwitz, and the rabbits were used for experiments which would later be tried on Jewish women in Birkenau. Mengele used to visit regularly to follow the progress of the experiments.

The farm was run by a German couple; the husband was an officer in the Wehrmacht, and his wife, who had chosen Zosia and me in Birkenau, was the chief supervisor of the farm. She rode a horse and ran the place with an iron hand. She could often be seen checking for dust on the windows of the chicken coops, in true German fashion.

The move to the farm was in many ways a privilege. There was no high-voltage wire fence, and the conditions were better than in Birkenau.

It was much cleaner, and the guards had regular positions there, so we got to know them. We could talk to them, and after eating they would often give us their leftovers. Most of the other prisoners working on the farm were women too, mostly Dutch women, Jewish Czech girls, and religious Baptists.

In spite of the improvement in our circumstances, we still lived in fear of punishment. Once I developed malaria and had attacks of very high fever. If the Germans discovered that a prisoner had malaria, they sent him immediately to the crematorium to avoid the risk of contagion. During roll call I hid in the latrine so that none of the overseers would notice how sick I looked, and I went to work with a temperature of 105 degrees.

Eventually the temperature plummeted to 94 degrees, and I became so weak that I knew I would not be able to survive without some nourishing food. Zosia endangered her life and stole eggs, rabbits, and other fatty foods for me. She even stole vodka and then conducted "business" with one of the Germans: vodka in exchange for a rabbit.

Zosia herself once became intoxicated. She pulled me aside and whispered, "Eva, I know that you are Jewish, but I love you anyway." I was flabbergasted, wondering what had betrayed my secret. The next day she tried to apologize, telling me that she had been drunk and that I shouldn't pay attention to anything she'd said . . .

I couldn't forget, and yet I stuck to her. She was all I had.

The Final Leg

When the Russian front began to move closer to Auschwitz, we were ordered to evacuate the farm, including the livestock. We worked under guard all night, packing and loading the entire stock and equipment of the farm onto wagons.

We marched on the road for weeks. At night we would stop at the nearest farm, kill some of our chickens, and cook meals for the Germans and for ourselves. As soon as the food was gone, we were loaded again onto the wagons. The Germans warned us that if we tried to run away, they would shoot us down. After traveling for another few days, we were brought to the Ravensbrueck concentration camp.

I spent three months at Ravensbrueck, working at building a fence. There was almost nothing at all to eat. Zosia and I saved our scraps and shared them. Her self-control was remarkable, and it was only because of her firmness that I developed enough will power to leave over slices of my bread "for the next day."

At the end of April 1945, in an almost dreamlike manner, Red Cross caravans suddenly drove into the compound. We were so numb by that time that we had little sense of reality; it was hard for us to absorb the idea that the war was over.

The caravan operation had been organized by the Swedish government. The vans picked up the prisoners from the Scandinavian countries first, then those from Belgium, Holland, and France. A second fleet of vans came for the Jewish inmates. The Polish inmates were the last to go, and I was among them, having maintained my Polish identity to the very end.

On the way we were transferred to a train, and the Red Cross staff began to distribute food packages. People were so hungry that they attacked the food without thinking, and many died soon afterward, for their weakened bodies could not handle the onslaught. Zosia, however, had kept her sense of inner control, and she took care of me, giving me only very small portions and forcing me to eat slowly. She monitored every bite I put into my mouth. Several times during our stops on the way to Sweden, she found ways to make a small fire in the field so that she could boil water and cook the food before she gave it to me. This was her final contribution to my survival.

On May 3, 1945, we passed Copenhagen, the capital of Denmark. Many Danes were standing on the platform, waving to us. When the train stopped, the Danish police literally carried us down from the wagons in their arms. Stands with food and drink were waiting for us. A few Germans could be seen in the distance, but nobody paid attention to them.

The Danes put us on a luxury ship to cross the sea to Sweden. When we arrived we were taken to a public bath. Our old, infested uniforms were taken away, and in the process my treasured photo of Antek, which I had kept with me for the past three years, was lost. This was the only sad event of the liberation.

Two nurses came around and washed us gently, handling us as tenderly as though we were babies, and after the bath they gave us beautiful new clothes. Then we went through a thorough medical examination.

That night I revealed to my friends: "I am Jewish!"

After the war Chavka Raban emigrated to Israel, where she lived in the Beth Lochamei Haghettaoth, a settlement founded by Holocaust survivors who were members of the resistance.

Chavka's brother Vovek joined the partisans after trying to get her out of prison and was killed in the Kielce area, dying heroically in a partisan action against the Germans. Chavka later went to search for his grave but was unable to locate it. Vovek's wife Rina and son Rafi managed to survive on the Aryan side of Warsaw. Rina found a doctor who surgically disguised the boy's circumcision, and after the war she remarried and emigrated to Israel. Chavka's mother and her brother Marek did not survive.

Laban Lebowicz, whom Chavka last saw through the keyhole of the prison cell in Krakow, was taken out of jail to be shot, but he ran away. When the Germans caught him he tried to fight them off bare-handed, and they shot him fifty times.

Antek Zukerman and Tzyvia Lubetkin both survived the war and were among the original founders of the Beth Lochamei Haghettaoth. They were also very involved in rescuing Jewish children who had been housed with gentiles during the war. Both Antek and Tzyvia passed away some years ago.

THE FRENCH UNDERGROUND

Miriam Chlebnowicz-Novitch
Paris, France

Miriam Chlebnowicz was born in 1908 in Yurtishki, a small town in the vicinity of Grodno, which had belonged to Czarist Russia before the revolution of 1917. Her childhood and youth were spent in Poland and later in France, where she became a member of the French underground during the war. Her original testimony was given many years ago to the Beth Lochamei Haghettaoth.

The Nazis were not the first people to disrupt our family life. It seems that we were doomed to be pursued by wars. During World War I my parents and my two brothers and I ran away from our hometown of Yurtishki to Russia proper, where we lived as refugees. When we returned to Yurtishki, we found a town devastated by combat. The houses — all wooden — had been burnt to the ground, and we had to start anew.

My father tried to earn a living as a tree merchant, buying trees from landowners and selling them to paper factories, but the business did not succeed. I remember hearing my parents talk about going to America, where my father's brothers lived, but my mother was against it. She did not want to be the poor relation and have to depend on others. My mother remained a beautiful woman in spite of her hardships, but she died young, and eventually my father remarried.

150

My father was a very handsome man and a very learned one. He did not receive a formal education, for Jews had no access to the schools, but educated himself at home. He even taught himself Hebrew, although the little Jewish education he received had ended in his youth. He grew up a staunch Russian and ran a household that revolved around the Communist ideal, but he never lost his passion for education. He continually pushed all of us to study, including me, even though formal learning for girls was not stressed at that time. He used to tell me: "I haven't got a dowry for you, so the dowry should not be in your pocket, but in your head. Learn, my child, just learn . . ." My father and his entire family in Europe perished during the war. All he left to me were his teachings and his name, Chlebnowicz, which I perpetuate along with my current surname, Novitch.

My family moved to Vilna so that I could attend a better school, and I enrolled in the Gymnasium Oks. This was a Jewish school, but the predominant language in which we studied was Polish, and we learned very little about Judaism. After I finished gymnasium, I decided to become a language teacher, but there was no possibility of getting into a teaching school because of the restricted quota for Jewish students. I had no choice but to do what many aspiring young Jews were doing then — I went to France to continue my studies.

I registered in a post-secondary school in a program for East European languages. I knew Russian well and managed to graduate in a very short time with a diploma which certified me to teach Russian, but I continued to study so that I could gain certification in other languages as well.

Earning a living was extremely difficult. I worked — without a work permit — in a factory which manufactured artificial jewelry. It was rigorous labor, and since we had no permits the factory owners took advantage of us and paid us less than the minimum wage. I also worked in a doll factory, drawing masks for the dolls. This was a painstaking craft, since each face had to be drawn very accurately and attractively, and because it was piece work, I made little money. Between these two jobs and the private lessons that I gave, I somehow managed to make ends meet and to continue studying.

We Jewish students were quite a substantial group of laborers at that time. We worked mostly for various Jewish factories and invariably for very low wages; but our major interest was to study — to be in contact with the wide world, to absorb western culture and the arts, and to be involved politically.

Through my work in the factories I came into contact with artists and members of the leftist movement, and I was naturally drawn to them. I frequented museums and stood on corners selling "La Humanita," a newspaper of the Communist movement. Our material circumstances were meager, and we thrived instead on ideals, on food for the mind and spirit. Although there were many leftists who were also strongly Zionist and who yearned for Eretz Israel, I myself never had any Zionist leanings until much later on, when I was incarcerated in the Vittel camp. And yet I always had some sense of contact with Israel. For a span of time I was married to an Israeli painter named Joseph Kastel, and we had a son named Boris (Boruch).

The leftist movement was not an isolated, radical venture. In fact, most of the young people who came to France to study and to work before the war joined the French left in the hope of improving the status of the Jews. They eagerly anticipated a leftist takeover of the government, a victory which they hoped would ease anti-Semitic discrimination. They also longed to bring their families to France from Poland and Lithuania in order to give them a chance at a better life. I too wanted to bring my brother to France so that he could learn and progress here.

And then suddenly, World War II broke out.

When the Nazis took over parts of France in 1940, many young students from the leftist circle, including the Zionists, joined the French underground and fought in its ranks. I too joined; it was a natural choice for me, as I identified completely with the aspirations of the leftist movement and its passionate desire to effect changes in the world. I was "permanent," meaning a steady recruit, and among many other tasks I worked in the press and publications division of the underground network. One of my most frequent functions was to deliver printed material about the resistance movement to people in Paris, who would then distribute it in designated sections of the city.

I usually carried four or five packages of leaflets at a time, and I used to wrap these around my stomach, underneath my dress. My extended belly and the large cape that I wore made me look very pregnant. I was constantly afraid, though, that the papers might slip from underneath my dress as I was walking down the street and disclose my mission.

My contacts were always waiting for me when I arrived in Paris. I never knew the names of these people to whom I handed over the packages; in the underground, the less you knew about your contacts, the better. I recognized them only by the signs I had been given. For example, I might be told to look for a person holding a green paper in his right or left hand, or wearing dark glasses or a flower in his lapel. Such arrangements now seem almost facetious, the stuff of spy fiction, but then they were a part of our everyday lives, and the danger was as real as the air we breathed.

On one occasion a friend and I were assigned to distribute literature directed toward women, encouraging them to join in the resistance and not to despair. My friend acquired a dog, which made her "deliveries" much easier; while walking the dog, she would surreptitiously slip the leaflets into the mailboxes at the gates of the houses along the street. I had no dog, and so my cover was not as secure. I usually walked from gate to gate, looking around carefully all the while to see if I could spot any informers, and then slipped handbills into the mailbox slots when it seemed the coast was clear.

We distributed literature in other places as well. Sometimes I would enter a kiosk and ask permission to use the phone, and then, while dialing, I would slip leaflets between the pages of the telephone book. We also left circulars on the metro benches where we had been sitting.

Distributing literature was not the only way in which we encouraged people to resist. In the beginning of the occupation I often used to approach Jews standing in ration lines and urge them to take off their yellow patches. It depressed me to see them marked like cattle. But they did not listen, cautioning me instead that people like me would cause trouble and disaster. Some even said that they were proud to wear the yellow patch.

No matter what type of activity I was engaged in, I was always terribly frightened. At any minute someone could inform on me, and those who disclosed a Jew or an underground member were generously rewarded by the Germans. Detectives and informers used to follow people around, looking into their eyes for signs of fear. They would pretend to try to help them, sometimes inviting young girls to have a cup of coffee with them in a cafe, with the purpose of ferreting out names. I was a pretty girl, and men frequently used to offer me coffee. I always had to be very careful.

I often had the feeling that I was being followed, and at such times I was afraid to sleep in my apartment, or even in one of my friends' apartments. I used to keep a toothbrush in my pocket and wander in the streets, where there was less chance that someone would track me down.

One strategy I devised was to memorize the timetable of the trains leaving Paris. I made sure always to be a bit "late" for the one that had just departed, arriving in time to see the tail end of the train pulling out of the station. I would wander in earshot of other people and begin to curse my bad luck, and then settle myself somewhere to wait for the next train. In this fashion I was able to stay in the terminal throughout the night, catching snatches of sleep on one of the benches.

Another of my tasks in the underground was to deliver letters from people who had been sentenced to death. Some prisons or camps allowed the sentenced people to write a last letter, while others did not; yet every person tried to leave a message behind. These might be written on a shred of toilet paper, a piece of wet toweling, or any other scrap that could be found. One of my partners somehow always found a way to get into the prisons. She would then meet me at the local train station and hand me the package of letters, and I would deliver them to the underground archives. During wartime there often was no clue as to the whereabouts of the addressees, but if the letters went to a central place, there was some slight hope that eventually they would reach their targets. I wasn't supposed to read those letters, but sometimes my curiosity overpowered me. I remember the declarations that punctuated those notes: "Long live France!"; "Liberty forever!"; "Death to the occupant!" Some added personal remarks like "Kisses to the family" and "Dear, I love you very much, and if I am destined to die, I would be happy knowing that you would start a new life for yourself . . ."

Although I worked for the general underground, many of the letters I carried were from Jews. After the war I tried to get in contact with the people to whom the letters were addressed, but I couldn't find even one. Jews routinely carried false identification papers and died under assumed names, and sometimes a Jewish name could be deciphered only with painstaking effort.

The money we received for our underground work wasn't enough to live on, so I decided to earn some money by teaching Russian. Early in 1942 I put a notice on the bulletin board of the public library, advertising myself as a Russian woman who would give private lessons in the language for a very low price. Fortunately, several French people answered my announcement, although I could never figure out why they were interested in learning Russian.

One man, however, did give a reason. He was a handsome SS officer in his thirties who came to the library, asking for "the lady who gives private lessons in Russian." The librarian was very afraid to arrange a meeting between an SS man and me, for her own sake as well as for mine, but she did relay the message and I arranged to meet the man on my own.

The officer told me that he was interested in learning Russian because he was going to the Russian front. He asked the price and wanted to know how quickly he could learn the language. From our short conversation I learned that he was an engineer in charge of a truck factory and that he lived on Ponderee Street, Section 16, in the most elegant quarter of the city. We set up an appointment in his house.

For the meeting I put on an elegant dress and dangling earrings, and set my long, jet-black hair high up on my head to give myself an East European look. When I arrived at the officer's home, a French servant-woman opened the door. She looked at me with suspicion, thinking that I was a "cheap" woman who had come to spend some time with her boss. However, she let me in.

Three little children were playing on the floor of the parlor. I forced a smile, but when I looked at them all I could think of was Avraimale.

Avraimele was a little boy who had been brought to me by the underground. I was asked to hide him in my apartment in the non-Jewish section of Paris until better arrangements could be made for him. I wanted to call him Jacques, a French name, but he insisted on remaining "Avraimale." He was a very sensitive and excitable child, completely bewildered by the circumstances and by the strange people who used to visit my apartment at odd hours, and he would frequently wet his pants. After several days the people who had brought him to me took him away, and I lost track of him.

To tell the truth, I did not believe the rumors going around at that time that Jewish children were being taken to their deaths. I did know, however, that they were being transported in trains, and I was worried for Avraimele; but I was never able to find out what had happened to him. All I knew was that his father, an underground activist, had been captured and killed . . . And here I was, standing in a German home, watching little German children playing happily on the carpet, and I had to smile at them. My heart ached for Avraimale, but I had to force myself to smile. The German engineer approached me with great politeness and led me to another room, where we began our lesson . . .

The German talked freely to me about his work. He told me that he was going to be stationed in Baku, Kavkaz, an area where there were many oil wells, and that a convoy of trucks had already left his factory for the Russian front. I listened carefully, recording everything he said in my memory; his was one of many stories that I later related to the underground.

In June 1943 I was arrested and taken to a solitary cell in a prison on the outskirts of Paris. Apparently the Gestapo had filled an entire file with material regarding my underground activities, from the time I had joined the movement in 1940 all the way to the present.

On August 10, 1943, I was transported to Vittel, a prison in eastern France not far from the resort town of Nancy. There the Germans had fenced in several hotels and tenement buildings and turned them into a concentration camp for foreign citizens, with the ostensible purpose of returning them to their mother countries. The prison was like a miniature ghetto; it was completely sealed off and policed, but the prisoners were not under lock and key and had a certain amount of freedom to move about on the grounds and to converse among themselves.

I was registered as a foreign citizen like the others, as I had a foreign passport, but I was known as a Jew and a leftist and was watched very carefully. My son Boris had gone into hiding elsewhere in France.

During my stay in Vittel I discovered that resistance does not end simply because one is not physically free, that great changes in the spirit can occur in the most dire circumstances . . . Here, in a sealed compound, I found that I was still able to continue my work for the underground; here, in a sealed compound, I learned the truth of the Holocaust; here, most wondrous of all, my true sense of Jewish identity was born . . .

When I had been in the camp two days, I was surprised to hear the chatter of children: our children — children speaking Polish! "Children! Where are you from?" I asked them. "We are from Warsaw!" they answered. The arrival of the children marked the beginning of a terrible revelation for me, for up until then I had had no notion of the truth of the ghettos and concentration camps, of the real atrocities that were taking place in Europe. My involvement had been purely political.

The children were not the last to arrive. In January of 1943 and later on in May, two groups of Jews from Poland arrived in Vittel. They were from Warsaw, Krakow, and Lwow, and held citizenship papers from several Central and South American countries. Among them was the poet Yitzchak Katzenelson and his son Tzvi.

It was hard for me to make contact with Katzenelson; he and his son were afraid to talk because there were so many spies and informers in the camp. However, once he found that he could trust me, the other rooms in the prison opened up before me as well, and the prisoners began to tell me about the destruction that raged in Poland. I listened and heard; I asked myself: "How is it possible that the Germans should annihilate an entire nation? Small children? . . . The Jewish world, of which my father, mother, and brothers are part? Such a beautiful world, with its greatness and its illustrious history and tragedies? . . ."

All this seemed so cruel and terrible to me that I thought I was losing my mind. I felt so despondent that I fell ill for a time and wished for death.

It was Katzenelson who changed my life completely during those days in Vittel. He opened my eyes to the horrors of Jewish persecution and at the same time drew me closer to my own people. Through him I began to shed my Communist sympathies and to develop a sense of true belonging to the people of Israel. We spent many hours together in the garden of the prison, and our conversations seldom deviated from the topic of the tragedy that had struck our nation. There were few instances when I saw Katzenelson smile . . . Any light moment was laden with sadness, for news of the suffering of the ghetto Jews and the horrifying slaughter in the death camps continually filtered in to the prison.

Katzenelson often showed me pictures of his wife, which he always carried in his pocket, and of his two sons: Yummele (Benyamin), a charming and smiling boy of eleven, and Ben Tzion, on whom all his hopes were pinned . . . "A great blessing is hidden in the soul of that boy. He is a poet of the future," he used to tell me. His oldest son, the eighteen-year-old Tzvi, who was here with him in the prison, was a bright and pleasant boy and used to describe life in the Warsaw ghetto for me. Once he drew me a map of the ghetto borders and explained the strategy of the armed resistance and the revolt of the Jewish underground.

Katzenelson had lived a life of want and distress in the Warsaw ghetto until his deportation, and yet he had continued to teach in the underground gymnasium established by the Dror movement, as well as in the framework of the "Oneg Shabbath," an illegal institute which collected evidence of Nazi atrocities. During his time in the ghetto he had composed more works than in the previous fifteen years. Of all those writings he had brought nothing to France, but he had writings and knowledge of all kinds in his head, and he frequently used to tell me stories from the Talmud.

He hated assimilation with all his heart and soul and had tried to do everything in his power to foster a strong sense of Jewish identity among the ghetto youth before he was deported. "The individual," he would often say, "is indebted to his mother nation. From the time he is born he is indebted to the society to which he belongs. He has no right to waste the riches which he has received as an inheritance from his fathers . . . On the contrary, he has an obligation to multiply those riches."

"We Jews," he once told me, "are like a man who has a mother, a wife, a family — yet he wanders all over the world in search of a person to understand him. If he has all, why does he have to roam around and bother everyone?" For Katzenelson the Jewish nation was everything.

One day I confessed to him that only thanks to his influence had I again found myself and my soul, and that from then on I would remain what I was born to be: a true Jewish daughter. "From now on," I promised him, "I want to devote my entire life to emulating the past, and I want to take an active part in building the future of our nation."

"The path that leads to knowledge of ourselves," he replied, "is the longest and hardest . . ."

Katzenelson wrote feverishly in Vittel, hoping to inform the world of the catastrophic destruction of the Jewish nation. I managed to smuggle many of these writings out of the prison by sewing them into the coat seams of a Frenchwoman who used to come in from the city to do the laundry. I asked her to hide the writings in her mother's house until after the war. Later on I also enlisted the help of a woman named Ruth Adler, who had a valid passport. She left Vittel as an exchange prisoner while the war was still on, and smuggled more of the poet's writings through to Palestine in the metal handle of her suitcase.

The prisoners in Vittel who held foreign passports thought for a while that they were immune from deportations, but they soon realized that they were vulnerable just like all the others. One night in March of 1944, the Germans confiscated the Latin American passports of most of the Jews in the camp, sending nearly three hundred of them to Auschwitz, where they perished. Among them were Yitzchak Katzenelson and his son.

Miriam Novitch remained in Vittel until the end of the war. Even there she continued her efforts for the resistance and managed to save a young Jewish girl from deportation by cutting the wire fence surrounding the prison and smuggling the girl out to a French woman, who reunited her with her father in Paris.

In 1946 Miriam Novitch came to Israel, where she wrote several books, including Sobibor. *She remained active in perpetuating the memory of the Holocaust until her death in 1990.*

IN THE CAMPS

❖

THE ODYSSEY

Leah Weis-Neuman
Kosice, Slovakia

Deportation

One spring night in 1944, a third of the Kosice Jewish population was ordered to assemble at the railroad tracks in the ghetto. There we were beaten savagely and forced to relinquish our belongings. Most of the townspeople were then pressed into freight wagons, eighty people to a wagon which was normally used to carry six horses. My parents and I, along with some of my close relatives, were ordered to go with the following transport, and we stayed in the train station that night.

The next morning was a regular springtime Monday, and the sun was shining brightly. Yet to me it was not a regular day. It felt more like Yom Kippur, before *Tefillas Ne'ilah*.*

Suddenly, two of our town boys came running out to the tracks. They had just escaped from a concentration camp and had smuggled out letters from some of the prisoners to their relatives on the outside. These two boys had undertaken the mission of delivering messages to any place in the occupied regions that they could reach on foot, and several people on the platform gave them letters. We too gave them several letters of warning for our relatives in Budapest, which was not under strong

*The final supplication of the Yom Kippur service, offered at the close of the day before the heavenly judgment is sealed.

162

occupation yet, and one for my brother, who had escaped to Russia at the beginning of the war. This was the last sign of life he would receive from my parents — if indeed he ever received it.

The transport was ready to move in the late afternoon. The villagers began to push and shove like demented creatures, shouting and screaming, trying to stay together with their families so that they would not be separated on the transport. All the while the gendarmes beat them with their rifle butts and forced them madly backward and forward.

I saw someone helping my mother to board an elevated wagon which had no steps. My father was not far from her, but I had gotten pushed back by a great cluster of people. I heard my father calling to my mother, "Do not fear, we are coming," and then he turned around to see what had happened to me, paying no attention to the brutal gendarmes who were clubbing him over the head with their guns. I wanted to protect him, but I couldn't. My parents and I were nearly the last ones to board, and by some miracle we succeeded in getting onto the same wagon. At the last moment a friend of ours, a doctor, brought us a box of medications and a case of jam. We sat on this case all through our journey.

Toward evening the locomotive let out a whistle and began to move forward. All through the night the guards shot bullets randomly into the air, and some pierced the roof of our wagon. We were terrified. Each car had one pail for the bodily needs of its eighty passengers. People began to relieve themselves unabashedly in front of others. We could not eat; we could not stand up without stepping on someone else. The doors were sealed shut and the car was airless. Unable to breathe and overwhelmed by fatigue and despair, many people broke down.

Before we left the wagon at the end of the trip, my father blessed me just as he had always done upon returning from *shul* each Friday night. But this time he added a blessing: "My little daughter, I know that there is no need to tell you how to behave in the future. May the Al-mighty give you strength to endure . . ." He could not continue. He and my mother and I stood hand in hand, crying.

I was so torn inside that I was unaware of what was happening around me, and before I realized it we were on the ground. My father wasn't with us anymore, and I held my mother's hand with all my strength.

Suddenly an SS man separated us. I ran back to my mother, but a German hit me over the head and chased me to another transport that was full of young girls. My mother then tried to come toward me, and the German started to beat and kick both of us. Until the end of my life I will see my poor, dear mother in my mind, stumbling and staggering back to the transport of the sentenced adults.

That day was 29 Iyar, April 1944. I knew that I would never see my parents again, and therefore I still keep that date as the *Yizkor* (memorial) day for both of them.

At that time I did not realize coherently that I would not see them anymore; rather, I had a premonition. It took several days until these occurrences began to sink into my mind, until I understood them as real.

The transport of young girls moved out, guarded by SS men and dogs. Some of the girls cried, others murmured prayers. On the road we noticed a trainload of young men going in the opposite direction, and further along we saw huge trucks filled to capacity with adults, many of them young mothers with babies. We tried to guess where all these people were headed. The optimists said: "The young people are going to work in factories or in the fields; the older people are going to do easy work in the camp itself." The optimists also said: "The smoke that we see and the odor that we smell does not prove anything definite."

We passed through a wooded area, and in the distance we saw many burning stacks. They seemed to be gigantic heaps of clothing or rags, but when we came closer we saw that under those rags were bodies of people, burning.

Birkenau

Soon we came to the main entrance of a huge camp called Birkenau. An orchestra comprised of prisoners was playing the Nazi hymn, and behind the wire fence neat barracks stood in rows, surrounded by flower beds. Our imaginations were too poor to understand what type of place this really was.

I had never seen a prison. I had read several books about concentration camps in Siberia and in Turkistan during the First World War, but there was no comparison between those accounts and what I was about to see with my own eyes.

Two beautiful young girls, dressed in black aprons and wearing black ribbons in their hair, appeared before us. In husky voices they questioned us and wrote down our names, birthplaces, and other statistical information. They then classified us under the group name "*Tzucht und Ordnung*" (Obedience and Order).

Further inside the camp, we went through another registration; our names and personal information were written down countless times. All the while, several girls dressed in the same black-aproned uniforms passed between the lines and asked us in furtive whispers if we knew anything about the Jews of Kosice, Prashow, Beredyev, Tefolczyn, and other towns. These unfortunate girls were Jewish prisoners too. They had been lucky enough to be given positions in the camp and were therefore decently clothed and fed, but there was no mistaking the distress in their eyes.

Some girls from our transport either had relatives in the towns they had mentioned or knew many people who had been deported from those areas in 1941, and we gave them whatever information we could. Then we began to ask questions of our own: "Where are we? What's the name of this place? Where are our parents and our brothers and sisters?" The answers we received were frigid and cynical. The girls shot looks at us as if to say, "What greenhorns you are! You don't know what's going on here? Should I tell you where your parents are now?" They did not have the heart to tell us directly what we would soon learn ourselves: that no one lasted in this place. Instead they said harshly, "You'll find out . . ."

I came upon a very pleasant girl, and I knew the family she inquired about. We conversed with great difficulty, for she did not know Hungarian and I did not know Slovakian. We had to use German, but were afraid to speak openly because the German guards were present. She whispered: "Stop asking about the parents and children. With time you will learn what the 'left side' is. They are there, and you are here. Eat everything you get, and think of one thing only: 'I'm young! I will overcome!' "

I asked her how long she had been here. She lowered her head; there were tears in her eyes, but she tried to hide them. "A long time," she answered. "We have no hope here. If ever the hour of liberation is near, they will finish us before it comes." To this day I am sorry that I never learned her name, and so I could not find out if she survived.

After the registrations were finished, we were taken to a building with many rooms. In the first room we were literally attacked by "barbers" who shaved our heads with a vengeance. Then we were pushed into another room which was already very crowded, and we were ordered to undress. In a third room, under the watchful eye of a young SS man, the other parts of our bodies were shaved.

At first we blushed; then we tried to convince ourselves that the SS man was not a human being. This did not suffice to allay our shame, however, when a group of SS men came to observe the scene, their faces full of loathing.

After the shaving we were thrust into a hall lined with several faucets running hot water. We enjoyed the shower for just a couple of seconds and were then chased out to receive clothes. We were given some kind of loose, baggy underwear, a pair of shoes — each shoe a different size — and a single, long, gray prison dress. My dress was so long that it reached my ankles, but I was simply glad that it covered my legs.

We were led out to a yard and ordered to line up in columns, five girls to a line. We were counted, then marched back into the camp and assigned to different barracks. My barracks number was 26.

At the entrance to the barracks we were met by several women in civilian clothing. Two of them seemed nice, but the others looked savage. They held whips in their hands and screamed at the top of their lungs, "*All into the barracks!*"

These "civilians" were our superiors, and each one had a different function. Most of them were Polish or Russian, and they had been in the camp since the beginning of the war or even beforehand, when Auschwitz was used mainly to house political prisoners. Some of them were former criminals, with the look of the underworld stamped on their faces; and though they themselves were captives, they behaved toward us with extreme hatred and cruelty.

Life in the barracks was a chain of maniacal rapidity, hunger, cold, and nervous tension. We were rushed from place to place, assembled, counted and recounted, all without any constructive purpose, and even at the end of the first day, many girls were on the verge of fainting. Yet I was glad that at least we did not have to stand outside in the cold, gusty rain. Our last order of the day was a short bark: *"Bedtime!"*

The beds were planks of wood attached to the walls, and in each small cell there were twelve, six on one side and six on the other. As we were about to enter the cells, we suddenly heard a pleasant and familiar voice; it belonged to a woman from our ghetto who had been a kindergarten teacher. Here she had been given the job of translator. She called out, "Climb up, twelve girls to each cell. Try to carry out all commands quietly and quickly; do not irritate them. Don't make the situation any more unbearable!"

We scrambled into the cells, maneuvering to stay with our own relatives or friends. This was of the utmost importance, for we understood from the hints of the veteran prisoners that our plight here might continue forever.

Somehow we did manage to organize ourselves and find bunks. Immersed in tears and fearful thoughts, I had almost fallen asleep when a sudden and threatening shriek pierced the hallway: *"Out to the appel! Schnell, schnell!"** We ran out to the rain-soaked yard and lined up in fives, the shortest girls in the first line and so on according to height.

First came the Blockelteste, the commander of our barracks, with her whip, and she counted us. Next came the Lagerelteste, the camp commander, who counted us again. Then came a woman SS officer who scrutinized each of us very thoroughly.

The roll call lasted an hour. By the time it ended, we were drenched, tired, and hungry. Finally we heard a command to return to the barracks, and we wearily found our places again.

After it became quiet, the evening meal was distributed. It was our first meal since we had left Kosice. Each girl received a dirty bowl filled with some green soup. We looked at it and could not tell what this soup

*"Quickly, quickly!"

was made of; it might have been nothing more than cooked grass. Along with the soup we were given what looked like a gray cake of soap, or perhaps a stone. We were told it was bread, and we were so hungry that even if it had been soap we would have eaten it.

After our "meal" we found out from the translator that the Birkenau camp was located right next to Auschwitz, and that it stretched over a very wide area where millions of people were imprisoned and exterminated.

And it was morning and it was evening — one day in Birkenau.

Before dawn had broken the chains of the night, we were awakened by yet another fiendish hollering: "*Get up! Get up! Get out of bed quickly! Quick! Quick to the appel!*"

In the moments of lunatic madness that followed, we were showered with a flood of lashes from the whips of the overseers. We were still disoriented from the deep sleep, from the influence of the *brum** mixed with our food, from the uncertainty of our dear ones' fate. It was one huge madhouse, each girl staggering, stumbling, crying, moaning, looking for someone she had lost only yesterday: her mother, her family, her individuality, her G-d. The confusion grew from minute to minute, a mixture of rising cries and shouts in a medley of languages: Hungarian, Yiddish, German, Slovakian, Rumanian, Polish, Russian. It was a new Tower of Babylon.

We were finally lined up outside the barracks, and again we were kicked, slapped, and beaten. We were counted and recounted several times over the next three or four hours. During that time a group of girls was chosen for an Ess Kommando to haul barrels of tea and soup from the kitchen. These wooden barrels were very large, and it took six girls to drag each one. A Sheiss Kommando was also chosen. This crew went around with pails to all the latrines and emptied the excrement.

Our *block*, or barracks unit, was "blessed" with a Kapo named Shlivinskaya, who had originally been a Russian war prisoner. She smoked a pipe and walked around with a rubber tube in her hand, which

---

*A substance mixed into the women's food to stop menstruation. After the war, most of the women who survived regained their menstrual cycle over varying periods of time, though some never did.

she used to strike her victims' naked bodies. She was a sadistic, merciless animal; but our condition deteriorated so rapidly that in a short time we became insensitive to her beatings.

After several days we learned that the block we were in was a solitary block which had been designated for scarlet fever and typhus patients. We had been brought here for experimentation. The Germans wanted to test how many of us would develop these sicknesses during twenty-one days of exposure to contaminated people, and they also wanted to eliminate anyone who was diseased.

We were visited periodically by a medical commission headed by the notorious murderer Doctor Mengele. Before the commission's first visit, one of the Jewish supervisors warned us: "Beware! The girl who gets thrown into the black auto* goes directly to the gas chambers. Those who are taken to the infirmary will never return. Anyone who feels sick should hide, and anyone who has temperature should not disclose it."

We followed her advice. When the commission arrived, we covered for the girls who were running a high fever. We tried to sneak them into rooms that the commission had already passed through and made sure their places were taken by healthier girls. Only in two cases we failed because the women were so sick that they could not stand up at all.

During those three weeks we were locked up in the block. We were forbidden to go out, and we did not work. The *brum* that they put in our food assured us a deep sleep, regardless of the conditions, yet our strength diminished greatly. I came to learn that crisis could create selfishness in the same measure as heroism, and both to an extreme degree; for in spite of the great self-sacrifice exhibited by the women when it came to protecting the lives of the sick, the severity of the conditions often made them behave cruelly as well. Those of us who tried to save a piece of bread for later were often disappointed because there were girls who stole crumbs from other starving girls. Sometimes the food in Auschwitz was distributed to each cell in a pot, with no utensils. The girls had to take turns drinking from that pot, and in order to ensure that no one got more than her share, they used to watch the throat of the one drinking to see how many swallows were taken. And none of this was

*The "black auto" was a closed black truck used to transport people to the gas chambers or crematoria.

out of innate malice; the unnatural fear and desperation of the times created unnatural character in us, both good and bad.

During the time that we were in quarantine I had great trouble digesting food. I felt faint from starvation, but whenever I tried to taste soup from that dirty dish, I became nauseated and could not force it down. Elizabeth Frankfurter, a neighbor from my hometown who was in the block with us, tried to convince me to eat and to guard my strength as much as possible, because when we returned home I would have to take care of my parents . . .

I'll never forget the festival of Shavuos. On that day we received goulash with potatoes. We didn't know what had happened; why were we suddenly receiving better food? We were suspicious, but we ate it with great appetite. We had barely finished when we received a secret warning from one of the kitchen personnel: "Do not eat the food because there is 'something' in it!" A half hour later this "something" began to work. We ran to the pails in the yard with terrible diarrhea and vomiting.

The Germans were smart. They knew the dates of all the Jewish holidays, which is why the food given before Yom Kippur was salty. Their calculations were meticulous.

We passed the first twenty-one days in quarantine, but we had become almost careless of our fate. The hunger grew. We talked with a fond nostalgia of the fat goulash we had received just a short time ago; it lived in our minds as a fantasy, a vision of nourishment, in spite of its aftermath. The dirt in the block was beyond imagination. We had not washed or changed our rags since our arrival in the camp. Worst of all were the "selections" which always took place during the night.

At each selection mothers were separated from their children, sisters from sisters, friends from friends. By that time we knew about the gas chambers. Many women suffered nervous breakdowns, others were driven to insanity. Each of us wondered constantly: "Where will I be tomorrow?"

At the conclusion of the twenty-one days, another medical commission arrived. They examined us and checked our temperature. We were warned not to talk among ourselves because there was one person in the commission who understood Hungarian. Afterward, rumors began to spread about the purpose of that visit, because the examination had been carried out in greater secrecy than usual.* The women began to guess what would be done with them now. Some said that most probably we would go to work, for "they" would not feed us bread and *brum* without using us; one would have to work in return. But what kind of work, and where? . . .

The following day we were led through the lager street to a public shower and latrine. When I passed the first window of the latrine, I suddenly felt faint. The window was painted on one side, so I could see my reflection in it, and I was sure that the person in the glass was my brother. "Eliezer!" I screamed out; but in the blink of an eye I was hit over the head, the line moved on, and the image disappeared. How could I have known that with a shaven head I would look exactly like my brother Eliezer? Since we had arrived, we had not seen ourselves in a mirror.

We were then returned to a regular block and were permitted for a while to go to the public shower unescorted. This was a random privilege, a fortunate caprice of the block chief, who was at liberty to abuse or "indulge" the prisoners as she pleased. The shower guard was a kind, middle-aged Jewish woman. She never talked to me, but whenever I passed her she would gently stroke my head. Maybe I reminded her of her daughter . . .

Around the shower barracks and latrine, a kind of "business" was conducted every day after the afternoon appel. We called it the "Wall Street of Auschwitz." Here the veteran prisoners clandestinely exchanged a spoon, an onion, or half a comb for a slice of bread or salami. Some of them worked in the kitchen or warehouses, and no one knew how they came into possession of their "wares." The prices on that market went up or down according to supply and demand. I too made exchanges there; for a long time I could not swallow my ration of sausage, which tasted like horse skin, and I would gladly exchange it for a piece of onion.

---

*An examination conducted "quietly" served the Germans well. It prevented mass panic among the prisoners, and it gave some subordinate block officials the opportunity to arrange unauthorized selections of their own.

Aside from business, one could make acquaintances in the latrine with prisoners from all parts of the world. Here I met girls from France, Holland, Italy, even from Hawaii. The Hawaiian girl told me that she had been studying in Paris when the war broke out. Her parents had begged her to come home, but she refused because she was curious to see how things would develop — and had wound up here.

I also met my two cousins, Martha and Eva Wilmani. They worked in a group called the "White Kerchiefs," one of several units assigned to sort the belongings taken from the people who came in with the new transports. Seeing my cousins and the other girls at the "market" gave me a sense of some kind of freedom, but it did not last long.

A few days later a lager curfew was called, which meant that every prisoner was confined to his block and could not even go out to the latrine. Right after the morning appel, a group of SS men and women arrived. We had no idea that there were doctors among them. They walked along the lines, scrutinizing us like cattle in a pen. Finally they chose a hundred and twenty relatively pretty, healthy, brown-haired girls, including myself, and ordered us to wait on the side. At the end of the selection they led us to the revier, the camp sick block. When I saw where we were headed, a heavy fear clutched at my throat; we had heard that no one ever returned from that place.

In the revier they wrote down our names in alphabetical order, and they took a sample of blood from each of us. Since my name was Weis I was the last on the list, and I had a chance to observe the other one hundred and nineteen girls. Each girl had become a living question mark; each pair of eyes asked silently: "What is awaiting me?"

They began calling names from the end of the list, eventually reaching mine. When I returned to the other girls in my block half an hour later, they were stunned to see me back. I reported that a woman doctor had drawn half a liter of blood from my right arm. Though I knew that in my undernourished condition I would not easily regain half a liter of blood, I was thankful that nothing worse had happened.

One afternoon ten days later, we heard a wild yelling: "*Appel! Appel! Outside! Appel!*" Until then we had been called to stand appels only at night. And now . . . what did they want now?

After we were all lined up, the same medical commission arrived, escorted by a number of revier workers who carried blankets, bread, margarine, and sausages. A table with a stack of files was placed in the center of the yard. The Blockelteste announced that those who heard their names called should come to the table. A massive silence engulfed the lines. Finally my name, Elizabeth Weis, was called. With trembling knees I approached the table, visions of horror racing through my mind.

I was handed a slice of bread, a pat of margarine, and a piece of sausage. "My G-d!" I thought. "What is going on?" Yet the saliva poured into my mouth and my stomach contracted at the sight of the food. I saw a smile on the doctor's face, and I calmed down a bit because I recognized her from the revier. There she had sat at my side, holding a jar into which my blood streamed through a rubber tube, and with the other hand pressing a stethoscope to my chest; but at least she had done her job in a gentle manner.

Now she was giving me a *tzulage* — an addition — and I began to tremble all over again. Extra food could only mean one thing: another half liter of blood!

They needed our blood for their wounded soldiers. G-d in heaven! Jewish blood for German soldiers! *Our* blood for German soldiers! When the drawing was over, I felt weaker than I had the first time, and very angry. We received a double portion of soup and were ordered to rest, and I burst out sobbing because I felt that my strength was leaving me. I was so weak that I couldn't run with the Ess Kommando, even though extra soup was awarded to those who carried the food barrels.

At that time one of our overseers was a Stubendienst, a secondary supervisor, who had come from Holland. I do not remember her name, but I cannot forget her bright and kind face. We called her "Moon." Once she was able to get some additional food for us, but because of the pushing and shoving it might cause she suggested calling an appel and distributing the soup while we stood in line. The SS woman in charge of the food allowed her to call the appel, but it did not help. The starving girls jostled each other aside to get a sip of that dirty liquid. For the German overseers, however, this was a pleasant sight; they enjoyed watching these wretched girls fight over a bit of food.

During that appel we were arranged in line according to height, so that everyone should be visible. I was the shortest girl and always stood in the first row, and therefore I was the first to be slapped and beaten when the line behind me wasn't straight or when a noise was heard in the column. But this time it was different.

To this very day I do not know what sort of expression crossed my face as I stood looking at that soup kettle before me. Perhaps it was one of desperation and pain. I remember that moment vividly, for there was cabbage in the soup, and I imagined the tasty stuffed cabbage my mother had made at home. For a second I found myself in a different world.

I awakened from my daydream when the Moon dragged me by the shoulder and pushed the ladle into my hand, saying, *"Du kleine, ouskratzen,"* meaning "You, little one, scrape." She was telling me that I could scrape the remainder of the cabbage from the bottom of the kettle. I had been so absorbed in my thoughts that I did not understand her and began to explain: *"Ich habe keine kretze* (I do not have scabies*)."* My misunderstanding came from the close similarity of the two German words *kratzen* and *kretze.* I was so moved by the Moon's kindness that as I bent over the kettle I began to cry. I licked and licked the remnants of the soup and cried; I choked from crying, yet I continued to lick . . . When I finished and was satiated, I felt a new desire to live.

Breslau-Hundesfeld

On August 9, 1944, we left Birkenau. Several SS men and a few civilians had come to our barracks the week before and chosen three hundred and sixty girls, registered us in alphabetical order, and divided us into three groups to be sent out in transports. We had no idea of our destination or of the fate that awaited us.

To our surprise we reached Breslau-Hundesfeld that same evening. The buildings of this camp were new, and in comparison with Birkenau — physically, at least — it was a better place. Twenty-four girls were assigned to each room, and each was given a separate *pritsche* and two blankets, as well as her own plate, cup, and spoon. The room also had two

---

*Scabies is a contagious skin disease marked by severe itching, which is caused by mites burrowing under the skin. Many Hungarian girls in Auschwitz contracted it.

tables, a couple of benches, and an oven. In the corridor was a common shower room and a bathroom consisting of a few rows of receptacles and faucets. Those girls with a sense of humor began to make jokes about our "luxurious" conditions.

Two girls from our transport—the sisters Lefkowicz, whose family had owned the restaurant in Kosice — were chosen as cooks. There was little food, but it wasn't bad. We did not receive any underwear or change of clothing, yet we felt that our lot had improved.

The work in the camp was extremely exhausting. Some of us were assigned to the Reinmetal factory, where we worked at machines on alternating twelve-hour shifts, one week at night and one week in the daytime. We also cleaned the entire camp, did the washing, and stood appel continuously. At each appel we were beaten and kicked and warned without end: "If you do not behave, Auschwitz is not far from here."

In the factory there were three sections, named after the managers: Richer, Lusha, and Dorneman. I worked in the Dorneman section at a metal-cutting machine. I was curious to know the purpose of these little pieces of metal. They must have been of great importance, because every hour a middle-aged man in a white coat and gold-rimmed spectacles checked our work and examined the pieces with a special instrument. I came to the conclusion that we were producing armaments parts.

This awareness horrified me: with our own hands, we were creating weapons which would be used against our people and against the free world!

Three of my good friends — Sarah Wieliczker, Clara Weisfeld, and Elanka Weinberg—worked in the same section with me and lived in the same room. We slept next to each other, and if one of us had a crumb of bread, it was considered common property. We also shared our thoughts and ideas. The four of us began to think of sabotage, and we let some of the other girls in on our decision. They accepted our plan and committed themselves with enthusiasm and understanding. We could not approach everyone, however — not because we did not trust them, but because some girls' nerves were on edge, and a dangerous undertaking might have damaged their health further.

Now the question remained — how would we turn our plan into action? If we did not make the right quantity and the right quality of the product, we would be punished for sabotage. If we worked at a slower pace, they would bring in more people to complete the production. The only other option was to turn the raw iron, copper, and aluminum we received into useless material. We decided that we would work diligently to create a good-looking product, but during the hour between inspections we would corrupt the raw material, either by carving very mild scratches into the pieces or by putting the different types of metal into the wrong piles. Fortunately we found other partners in our enterprise, and in time eighty girls from our section were involved in sabotaging the raw material designated for German weapons production.

In addition to political offenders, there were French war prisoners who worked in our factory as machine technicians. They were not as completely enslaved as we were. They walked to and from work without an SS escort; they had a canteen where they could exchange tokens for food, and they were permitted to read newspapers. They weren't allowed to talk to us, but even without communication they soon caught on to our conspiracy and tried to help us. Thanks to them we weren't caught by the German inspectors, and our project was more effective.

The French technicians were well organized. Three or four of them worked on each shift, passing between the rows and checking to see if the machines worked well or if they needed some adjustment. This afforded us the opportunity for a second form of sabotage. Our machines were never "all right" and always had to have something "fixed." All we had to do was hold a particular screw a bit longer or let it go a bit too soon, and the results were twofold; the machine parts broke more easily and the product came out damaged. While we carried out our plan, one of the Frenchmen would fix my machine while two of his friends kept the German overseers occupied by asking legitimate questions and making logical requests pertaining to the factory. These Frenchmen also had a natural ability, when necessary, to draw the attention of the SS women, preventing them from watching us too closely.

More than once our hearts stopped beating when an inspector or an SS woman unexpectedly appeared to check our work, but our powerful desire to persevere gave us strength to endure the tremendous pressure we had created for ourselves. After an exhausting shift, Clara Weisfeld and I would sit down in our room and figure out the "balance" of the day, noting how many girls had done sabotage and in what span of time. After a careful calculation we estimated that even on the less successful days, a substantial number of parts and materials turned into waste.

The Frenchmen, in addition to being our partners in sabotage, encouraged us to hold on because the war was coming to an end. If there was special news they related it to us while fixing our machines. The SS women, especially the blond beast who was our commandant, tried to make sure there would be no contact between us, and when the Frenchmen were around she walked between the machines continually, yelling at us not to talk. Sometimes we could catch only a few words or part of a sentence from our French friends. But this was our only fragile connection to the outside world, and the few bits of information we collected were desperately important to us.

One of the Frenchmen once approached my machine and "accidentally" spilled a can of oil on the table. In the oil he drew a map of the front. "Here are the Russians," he explained to me in broken German, with the embellishment of hand gestures. "Here are the English . . . and we are here. Do not fear, continue to break parts, we will help you. Soon we'll be liberated and you'll come with us to Paris . . ." He knew that if the Germans discovered his "map" he would pay with his head, and yet he did it to give us hope.

By that time we already knew what had happened to our parents and families. Our own future was uncertain, but as long as we still lived, we tried as best we could to give meaning to our lives and to take encouragement. Each Sunday evening after the appel we got together and talked. This was the most favorable time for a gathering, for Sunday management in the camp was a little slacker than during the week, and our Jewish supervisor would turn a blind eye to our talk. We organized groups, arranged cultural evenings, and sat around the table or on a bed and ate a "meal" together. We tried to forget where we were, at least for a while, and sometimes we even joked about our situation. Some girls talked about books they had once read, others sang sad songs in Yiddish or Hungarian, and all of us related episodes from our home lives. We described our families in detail so that in case we ever left this place, we would be able to recognize each other's relatives and send regards or hasten reunions.

But even with hope, the Sabbath and holidays were unbearable. The first holiday in Breslau-Hundesfeld was Rosh Hashanah. We talked about nothing except what Rosh Hashanah had been like in our homes, and all the while we wondered how we could celebrate it here in the lager.

That week my friends and I worked the night shift. On the night before the eve of Rosh Hashanah we went to the kitchen after the shift to get our ration of tea, and we asked the kitchen workers, who were from our group, to prepare a bit of hot water for us the next morning so that we could wash ourselves in honor of the holiday.

We woke up before the sound of the whistle, depressed and bitter at the remembrance of the homes we had lost and the families we might never see again. Almost every single one of us broke down and cried for hours. We looked into each other's eyes, searching for the support we so desperately needed; but we had no one, and it was very hard to accept the reality that we were all alone and yet we were forced to live.

Some time later I went to the kitchen to get the water we had been promised, still feeling miserable and with tears on my cheeks. Apparently the kitchen workers had told our overseer, who was Jewish, about the approaching holiday, for when she saw me she asked why I was crying. Then she called me into the kitchen, removed the cover from a barrel, and said, "Eat, little one, as much as you can." Before I could take a bite, I burst into another flood of sobbing. I cried and prayed to G-d from the depths of my soul, asking Him to help us.

At two o'clock that afternoon the whistle sounded, and we were called to the clothing magazine to get winter clothes and shoes. We walked, crying in silence as we thought of our youth, when children in every Jewish home had received new clothing for Rosh Hashanah. In the magazine our dirty rags were exchanged for clean ones: a skirt, a blouse, wooden clogs, and a winter coat.

After returning to our rooms, we swallowed our soup and went to work on the night shift, the soles of our new clogs clacking to the drill: "Left, one, two, three." I remember telling my friend Elanka Weinberg that the sound of the clogs was like the bumping of my heart, and involuntarily I pointed to the left side of my chest. Elanka looked at me with her big eyes and said, "Erzhi!* If we were chosen for the *right side*, let's not think of the left — let's think instead about what we will have tomorrow for 'dinner.'"

Yom Kippur, the most fearful day of the year, did not overwhelm us as Rosh Hashanah had, perhaps because we lived in the most fearful of times and saw death every day before our eyes. And yet we wanted to observe Yom Kippur too, so we decided to fast. This was a dangerous decision.

Our German commandant noticed that something was going on. She ordered us to assemble and told us that if we did not eat the "precious food" we were given for even one day, she would consider it sabotage: "The cursed Jews get food for one reason only — to produce weapons for mighty Germany, and not for you to live. If you do not eat, we will withhold all food, and you will work until you collapse and then be thrown straight into the crematory."

About a hundred of us from the Dorneman section discussed the commandant's warning. The girls differed widely in their opinions, and yet many decided to fast, regardless of what might happen.

On the eve of Yom Kippur we let only a few of our machines run to make a clatter, and at midnight as always we accepted our food. But the Frenchmen, who understood our silent signs, turned off the central switches which controlled the electrical surge to many of the machines, making it appear as though the main current were at fault. Then they left open the gate leading to the latrine, as if by mistake. While they occupied the Germans with talk, we each took turns going to the latrine and spilling out our soup before the commandant had a chance to notice. We were so happy that we had succeeded in fasting on Yom Kippur! Those who had been against the idea were embarrassed afterward that they had not participated.

*A pet name.

Winter arrived, and the fierce cold aggravated our lives even more. The appels were conducted at dawn, in the midst of the powerful winds and gusting snow. The water in the washroom froze. We were dressed in rags, and our clogs were always wet.

One night on the way to the factory the snow stuck to the soles of my clogs, and I stumbled with each step. When we arrived, I removed my clogs until the snow had melted from them, and I put my cold feet against the radiator, letting my machine run to create noise. It never entered my mind that the chief supervisor would discern this from a distance of thirty or forty meters, that he could detect one machine running empty amidst the hammering of so many others. But he did. He came over and saw me warming my feet at the radiator, and he began to scream, beating and slapping me from left and right. His face turned red and his mouth spouted saliva. The girls were frightened; our French friends ground their teeth in anger but could do nothing to protect me.

Even though they were totally helpless at such times, the Frenchmen tried in various ways to ease our lot and lift our spirits. In addition to relaying news from the front, they actually gave us little gifts from time to time. I remember that once on a Sabbath afternoon after "lunch" I returned to my machine to find a small package hidden in the pile of raw material that was prepared for polishing. I was frightened, thinking that it might be a trap, and covered it without looking at its contents. A few minutes later one of the Frenchmen came to my machine as if to fix something and began to talk in a fast whisper. He told me not to be afraid of him, that he had brought me the package as a present and that more would follow. Before I could thank him he disappeared. Afterward, every Saturday afternoon, I found a tiny package near my machine, and I wasn't the only one; almost all the girls received something. Sometimes it was a sandwich, or a few biscuits or candies. Once a girl received a mirror and a small comb, a present so characteristic of the Frenchmen.

Their genuine attention and goodwill were for our souls what this food was for our bodies. A trinket or scrap which in normal times would have been thrown into the trash were in those days so great that they were almost a dream, and I never forgot them.

These priceless gifts did not come only from the Frenchmen. Once when we arrived at the factory, several French and Czechoslovakian girls from the day shift were waiting to instruct us in a new work procedure. They were visibly moved at the sight of our torn rags and of the scraggly hair on our heads, which was in various stages of regrowth. The girl who was assigned to my machine was especially touched, and began to ask me about my background and how I had been brought here. She told me not to be afraid, but to go to the washroom and wait there for her. When I hesitated, she assured me that she would come right after me. In the washroom she pushed a big piece of bread into my hands and told me to eat it quickly while she stood and kept a lookout for an overseer. With tears strangling my throat, I ate the bread, thinking of my hungry friends with whom I would have loved to share it. I had hardly finished when a guard came looking for me. It turned out that two prisoners had run away, and after that night it was announced that no one would be allowed to go to the washroom without the permission of an SS guard.

The most precious gift that I remember, however, was one of an entirely different nature. One morning when I returned from the night shift, I discovered under my bunk a package and a note from my cousin, congratulating me on the occasion of my birthday, which I had completely forgotten. In the package was a slice of bread, a pat of margarine, a piece of cheese, and a second note containing a few words of congratulation — from our Blockelteste, Magda!

Magda apparently had made an inspection in our room and found my cousin's note. She had read it and added her own message to the package. It is almost impossible to describe my feelings at that moment. Magda was Jewish, but in the camps this did not always have great significance, since many of the Jewish supervisors had already lost their hearts. I was moved to the core of my being. This package lit up the darkness of the day and proved that in spite of all we remained human beings — capable of feeling, capable of something so ordinary as the pleasant warmth that accompanies birthday wishes.

I told my friends that I had seen in that incident the hand of G-d. My parents, Shmuel and Esther Weis, had always kept their home open to the poor and made sure that there was food on the table for them, and I believe it was in their merit that I survived.

Chanukah was approaching. I decided that we must find a way to celebrate; we were all tired and despondent, and our spirits needed refreshment. A week before the holiday I began to steal small amounts of the oil we used to grease our machines in the factory. I also went through the garbage, collecting cotton threads which we normally threw away after cleaning our machines, and I hid them under my mattress.

"What do you need them for?" a girl asked me. I told her of my plan and asked her to help me "organize" five uncooked potatoes. She was overwhelmed by my idea and through a contact in the kitchen manage to get the potatoes, at no small risk.

On the first night of Chanukah I cut one of the potatoes in half, carved a hole into it, and filled it with oil. Then I twisted my hoarded threads into a wick and placed it in the oil — and we had a menorah! All the girls came to my room that night. They sat on the beds while I lit the first candle and made the blessings. Together we sang the first stanza of *Maoz Tzur*, and we talked about the Chanukah celebrations in our homes. The first four evenings went by smoothly.

On the fifth night we were late lighting our menorah, and when the "lights out" whistle was sounded, the candles were still burning. In the complete darkness that enveloped the camp, the tiny lights betrayed us; the SS guard was sure that they were some kind of signal. She burst through our door and was stunned at the sight that met her eyes: the room was in prescribed order, the girls were sitting quietly and singing in a whisper. I jumped to my feet and saluted, though the blood froze in my veins. In my mind's eye I saw the punishment coming: twenty-four newly shaven heads! But even worse than that vision were the accusing eyes of my friends. Because of my reckless enthusiasm, they would all suffer now.

"What's going on here?" the guard snapped.

I regained my equilibrium and said, "Lady commander, this week we celebrate the memory of the Maccabim, who, with only a handful of Jews, defeated their many enemies!" I wasn't thinking when I spoke; the words just slipped out, as if a *dybbuk** had overtaken me. I think I was even more shocked than my friends. We breathed again when we saw the

*A *dybbuk* is the spirit of a dead person which takes possession of a living person's body.

guard leaving the room, but we could not understand it—she had simply left without another word.

The first to recover from this double shock was Sarah Wieliczker. "Erzhi," she said, "put out the flames." I did so immediately. We were really frightened, certain that a punishment awaited us. We just didn't know how severe it would be. I hid the rest of the potatoes and went to bed, but I could not fall asleep.

Sarah whispered, "Erzhi, are you asleep?"

"No!"

"Have you lost your mind? What did you want to prove with your speech?" she asked.

"I didn't think about what I was saying. The words came out by themselves. I didn't want to be a hero! Please believe me!"

"I believe you. But we are used to seeing you choose your words more carefully. Oh, well! If they only shave our heads, then it was worth it."

"Yes, but what would Zissi say if her 'hairdo' had to go?" I asked in all sincerity. Zissi was the coquette in our group, and she had taken great pains to arrange her hair once it began to grow back.

However, the most unbelievable thing happened: we weren't punished! That night the SS woman who had discovered us chose one of our girls to haul the food barrels. Carrying the food was considered a privilege, and we allowed ourselves to relax, for we knew that she would not take any action against us. But why she was so "good" we never understood.

It was a new *Nes Chanukah*.

Evacuation

The Russian air attacks became more frequent and more forceful, and yet we welcomed them in our hearts, for they brought us hope. We weren't afraid of injuries or death; we thought only of the liberation and freedom that the attacks promised. We called the bombs "Stalin's Candles" because they lit up the skies and terrified the SS men and women, which gave us a great deal of satisfaction.

When the first few attacks came, they rushed us all to the shelters.

Later on they kept us at our machines, turning out the lights and making us work by lanterns while they ran and hid in the shelters by themselves. Only once a bomb fell very close to the factory. Some of the girls were scratched lightly by flying debris, but in general we weren't caught up in the panic of the daily bombing.

Toward the end of January the Germans became very irritable. The Frenchmen too were on edge and whispered to each other, apparently unconcerned about what the guards would think. They told us that the Russians were drawing closer and that the Germans were about to flee. Discipline slackened; perhaps the overseers were beginning to think about what would happen to them if they were caught red-handed.

Sure enough, on Sunday morning we were ordered to turn off our machines and leave the factory. When we got back to the camp, we saw workers loading provisions from the magazines onto hand-drawn wagons. We were given food, which we realized was food for the road. Usually there was one loaf of bread for five people, but now there was one loaf for nine people. We were also given blankets to wrap ourselves with, and we secured them at the neck and waist with threads we had pulled from our mattresses.

Shortly before the evacuation a transport of Jewish women from a sugar factory arrived at the camp. Ninety percent of the women were in dreadful condition. The Germans loaded them onto a closed wagon and harnessed us to it. We were glad to push the wagon because we thought we were saving the women, but after a while we were ordered to abandon it in the middle of the road. The SS guards said that a truck had been ordered for the women, but it was a lie. No truck came. They were left to die of hunger and cold.

Toward evening dark clouds invaded the skies and a heavy snow began to fall. Our dresses were torn, and our blankets and shoes quickly became soaked. We were hungry, for we had already eaten our portion of bread, and the march weakened us further. Many girls developed fever and were on the verge of a complete physical breakdown, and yet our minds were occupied with one desire only — to see Germany defeated.

And indeed we did see the Germans in flight. We passed roads congested with all types of vehicles and masses of Germans, stumbling along with bundles on their backs, some riding on wagons drawn by horses or dogs, others on wagons pulled by hand. It strengthened our hearts to see the "mighty" race defeated. Let them taste the flavor of losing their homes!

At nightfall we reached a crossroads. We had no idea where we were. Suddenly we heard a command: "Half an hour of rest in standing position." Along with the darkness the frost increased. Our wet clothes and blankets froze on our bodies, and we began to tremble convulsively. After the rest, the march resumed.

No pen can describe the dread and terror of that night. Even at the hour of their own surrender, the uppermost thought in the minds of the Nazis was to drag us out and kill us on the road. They followed alongside us on horses and motorcycles and kept us marching all night and all of the next day on icy, broken, treacherous roads. Many girls broke down, unable to withstand the cold, the hunger, and the wounds of their frozen feet. The cruel SS women, seeing our woeful condition, gave periodic orders to remain standing. To stand in the freezing cold wearing clothes that have turned into ice is unimaginable torture. Girls who could not follow the "march and stand" rhythm had to leave the column.

I will never forget the last glances of those wretched girls. Some were frightened, but others were indifferent to their fate, the look of death already in their eyes. Immediately after they stepped out of line, rifle shots pierced the stillness of the frozen air. They were shot in the head right in front of us . . . They staggered to the ground, spreading their blood on the fresh white snow. On that frozen road, the space between life and death was only an eye-blink. Some girls did not want to go on living without their sisters or friends, and so they stepped out together with them, and together with them were murdered.

I envied those who did not have to struggle anymore. I was extremely weak and could barely walk on my frostbitten feet, but my cousin and another friend dragged me along like a sack of potatoes. I told them to let go of me, that I could not fight anymore. They had only one answer: "If you step out of the line, we go too. Do you want to take this responsibility on your conscience?" I told them that in any case they would fall victims because of me, and they replied, "What is fated is fated. But first you must strive!" They adamantly refused to let me slip or step out of line, and thanks to their steadfastness I held on.

We left the place of the massacre and kept on marching. There was nothing to eat, and we kept alive by licking the snow from the ground. Toward evening we reached a village and were pushed into a stable. It was warm and I yearned for a bit of sleep, but the Germans had their own plan; they led us to a granary filled to the ceiling with straw, and there was no place to lie down. Those who were too weak and exhausted to stand any longer fell to the ground, and others tumbled on top of them. The ones on the bottom screamed, bit, and pinched. I stood on my feet the entire night.

In the darkness I began to grope around in the straw, and I found one or two stalks that had grain inside. I took out the grain and ate it, and to me it tasted like the *manna* our forefathers had eaten during their wanderings in the desert.

At daybreak we left the farm. We marched for several hours until we reached a gigantic camp, which, we learned from other prisoners, was Gross Rosen, a principal extermination camp. In front of the gates were large barrels full of fire, and German soldiers were tossing documents and papers into the flames.

We were taken to a somewhat clean barracks with beds stacked one on top of another against the walls, four people to one bed. We also received a hot vegetable soup, which tasted delicious after days of starvation. We were permitted to sleep until the morning, and this was more than we had expected.

At the morning appel, several French doctors who were war prisoners came and checked our frozen feet. We were told that those of us who wanted to could go to the revier, but the doctors advised us in a whisper not to ask for it. Each morning while they dressed our wounds with ointment, they asked us questions and exchanged information with us about other camps.

We stayed in Gross Rosen for two weeks, standing appel in the morning and evening but doing no work. Before we left we were given old coats which had been worn by previous inmates. On the back of each one was painted a dark red cross. Then we were squeezed into open freight cars. People screamed and bit each other, fearing that they would freeze to death if they were not able to move. But nothing helped, and the train began to pull out. We did not get very far, though; the train would back up and then go forward a short distance, back up again and go forward. We heard that the railroad tracks ahead had been bombed and there was no way to proceed. Two soldiers dressed in heavy fur coats were guarding our wagon, and during that entire day of inching backward and forward they amused themselves by eating in front of us and drinking cognac.

After a while the train began to move ahead at an even pace. There was no place for me inside the wagon, so I stood on the outer brace and watched the passing landscape. We were traveling through a forest now, climbing steadily up the side of a mountain. I was transfixed by the awesome beauty of the surroundings. The snow on the fir trees sparkled with crystalline lights, but I had only one thought -- the world is drenched in blood, and nature carries on its routine and does not care to avenge the cries of the innocent.

All along the way we heard shooting, but we had no idea where it came from. We assumed the shots were meant to frighten the prisoners. After riding for several days without a morsel to put in our mouths, the SS soldiers opened the wagons and yelled, "Haul the food!" As always, I was the first to volunteer. The storage wagon was the first car after the engines, and as I walked toward the front of the train, I realized how long it was. What I saw on that walk will always remain an unhealed wound in my memory. On one side of me the ground was strewn with murdered people, the victims of the shots we had been hearing, and on the other side were the freight cars, filled with living corpses. Their faces were blue-green from beating and suffering, they were unshaven, their skin was totally dried out — they were dying people with living eyes, holding on to the last and thinnest thread of life. Half-frozen, hardly able to breathe, they screamed and made other startling sounds. Many of them, with open bellies and spilled intestines, were being dragged out of the cars and thrown into a pile.

As I ran alongside the train, carrying the food rations for our wagon,

I stepped into puddles. At first I thought it was only mud, but no! It was blood! Puddles of blood of murdered human beings!

And again we were pushed into the wagons; again the doors were bolted, the whistle sounded, the train moved forward in slow motion. We noticed fluid being splashed on the pile of the living-dead, and then rapid bursts of fire spurted up from it. Although it had been several days since food had touched our lips, we could not eat because of the flaming forks of fire before us. We looked in silence into the heart of blackness, into the soul of the night.

The train lunged into a gallop, swallowing landscape after landscape, but we became numb to our surroundings and unconscious of time; we could not differentiate between morning and evening, between caring and not caring, between life and death.

Suddenly the train stopped, and the SS men unbolted the doors with wild screams: *"Get down! Get down!"* We were frozen and dizzy; our heads were spinning from hunger and from the hellish visions we had seen. We did not have the energy to move quickly and stumbled over our own feet, but the Germans wanted us to run and beat us with their rifle butts, continually shouting, *"Schnell, schnell!"* The more they beat us the weaker and slower we became.

We marched silently and obediently in the thick darkness of the forest while they continued to beat and curse us. Finally we reached a cluster of buildings surrounded by a stone fence. Smoke was rising from the enclosure.

Mauthausen

In this camp the rituals we had been through before were repeated with the most dependable consistency. It was like revisiting a nightmare in vivid detail. We were marched into the camp, where they shaved our heads once again and herded us into a large hall that was warm and brightly lit. We were met by a group of SS men with dogs, accompanied by a number of young, beautiful girls, dressed elegantly in civilian clothing. Their appearance sent shudders through us, for in Auschwitz similarly attired girls had come to "escort" people to the place where experiments were done. We were ordered to strip and to go into a shower room, and before we could warm up under the hot shower, the beautiful girls came in and began to beat our naked bodies with rubber pipes.

When the beating was over, we received disinfected rags to wear. I was given a pair of long, gray men's underwear, a man's short-sleeved shirt, and a pair of shoes. When we were dressed, we had to dip ourselves into a pail filled with chlorine-water, and then we were chased, still wet from the shower, out into the freezing night.

Slowly the darkness began to lift from the horizon and the dawn showed us a gigantic camp, surrounded by the familiar high-voltage wire fence. In the distance we noticed a men's camp and tried to draw the attention of the prisoners by calling out to them. We asked them what place this was, and they shouted back, "Mauthausen!" Then they asked us who we were, where we had come from, and when we had left our homes, and we in turn asked them about members of our families. We searched them with our eyes, looking for our near and dear ones, but we saw no familiar face.

We were led to a block, where the Blockelteste gave us dirty, odorous blankets. Then she announced that we would not have to stand appel and that we were permitted to sleep. We lay down and immediately fell into a deep slumber.

Our guards were French women who were war prisoners, and in comparison to others they were fairly good. They did not make us work and let us sleep on the floor as much as we wanted. But the crowding and bedbugs and the groaning of the dying people were unbearable. We received no soup, only a decent portion of very black bread, which had not been made of flour but from the fallen dust of the mills or from some synthetic material. But it did not matter. We ate whatever we were given.

On the third night some of the girls were taken out of our block. We had learned that this camp indeed had an experiment section, and we feared that the girls had been taken there.

On Sabbath afternoon we were chased out to the courtyard, where a wagon filled with sacks of clothing was waiting for us. Three men jumped aboard and began to empty out the sacks. From one they took out coats, from the second bread, and from the third sausages. Immediately a war of fists and elbows began. I succeeded in grabbing a coat, fearing the cold more than I feared starvation. When the fistfight was over I went out to see what was left, and from the mud I was able to gather some bread which must have fallen from people's hands.

After only a week we were called for an appel and taken to the train station once again. We were loaded into regular passenger wagons, but the crowding here was just as severe as it had been in the freight cars. By the time I climbed up there were no more places to sit, and the guard would not let me sit on the floor. Just then I noticed a travelers' net above the seat, a strong netting used to store baggage, and I pulled myself into it and lay down. I was light enough and in no danger of falling out.

We traveled for several days, jerked continually by the forward and backward motion of the train; but this time, instead of shots, we heard explosions. After a while we passed a city that stood in flames. Those who were near the windows reported seeing road signs that said "Nuremberg." This was the city where the heinous "Nuremberg Laws" had been formulated.* Whenever we heard the word "Nuremberg," we had always wished: *"Farbrent zul zi vehren"* — "She should burn as in hell." Now I thought to myself: "Finally, Jewish wishes have found an open ear in Heaven."

We kept traveling through open fields, going on and on for many mornings and evenings, without food. One day the train halted abruptly. The guards jumped down and then came and counted us — but without hollering or beating. We also noticed that these were not SS men but soldiers of the Wermacht, the German army. Where had they come from? What had happened? Was it possible that the war was over? We had seen an outdoor pump and wanted to drink and wash our hands. One of our girls asked to leave the train, and she was given permission!

At first only ten girls were permitted to leave the train, but then they slowly allowed all of us to get down. We noticed a bombed-out train standing nearby, and when we came closer we saw that the wagons were full of large, frozen animal bones. We fell upon that "treasure," each of us carrying away as much as she could. One girl, a kitchen worker who

*The Nuremberg Laws, adopted by the German Reichstag on September 15, 1935, were the first major body of official anti-Jewish legislation. The edicts legalized the racist policies of the German state and effectively disenfranchised the Jews, placing them outside the protection of the state socially, economically, and politically, and leaving them at the mercy of the secret police.

had smuggled out a box of matches, lit a pile of dry grass, and we carried the fire to five places so that many girls could warm up. Then we began to scratch around in the earth in search of edible roots; but as always, before we had a chance to enjoy anything, we were chased back to the wagons, and the train continued its pitiless odyssey.

Again we had no water or food for days, and we lay on the floor, destitute and drained of strength. The bombs were the only thing that kept us alive. We were not worried that the bombs might kill us; we yearned only to see *their* end!

At one point I fell asleep in my net and dreamt that we were on the way to a very big camp and that the British would liberate us. I dismissed this as a mindless fancy of sleep, for I did not believe in fairy tales.

Bergen-Belsen

The last stop of our journey was Bergen-Belsen.

If we had had to endure only Bergen-Belsen, it would have been more than enough. If we had had to endure everything else that had befallen us, without Bergen-Belsen, that too would have been more than enough; but together they were beyond human strength. Yet it seems the Al-mighty had His own plan. To each person written down in the Book of Life He had given the ability to survive both.

The sun came out. We dragged our bodies into the camp — dizzy, starved, debilitated both physically and spiritually. We had to walk a long way before we reached a block. We passed women sitting in front of their buildings, doing nothing. They had been reduced to withered shells; their skin was dry and looked as if it were glued to their bones. They gazed around with bewildered expressions and kept scratching themselves. When we approached them, they told us that the blocks were swarming with lice and rats, adding, "And where there are lice there is typhus." They also told us that part of the camp was sentenced to a slow death. There were no beds, and the daily diet consisted of one slice of bread and half a liter of thin soup mixed with *brum*.

Our transport was divided and each group was assigned to a different block. For several weeks, day and night, we lay on the wooden floor. The blocks were so crowded that we hardly had enough space to sit next to each other. If one of us fell asleep and stretched her leg, she was awakened by the kick of her neighbor's wooden clog. There was no water, and the shower rooms and latrines were almost always closed. If one had enough strength she went outside to relieve herself, and if she was weak she used a tin can (G-d knows where she had gotten it from) and then spilled it out the window. But when her hand trembled, she often spilled it on the people around her.

During the first days of our arrival my friends and I volunteered to fetch the soup kettles, but after a short time we were too weak to do it. There were days when we did not eat, only because there was no one with enough strength to carry the soup barrels.

Each of us had received a number on arrival, engraved on a piece of aluminum which was tied with a string around our wrists. My number was 3333. Death cut down so many people that it became useless to count. The corpses were thrown out the window onto heaps. Every day men piled up these corpses on a high-walled wagon and deposited them in a dumping area inside the camp. The mound of bodies there was almost two stories high.

In Bergen-Belsen people deteriorated in front of one's eyes. They became yellow and developed diarrhea, their bellies swelled up, and they contracted intestinal typhus. I too fell victim to this disease. The color of my eyes darkened, my gums began to rot, and my teeth fell out.

The typhus swallowed thousands of people. I lost my two cousins, Clara and Erzhi Friedman, who were my best friends. Other friends succumbed too: Clara Fried, a quiet and shy girl; Clara Weisfeld, one of the most intelligent in our group; and Sarah Wieliczker, who had taken an active part in our sabotage attempts. Sarah used to tell us wryly that she always ran from Hitler but that he pursued her everywhere.

When she and Clara Weisfeld were dying, I pulled them into the shower room. Ironically, the shower barracks was not off limits in Bergen-Belsen — if any prisoner had the strength to drag himself there. And drag I did, pulling and tugging my two dear friends as hard as I could, and I waited there in the shower room with them until the last minutes of their lives. I saw their condition and did not want them to be dirty when they returned their holy souls to the Al-mighty.

Others were lost all around me: Freika Weiss; Clara Klein from Kosice, the richest and happiest girl among us, who had aroused our envy by telling us that she would go to live with her brother in Eretz Israel after the war; Fentchi Brown; Keti Dawidowicz, the nightingale of our group . . . all young, innocent victims.

The only one who remained when this entire group of friends had gone was Itza Frankfurter. She was in a different block, and when either of us had strength to walk we used to meet each other. Once, when several days had gone by and she had not come to see me, I felt that something must have happened. I summoned my last bit of energy and crawled on all fours to her block. She wasn't there anymore; neither were any of my other friends. The women in that building who were still alive were begging for a drop of water, each in her own language . . .

Liberation

This is how the British found us when they entered Bergen-Belsen on April 15, 1945.*

The first messenger of good tidings was a girl who worked in the kitchen. "The Germans raise a white flag!" she called out, but no one wanted to believe her.

Then others came screaming: "British tanks are behind the gates! British tanks are inside the camp!" Those who had some life in their bones jumped with excitement, but I was so wasted that I had no strength even to be happy.

Other prisoners soon began to shriek hysterically: "Come and see how the SS men and women officers, with badges on their uniforms, clean the corpses and dirt from the yard!" Joyless or not, this was something I could not miss. I dragged myself to my feet.

Minutes later British soldiers entered the blocks. Their faces were pale from the sights they had seen, and on every second step they stopped to vomit. They began to distribute candies, biscuits, containers with meat, and warm milk from clean pails. They had no idea what had gone on in the camps, and they were totally unprepared. They found them-

*The prisoners in Bergen-Belsen were so weakened by starvation and disease that over 14,000 of them died after the liberation.

selves facing a massive task: they had to arrange transportation, bring in medication and supplies, determine which people had contagious illnesses. It took about two weeks until they were able to organize and begin transferring people out of the camp.

During the first few days of freedom the camp looked like a big city after a revolution. People broke down barriers and grabbed anything they could lay their hands on: food, clothing, linen. Some people cooked, others sewed. They said: "Life has to go on." Others, like me, were only shadows of ourselves and could hardly stand on our feet. We just wanted to see our freedom; we were too weak to ask for more.

Finally the British registered us and began to transfer us to a clean army camp previously used by the Hitler Yugend. After having lived in filth for years, we were finally in a clean building with immaculate beds, each with two fresh blankets. We threw off our lice-infested rags and received clean clothing and real shoes.

We were liberated!

Wearily we dropped onto the beds and fell into a deep slumber. When we were awakened there was a second registration, at which time each of us received an identification card. Then a bell rang, and we were informed that everyone was to appear in the kitchen to get utensils and food.

We stood in line quietly. The British inspected us at close range and were shocked, for we looked like scarecrows. The scrutiny made us uneasy. A high-ranking official must have read my thoughts, for he took my arm and said in German, "Come with me to the window." No one had spoken to me so softly for a long time.

He ordered a woman soldier named Truda to give me a change of clothes from the clothing magazine, to allow me free access to the kitchen, and to satisfy all my needs. So much kindness all at once touched my heart, and I burst out sobbing.

I enjoyed the kitchen for only a very short time, for I became so swollen that I couldn't even go to the bathroom. I lay in bed, depressed and confused. All my friends were transferred to other facilities, and I was moved to a Red Cross hospital. Two doctors examined me there: Dr. Winterberg from Austria and Dr. Pekert from Czechoslovakia. Both were liberated prisoners who had now become directors of the hospital, and they were not only excellent physicians but also wonderful human beings. They instructed the head nurse: "All that can be done for her now is a diet! A diet! And once more a diet." The head nurse accepted the order, while I instinctively lifted my shoulder. It was an involuntary movement, but the doctors understood it as a sign of resignation, and one of them began to lecture me: "If you endured such a hell, then you must be a person of strong character. If under all those conditions you did not break down, then I beg of you, have a bit more patience. You will recuperate. You are young, and you will return home." I doubt if he really believed his last few words.

I burst into tears and explained that I knew what had happened to my parents and my "home," that I was lucky simply to see the defeat of Germany and the liberation of a remnant of the Jews. Now I was ready to die in peace.

"Life goes on," he said. "When you feel stronger, you'll look differently at the world."

After the swelling had gone down and the diarrhea stopped, I weighed myself. The scale showed twenty-seven kilograms — about sixty pounds. The nurses began to nourish me gradually, and two months later, when I was well enough to travel, I got a release. Elanka Weinberg helped me to put my blanket and one or two meager belongings I had picked up on the way into a knapsack, and together we went to another building in the compound to wait for a transport which was to leave in a day or two.

The next afternoon the hospital invited me to a festive meal. During this pleasant occasion I became dizzy, my vision darkened, and I felt a terrible pressure in my chest. Moments later I fainted. When I regained consciousness, I found that I was paralyzed; my fingers had contracted, and my face was twisted and numb. In a flash all the doctors and nurses were around me. One of them took my temperature and announced in alarm: "Over forty-one!"* Soon a delegation of Canadian doctors flocked to my bedside. They did not examine me but only talked among themselves, and apparently they thought the paralysis had affected my

*Forty-one degrees Celsius is equivalent to almost 106 degrees Fahrenheit.

mind, for Dr. Winterberg asked me to count to ten. I began to count in English, exerting myself heavily because I wanted to prove that my comprehension was still intact. Their faces lit up with relief.

They checked my temperature countless times. Within a short while the thermometer had plummeted below thirty-six, and I began to improve. My face straightened out, my fingers regained their function . . . yet I remained weak and depressed, fearing that the sickness had somehow left me defective and that I would never be able to work again. The doctors concluded that the entire episode was due simply to general weakness and a calcium deficiency, and they tried their best to convince me that I was not seriously ill or impaired. I was given doses of calcium in every possible form — powder, pills, milk, and cheese — and my strength began to return very slowly. The doctors cared for me with great devotion. They showed me off with a sort of protective pride to each arriving delegation, introducing me in jest as the "flaming thermometer." In the best sanatorium I would not have been treated better, but I was impatient . . .

My people were leaving, each taking off in a different direction. I was afraid that if I returned home too late in the fall I wouldn't be able to prepare myself for the coming winter. I hoped desperately that my brother Eliezer would return from Russia before me and that I would find him there when I arrived.

When I was finally well enough to be discharged for the second time, I left the hospital in an International Red Cross train. I was thankful to the British for providing me with such wonderful care, and I would never have believed then that only one year later this same nation would shoot at us on the open seas — shoot at those whom they had just liberated, at a downtrodden people who were on their way to build a homeland.

The train brought me to Pilzen in Czechoslovakia, where we stayed for several days, then continued on to Pressburg, and from Pressburg to Budapest. Budapest was still under the control of a civilian government and was therefore a good transfer point; the train tracks there had not been bombed, and it rapidly became an exchange post for family information. All along the way, with a heart full of pain, I inquired after my relatives.

Most of them were missing, but fortunately not all, and those I found opened their homes to me with a warm welcome. I learned from them that the packages we had sent to my brother in Russia had come back to them, and I began to doubt that he was still alive. All that remained for me was the hope that somehow, someday, he would return.

I stayed with one of my aunts in Budapest for two weeks, and then I left for my hometown of Kosice, where I had been born and raised. All the inmates of the concentration camps were free to ride the trains now, and many forlorn and weary people crowded the platforms, trying to get back to homes which now existed only in memory.

For me, coming home was like pouring salt on a fresh wound. I went from house to house, trying to find out information about my family. I remember looking in the window of one home that I passed, and hanging there I saw curtains which I had crocheted with my own hands. I knocked on the door and asked the woman of the house very politely if she would mind giving me back the curtains. In answer she pointed to her stove and burst out angrily, "Get out of here or I'll throw this hot pot in your face!"

In another house the woman asked me: "Tell me, miss, where is your mother?"

I answered with a question: "Don't you know where all the Jewish mothers were sent to?"

She looked at me for a moment and then replied, "Yes, yes, girl; wouldn't it have been better for you to remain there instead of coming back alone?"

I wandered in the town for four months, waiting for someone to return home. Luckily I found some gold that my father had hidden in the ground before the Germans captured our town, and thanks to that I did not have to resort to charity.

None of my family ever came back.

Leah Weis left Hungary two years after the war and emigrated to Israel, where she married Issur Neuman. She originally gave her testimony to Moreshet, a Holocaust research institute, in 1947.

THE TRAP

Chaya Stall
Told by Golda Danielewicz
both of Kolo, Poland

Chaya Stall was one of the very few remarkable people one would be lucky to meet once in a lifetime. Though only a young girl, she had a tremendous influence on all those who came in contact with her during the war.

Among the first decrees that the Germans issued in our town of Kolo was the prohibition for Jews to trade or come in contact with non-Jews. Once on market day, when the peasants came into the town to sell their goods, Chaya approached a peasant woman to buy an item she had for sale. The woman refused to trade with her, saying that the Germans had forbidden selling anything to a Jew. Chaya's pride was injured, and without thinking she replied: "The Germans will perish, and the Jewish nation will live forever!" A Pole overheard this remark and brought it to the attention of the Germans, who immediately arrested Chaya and sentenced her to death. However, thanks to an exorbitant sum of money paid by the Judenrat, her sentence was commuted to slave labor.

I first met Chaya in 1942 in the labor camp Univrotzlav. We suffered terribly there from the cruelty of our Polish overseers; yet all during that time Chaya encouraged me, saying, "Goldi, raise your head high! We have to hold on, the end of the Germans will definitely come! You've got to be strong!"

198

Such confident words had an untold influence on all of our girls. Though death reigned among us and every few hours another girl returned her soul to her Maker, Chaya's encouragement was a foundation of strength on which we leaned heavily. We were sure that if only one of us survived, it would be no other than she; but fate decreed otherwise.

Several of us, including Irka Lisk, Hinda Schwartz, Ludka Tchiplitzka, and Chaya Stall, were once assigned to the back-crushing task of transporting heavy bricks and stones. Our Polish overseer, Zintera, was a vicious sadist. He left us alone on the detail for an unusually long time, an uncharacteristic oversight. Guileless and unaware of his purpose, we sneaked out to the village to "organize" a bit of food, for we were always terribly hungry.

When we returned to the barracks, we could smell in the air that some sort of disaster awaited us, and we realized a bit too late that we had been tricked. The German block chief began yelling at us barbarically, demanding to know where we had been. The other girls and I received a merciless beating. But when Chaya Stall entered the barracks, he did not even ask her any questions; he began to slap her face with all his might and did not stop until her eyes dropped from their sockets.

Chaya was mortally wounded. She was completely blinded and suffered excruciating pain. When I approached her afterward, she summoned all her remaining strength and said in an energetic voice: "Dear Golda, I know that I will soon leave this world, but I believe that you will survive. Please swear to me that you will not be silent, that you will let the world know of the German atrocities. They must never be forgiven!"

I bow my head to the memory of a courageous and heroic woman; and with this story I carry out Chaya Stall's last wish.

A REQUEST IN BIRKENAU

Rabbi Aviezer Burstyn
Brother of Chava Burstyn
Goworowa, Poland

In Auschwitz I was selected to the Sheiss Kommando, the sewage workers' unit, which consisted of eleven people and was one of the most "distinguished" assignments given to prisoners. Its function was to remove the human waste from all privies and pits in the camp, including the crematoria area, the women's camps, and the Effecten Lager (one of the classifying units where prisoners' goods were sorted). Although the job itself was demeaning beyond description, the members of the kommando had the special privilege of moving freely with the sewage wagon through all of the forty divisional camps in Auschwitz, a right not allotted to many other "important" kommandos. We also had one other advantage: we were exempt from standing the morning appel, the vicious pre-dawn roll call that persisted for two full hours even in the severely cold winter months.

I had an additional personal privilege: our Kapo, Eizik, was Jewish, and he allowed me to pray each morning. Although he used very foul language, as did most of the Kapos, he spoke to me with restraint and respect and used to call me *"rebbele."* I suspected he did this because he came from our region and might have known my father, who was the rabbi of our town of Goworowa. Eizik was not bad by nature, but he behaved crudely in order to fit in and be accepted by his German superiors, and in the process his character deteriorated. Unfortunately his story was not an uncommon one; before putting them in charge of blocks, the Germans often brutalized these Jewish prisoners in order to destroy them morally and make them better agents of persecution against their own people.

Because of the Sheiss Kommando's ability to move freely among the camps without suspicion, we were able to give assistance to many of the inmates in very unique ways. We relayed information whenever we could, sending regards from the men's lager to the women's lager, and from parents in one camp to their sons and daughters in another. We were also able to obtain needed items and to pass them on secretly.

We saw every part of the camps, and we were acutely aware of the prisoners' suffering, even more so than they themselves. We knew that out of all the prisoners, the women in Birkenau B suffered the most. Birkenau was a subdivision of Auschwitz adjacent to the crematoria; the B stood for Brzezinki, the non-Jewish village in Poland which had previously stood on the site and which had been completely evacuated in order to annex its land to the camp. The Jewish girls there were literally crushed by their monstrous SS overseers, who created inventive forms of torture to degrade them. One of their tactics was to give large, oversized clothing to the more petite girls, and short, tight dresses to taller women. No undergarments were given; no rips were repaired.

Though our own lot was depressing, our hearts cried out at the wretched condition of our unfortunate sisters. We tried as best we could to help and encourage them and others in the different blocks, and sometimes we were even able to offer material assistance through our collaboration with the Effecten Lager.

The Effecten Lager was in a "prestigious" category of its own; it was completely locked and barred, and even many of the German officials weren't permitted to enter it. In this lager were concentrated all of the more valuable belongings of the Jews who had been brought to Auschwitz from the entire continent of Europe. Fifty young prisoners, men and women, worked at classifying the items, and they were allowed no contact whatsoever with any of the other prisoners. Their work was of great importance to the Germans, for the goods they handled included jewelry, medications, special foods, high-priced drinks, fancy linen, and books. Every single item was catalogued individually. Huge cases filled with jewelry, ornaments, gold, and diamonds were packed by Jewish hands and sent off frequently in transports to Germany.

Between shipments the items were stored in huge warehouses: some for men's, women's, and children's shoes; some for knitted items such as dresses, shawls, and sweaters; some for all the hair that had been shaved off Jewish women before they were forced into the gas chambers.

The workers in the Effecten Lager did not resemble the other prisoners of Auschwitz. They were not emaciated, for they ate well from the wealth of food they handled, and they were decently dressed. Their motto was: "Bedeck yourself and eat today, for tomorrow you will die."

We often joked that our Sheiss Kommando was equal in importance to the Effecten Lager. The SS men never approached the Effecten Lager because they did not want to fall under the suspicion of stealing from its treasures, and they never approached us because of the stench we spread! In fact we had a greater advantage, for while we could move freely from camp to camp, the effecten workers were imprisoned in a "golden cage."

When our kommando first arrived at this lager to empty the sewage, we thought we had fallen into a fairy-tale world, a world of fantasy and imagination. The people who worked behind these sealed doors were kind, helpful, and generous. They never refused any of our illegal requests for food or clothing for needy inmates. They were also courageous and had developed their own methods of sabotage. One young girl, who introduced herself to me as a relative of the great Torah scholar Reb Menachem Zemba of Warsaw, confessed that she and her friends had already burned thousands of dollars worth of paper currency that they had found among the possessions they were sorting, in order to keep it from falling into the Germans' hands.

Each time we came to the Effecten Lager, we asked for a certain amount of clothing, especially warm sweaters and socks. We hid these in our work pails and passed them on to the women in Birkenau B, who were grateful beyond words.

But not all the girls dared to ask us for help. They still had pride, and many of them would rather freeze and starve than to ask for help from a fellow prisoner, especially a boy. They were also afraid of our Kapo, Eizik, who always spit out his foul language in their presence and chased them away from the sewage wagon.

One day while I was working in the Birkenau B lager, I noticed a young girl walking hesitantly toward the wagon. She took a few steps and then lost her nerve and turned around to go back. Seeing that she wanted something but was too shy to ask, I walked over to her.

The girl was about fifteen, with flaming black eyes, a dark complexion, and a frame that was skin and bones. The entire world's suffering was expressed in her face. Something about her suggested that she came from a pious Chassidic family.

"What do you need?" I asked her quietly.

She lowered her long eyelashes and whispered what sounded like "Sweater."

I felt very sorry because we didn't have any sweaters with us that day. But I promised her that the very next day I would fulfill her request.*

The next morning when we went to work in the Effecten Lager, I "organized" a sweater of the best quality wool and stashed it secretly in the wagon. The girl was standing at the gate of her barracks later that morning, and she waited patiently until Eizik walked away. Then she came running to me.

"Here is the sweater you asked for," I said, holding it out to her. But she remained standing, as if perplexed, and I could not understand her response.

"I did not ask for a sweater . . ." she replied finally in a sad whisper. "I asked for a . . . *siddur* . . . a *siddur* to pray every day . . ."

I realized that I had not heard her correctly. She had not wanted a sweater to warm herself; that was of secondary importance. She had wanted a *siddur* in which to pray, to pour out her overflowing heart before the G-d of Israel.

The following day the girl received her *siddur*.

*A "new" sweater would not have been noticed in particular by the block officials. As many as 2,500 girls were placed in one unit, and from the Germans' perspective they had no individuality. Such a sweater would have been inconspicuous among the varied and mismatched used rags that were given to the girls to wear.

At the end of the war the Germans began to evacuate prisoners from Auschwitz as well as from other camps. Aviezer Burstyn was aboard one of these transports when the British caught up and liberated them. He became an officer in the American Joint Jewish Distribution Committee and later moved to Israel, where he established a trade high school for boys in Chaifa. Rabbi Burstyn now lives in Jerusalem.

A SIDDUR IN AUSCHWITZ

Golda Katz-Kibel
Lask, Poland

In 1942 Golda Katz was deported from her hometown of Lask to the Lodz ghetto, where she worked in several different workshops. She was deported to Auschwitz in 1944 and was placed in a block where most of the other girls were Hungarian.

The women in Auschwitz suffered most cruelly, and at the hands of more than one oppressor. The Kapos as well as the Stubendeinst, both Jewish and non-Jewish, abused us ferociously, beating us and withholding our food for the smallest infringement. But in between we existed. When we met friends, we inquired about other friends, and we made the acquaintance of many women from other towns and countries. To me, the Hungarian girls who were in my block stood out among the others.

They were very different from us in several ways. For one thing, they were not walking skeletons. During all the years that we had been vegetating in the ghettos, they had lived a normal life. They hadn't known the multiple curses of cold, cruelty, sickness, and malnutrition; they hadn't been exposed, as we had, to curfews, deportations, and death. I remember how amazed I was to see that they could not eat the soup they were given. They were too new to such deprivation and could not force down their throats the ugly slop that constituted our "meals" in Auschwitz. They would often give away their soup to other girls.

But what impressed me even more was their unshaken belief in G-d, the tenacity with which they clung to religion. I hadn't realized until then the enormous impact that constant suffering and starvation can have on the mind as well as on the body. We were not on the level of these Hungarian girls, but we admired them greatly. There was a certain innocence and simplicity about them, and they were able, in an almost supernatural manner, to hold on not only to their faith but to their illusions. This may have been due partly to the fact that Hitler's fortunes were declining by the time the Hungarians were deported in 1944, and so they hoped for an end to the war any day; but it was probably due largely to their lack of exposure to suffering. Many of them did not even want to believe that their dear ones had gone to the crematoria, in spite of the continuous clouds of smoke that rose from the compound and the constant smell of burning flesh and bones.

Because of their delayed acceptance of the bitter truth of the death camps, many of the Hungarians did not have the foresight to regulate their work rhythm and thus conserve their energy, and their health deteriorated to such an extent that they were unable to withstand the frightening conditions in Auschwitz. But their spiritual strength and fortitude is something that will remain with me always.

In one of the transports which arrived in Auschwitz before Passover of 1944, there was a Hungarian girl from a Chassidic home whom I remember well. She soon became the talk of our lager because she had a *siddur*.

For a religious girl or boy, a *siddur* in the concentration camps was much more than just a prayer book. It was a precious link to the past, to the home from which he or she had been severed — and it was also a link to the future. For others who knew of its existence, the *siddur* provided a sense of meaning in a destitute world, a beacon which the Nazis had no power to extinguish.

No one knew how this young girl had smuggled her *siddur* into Auschwitz, but everyone knew that it had been a present from her father.

On the inside of the front page was affixed a tiny, handwritten calendar specifying the Jewish holidays and the days of the New Moon. All the girls in our barracks knew about the *siddur*, and they kept it in the greatest secrecy.

When we were sure that our overseers had left the block for the night, the girl would take out her little *siddur* and read selected chapters of the Psalms of David for us. She read beautifully, translating and explaining to us the meaning of each Psalm. We listened to her without breathing. As she continued to read she grew in our eyes, and we saw in her the prophetess Deborah. Her words were like a balsam, a wondrous medicine that encouraged and comforted us. At those hours the beautiful verses aroused hope in our hearts and a desire to live.

We consulted her little calendar to find out about the approach of the holidays. On the day before Passover she told us that she would like to arrange a *Seder* the next night, as the Marranos, the forced converts, had done in Spain. We asked her how we could possibly do this, and she replied that each of us should visualize all the traditional accessories of the *Seder* ceremony; that each of us individually should imagine herself drinking wine and eating *matzos* and all the other dishes we had always eaten in our homes on the night of Passover. She said to us: "Each of you will light the holiday candles in your imagination, and then I will read the Haggadah from my *siddur*. In my mind I will make a blessing over a goblet of wine, and you will lick the tip of your finger as though you were drinking the wine from my *kiddush* — and you'll say *Amen!*"

Never in my life would I forget that *Seder* night. Our ceremony continued nearly until the morning. Because of the late hour and the fear that we would be discovered, the girl skipped several parts of the Haggadah, but she finished with "Next year in Jerusalem."

Golda Katz-Kibel was transported from Auschwitz to the Birenbaum camp in Germany, then to Gross Rosen, and finally to Bergen-Belsen, where she was liberated. After the war she settled in Chaifa, Israel, where she lives presently.

CANDLES

Miriam Weinstock
A small village in Hungary

A melancholy autumn sky hung over the German camp Alendorf. Birds sped away haphazardly through the stormy winds, and yellowing leaves sank down feebly from the naked trees. The dismal skies cast a heavy sadness into the hearts of thousands of Jewish women slaves who were working in an ammunition factory under rigorous guard. The visits of the SS kommando to the factory always ended in severe punishments, and life was hazardous for the women; yet a small, unexpected whisper had the power to light up their hearts. The news I heard that day shocked me beyond my wildest imagination.

"I've got candles! Candles for the Sabbath. Would you like to light Sabbath candles?" one of my fellow workers whispered in my ear.

I could only look at her in astonishment.

"Don't you believe me?" she continued pleadingly. "I've got real Sabbath candles! In the factory I found grease. I dissolved it here in this box. I've got real candles!"

This information set my heart on fire. Can you possibly imagine what it is like to think of seeing the spark of Sabbath candles in a bottomless well of darkness? I forgot the hunger, the SS guards, the high-voltage wire fence, the machine guns surrounding us. I was in a daze.

"Yes, of course I believe you," I answered.

"You do not fear?"

"I fear the Al-mighty," I said calmly. "I want to carry out my obligation as a Jewish daughter."

That evening she gave me two candles. They were very awkwardly made, but for me they were a priceless treasure. I saw in them my child who had been so brutally torn away from me; I saw in them my own childhood; I saw my mother covering her face with her hands as she said the blessing. I felt as if I had regained part of my lost soul. I thought: In what lies the power of these candles? How could these crude little mounds of grease kindle in my heart such a roaring fire? It was a sensation I cannot explain, but somehow I felt that the souls of all Jewish women of the past and present had an inseparable bond with candles. I hid my precious pair in my bundle of rags, together with the piece of black bread I had saved for someone in the block who was ill. My little bundle had a double purpose now.

The Sabbath was still two days away, but the gloom and despair of those hours was threaded through with a shining expectation, pierced by the words of our sages that I recalled with hope: "Remember the Sabbath day to keep it sacred." I also remembered the Talmudic teaching that if one finds a special food which will not get spoiled or an item of value, he should set it aside for the Sabbath. Even here in the camp I was able to honor this special commandment; for what better way could there be to consecrate the Sabbath than with candles?

That Friday evening after our shift in the factory, fourteen girls gathered in my room to welcome the Sabbath. The room was empty except for an old box and the sleeping sacks which lay on the floor. I placed the candles on the box and asked the girls to say *Amen* after I made the blessing. They were astonished, but they looked at me with respect and admiration. One of them said, "Just as my mother used to do . . ." The others only shook their heads, for tears had stifled their voices.

I lit the candles and passed my palms over them, but before I had a chance to cover my eyes, heavy steps were heard in the outside corridor. For a split second our hearts stopped beating. I covered my eyes and hastily made the blessing, adding under my breath, "G-d Al-mighty! It is clear to You that what I did was not for my pleasure or honor, but for Your reverence . . . in reverence of the holy Sabbath . . . for all to know and to remember that G-d created the heaven and earth in six days, and on the seventh day He rested . . ." I pieced together whatever prayers I could remember and begged G-d in my heart not to let the others suffer because of the terrible risk I had imposed on them.

I had barely finished when a command was shouted: "Out to the waiting trucks!"

All the girls ran out, and I wondered in alarm if they were running toward their punishment. I followed them into the compound, and I saw that they were unloading loaves of bread from the truck. A shipment of bread had come and we had been ordered to carry it to the kitchen . . . I raised my eyes to Heaven and thanked G-d for the miracle that had happened in front of my eyes.

Miriam Weinstock remarried after the war and now lives in Tel Aviv.

NOTE: Many women in the concentration camps, most notably the Hungarians, exhibited enormous self-sacrifice in their effort to light candles. Some of them, such as Miriam Weinstock and Leah Neuman (see "The Odyssey"), created makeshift candles by saving bits of grease and oil from the factories they worked in or drops of margarine from their rations. In Auschwitz candles could be obtained in the Canada Kommando. The task of this kommando was to collect and classify all the belongings which had been taken from the prisoners upon their arrival. The Canada workers were not allowed to use any of the items they handled, but many who were reluctant to give up the Sabbath tradition risked their lives and smuggled out a few candles to those who were prepared to light them.

Lighting candles in the camps was not just the maintenance of a tradition; it was a profound emotional experience. Many non-observant girls, such as those in this story, often gathered around to watch the lighting and to listen to the others singing songs in a whisper.

This phenomenon existed in our own circle. Mrs. Ryvka Weiser, a friend from our hometown who was to become my sister's mother-in-law after the war, told me in an interview that she never missed lighting candles all the time she was in Auschwitz. She lit them in a corner of the barracks or sometimes under her bunk, and she also tried to avoid working on the Sabbath. Whenever she was caught she was beaten and deprived of bread, but she was firmly determined not to violate the Sabbath, and her daughter and friends did their best to shield her from the overseers. — A.E.E.

THE TRIAL

Jonah Emanuel
Amsterdam, Holland

My mother and I were interned in one of the "family camps"* in Bergen-Belsen, which were designated for Jews holding foreign passports. On Tisha B'Av of 1944, the entire camp was punished and no food was distributed, not even to the elderly or the children. My mother endangered her life and cooked a "porridge" of water for Batia, my baby sister, who was three and a half years old. The Jewish guards caught her in the act and decided that my mother had to appear before a "court."

The camp justice system required that in addition to the punishment imposed by the Germans on "transgressors," the Jewish guards had to

---

*Many families with money or communal status had illegally obtained Latin American or other foreign passports during the war in the hope of more lenient treatment. The Germans sent these people to "transit camps," principally Vittel in France and Bergen-Belsen in Germany, which had been opened in 1943 specifically for this purpose. The inmates in Bergen-Belsen were kept in a separate compound for the benefit of Red Cross delegations, who used to come occasionally to make inspections and to insure that the camps were just "working" camps. The Germans wanted to show that these "legal" foreigners were being treated fairly and that their internment was merely a political measure. Many of these barracks even had flowers planted in front of them.

The conditions in the "family camps," although far from satisfactory, were not as dismal as in the camp proper. Men and women were housed separately but were allowed to meet during the day, and families were allowed to eat together. Living, sanitary, and nutritional conditions were poor, but since the inmates were kept for demonstration purposes, selections were made from among them much less frequently, and for a time they were deceived into thinking that they were being held for exchange for German prisoners. A small percentage did reach freedom through exchange, but the majority did not; the Germans quickly discovered the invalidity of the passports and sent the holders to their deaths.

mete out a punishment of their own. For this purpose there existed an "Interior Justice Court," where the Germans could enjoy watching the Jews punish their own people. My mother's court appointment was set for Friday evening, the night of *Shabbos Nachamu*.

Ordinarily a "trial" of that kind was very complicated and could drag on for a long time. The process involved various activities by the Jewish plaintiff, the witnesses, and a panel of jurors, after which came the advocate's speech and finally the sentence of the judges. However, my mother's case took very little time. Her sentence was pronounced quickly: no bread for the next two days.

During the proceedings my mother had relinquished her right to deny part of the exaggerated accusations. She even gave up the right to have an advocate request a lesser punishment. In the family camp, the men were permitted to meet with the women during the day, and when I next saw my mother I asked her why she had surrendered these rights so easily. Her only answer was, "I preferred to accept the punishment rather than to prolong the process."

I did not understand this. I asked her again: Why had she not taken advantage of her right to deny part of the false accusations? Why hadn't she pointed out that on the day she had cooked the porridge for her child, there was no food distribution at all? I felt that my mother was annoyed with my questions, but I could not hold them back.

Seeing that I was insistent, my mother finally explained: "In addition to the judges, there was a plaintiff, an advocate, and a secretary who wrote a protocol. Every additional word I said would have been recorded by a Jew. And wasn't it Friday night? Because of this I was silent. I told myself that it would be better to starve a bit longer than to cause a Jew to write on the Sabbath."

Jonah Emanuel was a teenager at the time of his internment in Bergen-Belsen. He and two brothers were the only survivors of a family of eight children. After the war they emigrated to Israel, where Jonah married and wrote his memoirs.

THE ENGINEER

Chava Bronstein
Senz, Hungary

The Reinikdorf camp in Berlin was located in an industrial district. It had been built in the form of a triangle and housed three thousand women prisoners who worked in the *Argos Verken*, a factory producing aircraft parts.

When we arrived at the camp, we were "welcomed" by SS soldiers and women overseers who divided and classified us.

"Which of you has higher education!" one of the overseers yelled.

I did not know exactly what this question meant, but on sudden instinct I dragged out the four other girls in my line, and we presented ourselves to her.

"We need a total of twenty women like this!" she roared again. Other volunteers joined us. We arranged ourselves into four lines of five and were then led to the aircraft factory.

"They are assigned to polish cylinders!" thundered the overseer to the guard at the gate.

"Section 115," the guard said phlegmatically; this was no occasion of any importance to him.

And so our work of polishing exchange parts began.

At first I wondered what the overseer had meant by asking for women of "higher education." Was she joking? Were the Germans simply intending to demean us by forcing the better-educated people to perform menial work? As time went on, I began to see that there was very little rhyme or reason to many of the orders we received, and in fact some of them contradicted or bore no relation at all to previous orders. This was by design, for one of the Germans' prime motives was to confuse, to keep us in a continual state of mental and emotional chaos in order to render any type of resistance ineffectual. The only thing that was very clear to us was that they wanted to destroy us.

Winter had already set in when we came to Reinikdorf, and the ferocious cold penetrated our bones. We had each been given a single loose, shapeless dress and a pair of wooden clogs, and to this meager attire the Germans now grudgingly added coats, realizing that if we froze to death we would be of no use to them. The coats had originally belonged to prisoners who were now dead, and they were in such poor condition that it did not pay for the Germans to ship them out for their own use; but for us they meant life, and we thanked G-d for them.

The distance from the camp to the factory was short, and we were marched there each day on foot. Our overseers made us sing to the rhythm of our stride, and so we taught each other whatever marching songs we knew — some in German, some in Hungarian or Slovakian.

On these daily marches we observed our surroundings: a simple stretch of ground covered with a white mantle of snow, capped by the same sky that had rested above us in our town. There was nothing unusual in the scenery, and yet glimpses of a distant landscape beyond the enclosure reminded us that we had been completely severed from the planet we had once known.

In the distance we could see small houses. In each there surely revolved a normal life: a family with a father, mother, and children . . . I felt a strange shudder of isolation run through me. Why had we sunk to such a low level of life? For what sins did we suffer so much? Birds were able to find shelter beneath rooftops, even dogs had their doghouses, but we . . . we were now encaged in a place of no shelter, trapped and humbled. And why? Because we were Jews.

Was I suffering only because I was Jewish? If that was the case, then

I would make sure the wicked ones did not succeed in breaking me.

The women around me sang because they were forced to. But I — I marched in a different world. On that walk a decision ripened in my mind: I would not break down, no matter what. I touched the small *siddur** I had secreted in the pocket of my robe and thought: G-d must help us. With His help we will get out of here, and we will tell the world the true nature of the German culture: of their doctors, so admired and respected, who were now turned into murderers and sadists, bereft of conscience; of a people who invented ingenious forms of torture to satisfy their own diabolic lusts. Was this the culture to which all European nations prostrated themselves, absorbing its language and customs, emulating its elaborate veneer of politeness? Did anyone really think that eating with a knife, fork, and napkin built a human being inside a person? . . .

I marched in my torn coat and wooden clogs, and I trembled from the cold. I was fourteen years old then, and I was hungry and humiliated, yet I thanked G-d for being strong inside. The Germans, hoping to crush my faith through the evil hand of degradation, instead succeeded in strengthening my belief in the Al-mighty. I looked and actually saw the hand of Providence in many events.

The industrial section of Berlin in which our camp and factory were located was exposed to constant air-raid attacks. The British and Americans took turns bombing us, and raids could be expected at any time of the day or night. The bombings frightened and infuriated the Germans, and they discharged their fear and anxiety on us, beating us and yelling like wild animals. We, however, were calm and composed, for we had nothing to fear. We felt that if we were fated to die from a bomb, then at least our suffering would come to an end.

One morning while we were at work in the factory, the air-raid alarm sounded. The Germans began rushing us back to camp, hustling us out amidst whips and blows, afraid that in the confusion some of us might escape. As they pressed us into shelters, the floor and everything on it

---

*Only a handful of people had access to religious articles in the camps. Chava Bronstein's possession of a *siddur*, although certainly exceptional, would be understandable in a place like Reinikdorf, where she had some contact with workers who were brought in from the outside, and where the strip-and-search process was not as severe as in Auschwitz and some of the other camps.

bounced and swayed like a swing in the wind, and the benches began to jerk loose from the floorboards. It was a terrible and surreal feeling. The impact of the explosions sent us hurling back and forth, and we toppled over each other. Some girls said the *Viduy*, some cried out *Shema*, others began reciting Psalms by heart. Suddenly another close explosion, more powerful than the previous ones, split the choking air in the shelter. This time we completely lost our balance.

After the air raid we learned that the camp next to us had been hit, and none of the three thousand Russian and Netherlands war prisoners had survived. A bomb had also fallen on our revier, but it did not explode.

We had seen a miracle in front of our eyes. We recited the *Bircas Hagomel*, the blessing offered by those who have been saved from catastrophe, and then we burst into passionate song: *"Lo amus ki echyeh va'asaper ma'asei Kah*—I shall not die, for I shall live, and I will recount the deeds of G-d."

This was only one of several open miracles that we witnessed in the concentration camp. There, in the depths of hell, we learned to believe that those who were destined to live survived, no matter what the circumstances, and those who were destined to die perished even after the war.

Our work in the aircraft factory was exhausting. Each shift consisted of twelve hours, and the cold and hunger were so severe that many girls fainted on duty. We revived them with a bit of water and hid them behind machines, away from the eyes of the German overseers. The hall was enormous and contained so many dozens of machines that it was possible occasionally to protect girls in this manner, but the risk was great, for anyone found not working would have been accused of sabotage and punished severely; even those found sitting or resting were beaten.

Once, one of our friends began to have convulsive shivers. She was running a high temperature and could not stand on her feet. I hid her behind my polishing machine. Just that day our section was undergoing a thorough German inspection, and I feared that she would be discovered. I was so tense that I could not concentrate carefully on my work. The needle of my polishing machine missed its target and made a deep scratch in the middle finger of my left hand. My friend, thank G-d, was not caught, but for me the episode was not over. My hand swelled up, and the pain became so great that I could not breathe.

In the morning I decided to go to the revier, regardless of the danger involved. The revier was not a hospital in the normal sense; it was more or less a dumping ground for the sick, almost all of whom were soon sent to the crematoria. But there was some slight chance that a bit of medication could be wheedled out of one of the personnel there, and in any case I had no choice. On my way to the revier, I prayed that the kommando who dragged the dead and the sick to the crematory would be absent when I arrived.

The nurse who tended to the sick took one look at my swollen hand and shrieked, "*You might die from the infection in your hand! The pus reaches all the way to your shoulder!*" Then she took out a regular kitchen knife, and without disinfection or any anesthetic, she cut a deep incision into my finger. The pain was so excruciating that I fainted. She slapped me forcefully twice in the face, and when I came to she continued the "surgery," making two more cuts while continuing to slap me with her strong palm so that I would not faint again. Finally she bandaged my finger with a piece of white cloth and told me to disappear.

As I was leaving the revier, sirens sounded, and again we had to rush to the shelters. Now any slight push or shove caused me torturous pain. Trembling, I sat in the shelter pressed against the others, whose movements drove me into agony.

Yet that very day, something much worse than my own pain was about to take place: an event so macabre, so evil, that the memory of it still shakes my soul.

One of the prisoners in our camp was a gorgeous girl with blond hair and blue eyes, whom we called Dolly. Because of her beauty the Germans had chosen her to clean their rooms, in return for which she was given a bit of food, a better dress, and shoes that weren't torn. Dolly's mother was also in our camp; she was a noble soul, and she too was magnificently pretty. She worried about Dolly day and night, anxious for the welfare of her only daughter. Whatever little food she received she shared with her child, and as a result she grew weaker from day to day.

Finally she had to be taken to the revier. This happened on the very day of my "surgery," the day when the sirens wailed.

The Germans, as I have mentioned, were dreadfully afraid of the air attacks. Each time the sirens sounded, they ran like mice to the shelters, and they always emerged angry and irritable. To release their anxiety they looked for amusement, and on this particular day they wanted special entertainment; it seems that whipping the girls no longer provided enough satisfaction.

After the sirens had died down, they ordered us to stand in line and watch the "performance" that was about to take place. Dolly's mother was brought from the revier, and they called the girl and commanded her to push her mother against the high-voltage wire fence. Terrified, Dolly refused. They then threatened to push the two of them together against the fence if she did not obey.

I closed my eyes. I could not look at that scene.

That beautiful girl, who had served them every day, cleaning their room, washing their clothes, shining their boots — and who had benefited, so we assumed, from special privileges — was for the Germans just another fly to be picked off. As I stood there, I was no longer aware of the terrible pain in my hand; it had been washed away in a flood of dizziness and nausea.

We heard the roar "Disperse!" I could hardly drag my feet back to the block. I fell down on my bunk and cried and cried and could not stop crying. I had not cried that much since they had taken away my father. The pain inside me was many thousands of times greater than the wound in my hand . . . a pain almost impossible to bear.

The next day I went to work. My hand was still swollen and full of pus, and I could not touch anything with it, but I was afraid to go back to the revier. One never knew when the death kommando might appear for a sudden selection and take all the sick people to a place from which there was no return.

I summoned all my courage, stood in front of my machine, and pretended that I was working. That morning a Yugoslav engineer came to inspect our work, and there were rumors that he was a captive working for the Germans. He was dressed in civilian clothes and walked around the machines with the air of a specialist, saying nothing but giving instructions by means of signs.

When he approached my machine, a sudden nerve infused me. I explained to him in Slovakian, a language similar to his native Serbian, that I was unable to work because of the injury in my hand. I said that I had come to work today only because I feared that if I stayed away my injury would be discovered, and they would take me to the crematory. Then I asked him if he was able to work for the enemy with a clear conscience, knowing that his friends and brothers were fighting them.

He looked at me wordlessly and left. The next day one of the overseers called me into his office and handed me a tube filled with ointment, as "an award for diligent work." Tucked underneath the cover of the tube I found a tiny piece of paper, on which was written: "I am with you. Tear up this note — Engineer."

I applied the ointment to my wounded hand, and the pus slowly began to drain out. Within a few days the finger was healed. A great relief flowed through me, and I whispered a prayer of thanks to the Al-mighty for this new miracle.

From that time on the engineer was especially kind to me. He even closed his eyes to my sabotage. Many of us quietly damaged the exchange parts we were handling so that the Germans would not be able to make use of them. I don't know where I found the strength and tenacity to continue my sabotage even under the eye of this engineer, whose identity I could never clearly ascertain. But he restrained himself and never reprimanded me for my "poor" workmanship.

Until this very day I haven't figured out if the engineer was a Nazi whose steel heart was somehow moved for a moment by my plight, or if he was a partisan planted in our factory. But in either case, it is clear to me that he was a messenger of G-d who came at just the right time.

Chava Bronstein remained in Reinikdorf until the end of the war. She raised a family and is now a published poet and the principal of a Bais Yaakov seminary in Sanhedria Hamurchevet in Jerusalem.

FELA

Leah Schnap
Margareten, Hungary

When we descended from the wagon in Auschwitz, my mother tightly grasped my hand and my little sister's hand. She held onto us with such force that the SS man had a hard time separating us. I vividly remember my mother's despairing voice. Even after I was far away and had been swallowed in the crowd, it reverberated in the air, like a distant echo of thunder. That voice pursued me for a very long time.

I was ten years old, lost in a gigantic crowd of people who thronged the square. Together with a thousand other young girls, ranging in age from two to sixteen, I was led to an enormous children's barrack: Block Number 8.

For weeks none of us could touch the food we were given; it wasn't suitable even for animals. We cried and moaned, repeating the magical word: "Ima!* *I-ma-le! I-ma-le . . .*"

It was not very long before the cold, hunger, thirst, and appels weakened our little hearts physically — and immunized them emotionally. We became accustomed to the demented lifestyle in the hell called Auschwitz, and some of us even became precociously adept at the art of survival. We learned to dodge and run after a single morsel of potato peel; to burrow in piles of garbage; to look for "goodies" among filthy debris;

*Hebrew for mother.

to scrape off food particles stuck in the corners and cracks of pots. Those who could not learn these tactics sooner or later ended up in the crematorium.

One night I developed an extremely high temperature, and a terrible burning pain began to throb in my ears. My dry lips began to crack and bleed, and my ears oozed pus. The pain was excruciating, and I thought I would lose my mind. Just then an appel was called: *"Out to the appel! Only the sick remain in the barracks!"* I heard this shouting as if in a daze.

By that time we already knew what happened to the sick, but I was so ill that I did not care. I lay down on the cold floor and resigned myself to my fate. Anything would be better than this terrible pain; even death would be a welcome end . . . anything to get rid of this unbearable pain! *"Ima'le, Ima'le! . . ."* I sighed and groaned. I stretched my hand in the direction of my mother's screams, which still rang in my ears.

Suddenly a pair of gray eyes, flooded with sadness and compassion, stared at me from above.

"Out to the appel! This is not a place to be sick! No one is sick here!"

"Oh, please, let me be!" I begged. "I do not want to go, and I do not care . . . just let me die . . ."

But instead of leaving me alone, the woman lifted me up with her strong hands, saying fiercely: "You've got to live! Do you understand?" Then she literally pushed me outside.

This woman was Fela, our Blockelteste, who was responsible for all the children in our barrack.

At the end of the night appel we were ordered to return to our blocks. By this time we were half frozen. Fela carried me like a baby to her private corner at the far end of the room, put me in her bed, and gave me hot tea. After I had rested a bit, she gently cleaned out the pus from my ears, and as she worked she caressed my shaven head. Then she told me of her own unhappy ordeal.

Fela was a veteran in Auschwitz; she had arrived here with her mother four winters ago. When her mother became ill and could not endure the suffering any longer, Fela, with her own hands, had put her on the truck which carried the sick to the crematorium . . .

Now Fela said to me: "But you — you are young children. You must fight, you must struggle for your lives! Because some Jews have to survive . . ." She repeated this over and over again.

From then on, day after day, she cared for me with the devotion of a mother. I wasn't the only one to merit her attention; Fela worried about all the girls in the block as though they were her own children. At night before we went to sleep she walked from bunk to bunk, talking softly, kissing and hugging us, making us promise that we would not despair, that we would keep fighting.

Two months after my illness I was transferred to another labor camp, where I suffered indescribable hardship and anguish. It is unnecessary to put down the details of everything that happened there. All I can say is that it was in Fela's merit that I survived the war, for her strong gray eyes followed me everywhere and kept me from collapsing.

The war's end did not bring our troubles to a magical close, for we, the young survivors, remained forsaken orphans, and we lived a life of bereavement and loneliness. Although there was nothing to compensate us for the loss of our families, there were people who did try to help out. One of the most important events of our new lives was the establishment of a children's home in the district where we had been liberated, and from time to time we had small festive gatherings there. Such children's homes sprang up spontaneously in many places, one of myriad relief efforts that helped people of all ages to get back on their feet after the war. In these homes one could meet friends and receive a meal, small sparks of consolation in the empty life we now faced — a life that demanded attention to daily activity in spite of the ache in our hearts.

No matter how good or bad I felt, I never stopped thinking about Fela, the noble soul who had cared for us so tenderly in Auschwitz. It pained me that I had lost contact with her and did not know where she was, or even if she were still alive.

Twenty-four years had passed since I left Fela. I had emigrated to Israel and settled in Chaifa. When the Six Day War broke out in 1967, my son was studying in a yeshivah in Jerusalem, and I begged him to come home: "In wartime a family ought to stay together!" I pressed him, thinking of my own war, of the mother I had never seen again.

"Mother," my son said, "please don't insist, for I cannot leave Jerusalem — and precisely because it is such a terrible war. Here everyone is needed, and everyone helps out in whatever way he can."

When the war ended, I was among the first people to visit the freed city of Jerusalem, and I went straight to my son's yeshivah. As I stood on the grounds, I was dazzled by the sweet sound of Talmud study which came from the building. This melodious sound was for me a most pleasant greeting . . .

My son came out and welcomed me with a blessing. "Mother," he said, "now I'll show you our Jerusalem: Jerusalem of Gold."

I felt exhilarated. For the first time in my life, standing there outside the yeshivah building, I felt that this alone had been worth my struggle to survive in the Nazi hell. I was so absorbed in my thoughts that for a moment I forgot myself, and when I came out of my reverie, I noticed a pair of sad, gray, tired eyes staring at me. I became spellbound and stood frozen to the spot. When I had regained my composure, I was able to utter only a single word: "Fela! . . ."

"Block Number Eight," she whispered in a calm and sweet voice.

My son could not understand the sudden change in me. He looked at both of us, stunned, ignorant of the dizzying images that were reeling through my mind, of the reason why tears gushed from her eyes and from mine. I began to tell Fela all that I remembered of those days, and she just looked into my eyes and nodded in understanding . . . Then she invited us to her house.

Fela told me during the visit that she had come to Israel after the liberation and had gone to work as a nurse in the Hadassah Hospital here in Jerusalem. When I asked her about her job, she replied: "Day and night I care for my children."

"What kind of children?" I asked.

"Wounded soldiers," she said in a quiet and compelling voice. "Today all the wounded soldiers are my children . . ."

Fela had not changed a bit. Even Auschwitz had not destroyed her beautiful character and deep compassion for others. She remained the same Fela . . .

ESCAPE FROM AUSCHWITZ

Mala Zimetbaum
Antwerp, Belgium

This account is a compilation of the testimonies of several prisoners of Auschwitz, primarily that of Mala's cousin, Giza Weisblum, and the recordings of the Polish Jewish historian Ber Mark.

The story of Mala Zimetbaum is told, with varying details, in almost all books on Auschwitz. In the Polish literature of the Nazi death camps, the history of Mala and Edward Galinski, the young Polish prisoner with whom she attempted a courageous escape, takes a prominent place, and in fact their lives and actions have been crowned retroactively with a halo of quixotic heroism that almost surpasses reality. The Polish literature, however, exhibits little knowledge of Mala's life and her activities in Auschwitz prior to her escape, erring even in facts as basic as her birthplace. One of the Polish narrators, for example, relates that Mala was the daughter of a rich diamond merchant from Antwerp; actually, her father worked in the diamond business but only as an agent, and the family was not wealthy. None of the Polish people who write about Mala were present at her hanging, for the SS guards forbade anyone except Jewish women to be present at her death.

Jewish attestation regarding Mala, however, throws a keen light on her background and character. There are two reliable sources of Mala's history: her cousin, Giza Weisblum, and a Polish boy named Waclaw Kielar, who was Edward Galinski's most intimate friend. From their descriptions we get a clear picture of Mala's personality and her involvement in the Auschwitz underground.

Giza Weisblum was born in Tarnow, Poland, and emigrated to Belgium, where she joined the Zionist Youth resistance organization. In 1943 Giza was deported to Auschwitz, where she met Mala. She followed her cousin's activities in the camp closely and witnessed her escape and her tragic death. Waclaw Kielar, the Polish witness, also knew Mala in Auschwitz, although he was closer to Edward Galinski.

Mala Zimetbaum was born in 1920, in Brzysko, Poland. Her family later emigrated to Antwerp, Belgium, and settled at 7 Marinos Street, in a section where poorer Jews lived, and here Mala was raised.

Mala's father was a diamond factory employee, and the family lived quite modestly. When Mala was still very young her father became blind, and as a result the children all had to go out to work. Mala's sister Estush (Esther) became ill and died, and only three sisters and a brother remained. Mala was hardened at an early age by the double blows of poverty and family crisis, but she was by no means cowed. She joined the Zionist Youth organization in Antwerp and began to absorb the spirit of high ideals so prevalent among the young people of that era.

At fourteen Mala had to interrupt her studies and take up sewing to sustain the family, and after the German occupation of Belgium her responsibilities increased greatly. It was she who carried the yoke of her family's existence on her shoulders.

The German hand closed in on Antwerp, and in 1942 Mala traveled to Brussels to rent an illegal apartment for her family. Upon her return to Antwerp, she accidentally fell into the trap of a Jew-hunt in the railroad terminal and was sent with several other Jews to the Malin Camp, a concentration center from which frequent deportations took place. Her parents were arrested shortly afterward and brought to Malin as well.

Mala planned to escape the camp but she did not succeed. She and her parents were deported to Auschwitz, and at the first selection her parents were sent to the gas chambers.

Mala's attributes were quickly assessed by her captors. She knew several languages — German, Polish, French, Flemish, and Yiddish — and also had a very pleasant appearance. Mandel and Drechsler, the two sadistic women who were chief overseers of the women's concentration camps in Auschwitz, chose her to serve as a translator and courier. A number of Jewish Slovakian girls were also selected as couriers. Their task was to deliver messages, orders, and reports, as well as to help the German overseers in managing the camp.

Upon their arrival in Auschwitz, many prisoners were forced to send home calming letters to their relatives and friends, assuring them that they were working at regular jobs and were well. Mala too was forced to write such a letter. However, she dared to add one sentence to the prescribed contents, a slim hint to her true situation. Her relatives in Belgium received a postcard from her which read: "I'm all right. I work and I am well. All the others are with my sister Estush." Mala's sister had been dead for several years. Regrettably, the hint did not benefit her relatives, for many of them later arrived in Auschwitz.

As a courier, Mala was permitted to move freely among the sections and barracks of Birkenau, the largest division of Auschwitz, and she also had access to the rooms of the block chiefs where transfer documents were stored. Agile on her feet and possessing an unusual gift of invention, she capably and carefully used her position to help as many people as she could. She was able to transfer weak women to easier work; to acquire medications and distribute them among the sick; to provide bread in secrecy; to smuggle paper and pencils to prisoners so that they could write to their relatives in other parts of the camp. She also changed the numbers of the death lists when she could and tried to save as many people as possible from selections, all at great danger to herself.

Mala used her influence in other ways as well. She would often reproach the Kapos for being hard on the inmates. "Here we are all equal," she would say to them. "We are all prisoners, and we all share the same fate!"

In the beginning Mala acted entirely on her own. Later, her cousin Giza Weisblum coaxed her to join the organized resistance movement, and from then on her activities were carried out in the framework of the underground. Her work as a courier took on a special character; in addition to the practical assistance she provided, her appearance and optimism alone aroused hope in the hearts of despondent prisoners. Mala evolved into a living spirit and her name became well known among the prisoners, especially the women from Belgium.

She also kept an extensive watch over everything that went on in the camp. Because she had access to the rooms where documents were stored, she was able to gather bits of information about developments in the outside world. When, in 1944, she came upon the shocking facts of the extermination of Hungarian Jewry, the decision which had been germinating in her mind for some time was sealed: she must escape from the camp and let the world know the reality of Auschwitz. In spite of the almost-daily attempts at escape that were made by the prisoners and the fact that virtually all of them were caught and killed, she was not daunted.

Mala became acquainted with a young Polish prisoner named Edward Galinski, or Edek, as he was known, a native of the vicinity of Krakow. He had been one of the first prisoners in the camp and worked as a fitter, installing and repairing plumbing parts and other equipment. Thanks to his job, he also had free access to most areas of the camp and knew a great deal about its layout and operations. Edek and Mala began to devise a plan of escape for the sake of alarming the world to the truth of the concentration camps. Originally Edek had planned to escape with his Polish friend, Waclaw Kielar, but when Waclaw learned that Mala was to come along, he refused to risk complicity with a Jewess. He also felt that since Mala was a woman she would inhibit their ability to travel quickly, and so he withdrew from the plan, hoping to follow them later. Mala and Edek decided to undertake the escape on their own.

Mala did not reveal her plan to anyone except her cousin Giza and three Jewish Slovakian girls who were also couriers: Leah, Pola, and Herta. They were Mala's admirers and greatly encouraged her. Edek revealed his plan to two friends besides his confidant Waclaw Kielar: a fellow Polish prisoner named Jurek Sadczekow, and a civilian worker named Anthoni Szymlak who lived in a village not far from the camp and who helped Edek to organize the escape.

Kielar had a friend who worked in the Canada Kommando, a sorting unit where the belongings of the prisoners were classified. This friend "organized" some money for him from among the clothing he was sorting, and Edek used the money to bribe an officer in order to obtain an SS uniform and a revolver. The transaction took a number of weeks, but Edek finally did receive both items. It was planned that on the day of the escape Edek would wear the uniform, and Mala would disguise herself as a male worker; she would wear Edek's overalls on top of her own clothing and carry a lavatory basin over her head. Mala secured a document from the block chief's office and forged it to the effect that the "SS" man was leaving to transfer a prisoner to a work site outside the camp. The lavatory basin, of course, was to hide Mala's face since she was well known in the camp.

Mala and Edek escaped on Saturday afternoon, June 24, 1944. They chose a time when the guards were changing their posts and most of the SS men had already taken off for the weekend.

That day, in both the women's and men's camps in Birkenau, the sirens began to wail at the appel. The interrogation and torture of three Jewish courier girls elicited no results. Two weeks went by, and the Germans were unable to come upon the trail of the escapees.

Mala and Edek traveled by foot and managed to reach the Zywiek mountains, near the Slovakian border; but when they tried to cross the border, they were caught by a German patrol, jailed in Bielsko, and then sent back to Auschwitz. The source of this information is a note that Edek himself later wrote to his friend Kielar, and it is most dependable. Many other versions of this capture surface in the literature: that Mala and Edek were caught in an inn in Katowice; that they were found in the restaurant of a German hospital in Mislowice; that the chief of the women's camp in Birkenau, Maria Mandel, discovered them in a train wagon. Edek's account, however, is the truthful one.

Mala's escape had aroused hope and joy in the hearts of the Jewish prisoners, especially the women, and her capture caused a great depression. Many people were disappointed not only because the attempt had failed, but because they feared that Edek or Mala would not be able to endure the torture and would implicate others in their circle. This fear, however, was groundless. Giza Weisblum received a note from Mala, smuggled out of the bunker of Block 11, the infamous Auschwitz torture chamber where she was being held. It read: "I am prepared for everything. Now I know for sure that *their* end is near. Be strong! Remember everything!" Mala's short note contained much information. She hinted at the news of the war which she had heard during her weeks on the road; she stated that she was prepared to die in spite of the torture, which meant that she would protect her friends' identities; and she encouraged her fellow prisoners to remember everything that their oppressors had done to them and to keep up the fight.

Waclaw Kielar also received three separate notes from Edek, which were smuggled out from Block 11. In the first, Edek wrote of the capture; in the second he said that the interrogators were now using torture; and in the last he informed his friend that Mala remained strong, and that she had not disclosed any names. Both were awaiting sentence.

August 22, 1944, was the day set for Mala Zimetbaum's execution in the women's camp. There was no scaffold, and the prisoners wondered what kind of death had been prepared for her. After the appel came an order: "All Jews to the square between the kitchen and bathhouse!"

All of the women in the barracks near the execution square were quickly assembled. Mala was brought out to the square. She marched proudly, her head raised high. Behind her walked the chief executioner.

While Maria Mandel, the camp chief, was reading the sentence aloud, Mala quietly slid her hand over her hair, pulled out a hidden razor blade, and swiftly cut her own veins. The prisoners froze in shock. Riter, the execution official, noticed and grabbed Mala's wrist. She slapped him with her bleeding hand. Riter shrieked: "You want to be a hero?! For that *we're* here — this is *our* job!"

"Murderers, soon you'll pay for our suffering!" Mala shouted at the top of her voice. "Girls, do not be afraid! Their end is near! I'm sure now. I know it, I was outside, I was free!"

Riter struck her with his pistol and she staggered to the ground. (Some witnesses claim that it was Rapportfuhrer Taube whom Mala slapped, and that he nearly trampled her to death afterward.) Instantly a stretcher was brought and she was carried to Block 4. A massive confusion and tumult arose, and the Germans ran to restore order.

Mala's last hour of life was witnessed and reported by her cousin Giza Weisblum, as well as several other prisoners in Block 4 who were with her. Mala lay on the stretcher and continued to talk, in a voice growing weaker with each moment: "Do not cry, the day of revenge is near! Listen! Remember everything they did to you!"

"Silence, you swine!" roared Riter.

"I was silent for two years, now I'll talk!" she whispered with her last bit of strength.

The SS man pasted a plaster bandage over her mouth and said to Mandel, "Now she'll be quiet!"

Mala, still alive, was then placed on a hand wagon and taken to the gas chambers.

Other eyewitnesses also have vivid recollections of Mala's last moments. Sarah Goldberg, a friend of hers, speaks of Mala's gray face and of the way she continued to stand proudly in the square in spite of her cut veins; and a Polish eyewitness relates that she heard Mala cry out: "I know that I'm going to die, but this is unimportant. It's important that you (Germans) will perish soon. Your days are numbered. Nothing will help you, and no one will save you!"

Edek Galinski was executed on the same day as Mala. He was hanged in public, in the presence of many of the male prisoners in Birkenau. At the last moment, before the SS guard finished reading the death sentence, Edek, whose hands were chained with wires, thrust his head into the noose and tried to shove the stool away with his foot. It seems that both Mala and Edek had resolved not to let themselves be killed by the German executioners, but rather to die by their own hands. Edek's executioners, however, were quick. They caught him before he pushed the stool away completely and managed to hang him. Before he died, Edek cried out, "Long live Poland!"

There is only one small remnant of this episode which remains today: a small pencil portrait of Mala Zimetbaum sketched by one of the prisoners, which now hangs in the Auschwitz Museum. It is a reminder of the awesome courage and fortitude that flowered against hope in the poisoned swamps of Auschwitz.

THE AUSCHWITZ REVOLT

The following account of the Auschwitz revolt combines outside research by Anna Eibeshitz with the testimonies of Fajga Segal-Finkelstein (Vilna, Poland), Mala Weinstein (Brussels, Belgium), and Leah Gutman (Sosnowiec, Poland), who were members of the Auschwitz underground.

In spite of the general view of Jewish resistance to the Nazis as passive at best, an underground did exist even in Auschwitz, the most massive and brutal of the death camps; and its efforts, especially in light of its severe limitations and narrow prospects for success, were ferocious. One of the first and foremost projects of the Auschwitz underground was the destruction of the crematoria. Explosives were accessible — though, of course, at an exorbitant risk — from the Union ammunition factory, which had been erected in Auschwitz during the last stages of the war, after many other munitions factories in Germany had been bombed.

The factory was in total seclusion, and the workers, mostly Jewish girls whose job was to produce gunpowder for cannon shell, were under constant and strict guard. The pavilion where the gunpowder was produced was more isolated and under closer watch than all the other sections of the factory.

231

The revolt was orchestrated by several men in the Sonderkommando,* the "special" unit that worked in the crematoria. They elicited both Jewish and non-Jewish cooperation, and their network of information and transference of stolen explosive materials extended to many sections of the camp. These links varied from day to day, and intermediate groups were often "blinded," kept unaware of the activities of other units, in order to protect as many people as possible. Many groups of workers, especially those in the munitions factory or in other sensitive positions, were forbidden to have communication with each other, and their networking took place either through code signals or with the assistance of those groups, such as the plumbing and sewage kommandos, whose workers could move freely among the camps.

In addition to the planned destruction of the crematoria, the underground was active in many ways. Among its members were engineers who actually created their own crude radios and managed to circulate news of the war to other prisoners in the camp. The underground also extended continual help to inmates in need by giving out bread, hiding people from selections, obtaining aspirin for the sick, and boosting morale. Every act they undertook was at mortal risk, for most of them were under the close scrutiny of their German overseers and were not even permitted to talk amongst themselves at work.

The first people the Sonder workers approached with their master plan to explode the crematoria were the girls in the gunpowder pavilion. These girls lived in terror of the SS and were extremely reluctant at first

---

*The men in the Sonderkommando worked in a world of terror beyond the scope of human imagination. They witnessed the greatest evil of Auschwitz and were unable to help.

The Sonders' task was to sort and dispose of the bodies of all the victims of the gas chambers. They would enter the chamber after a mass gassing and first hose down the mound of dead bodies with a strong torrent of water in order to remove the excrement. Then they separated the bodies, shaved the victims' heads, and searched their teeth and private parts for hidden gold and diamonds. Finally, they loaded the dead on elevators and delivered them to the crematoria. Often, the Sonders recognized their own parents and relatives among the victims.

The Sonders were chosen for their positions and had no say in the matter. They were fed and clothed well and were never allowed to leave their posts. They were not permitted to live more than four months after they had been on the job; they knew too much. At the end of their term they were murdered and replaced by a new group of prisoners. No Sonder ever escaped. Those who tried were caught and thrown alive into the crematorium.

Three Sonder workers—Zalman Gradowski, Zalman Lowenthal, and Rabbi Aryeh Leib Langfus— buried diaries in the ground near the crematoria, which were discovered and published after the war.

to get involved, but in a short time they became prime movers in the revolt. One of them was Ela Gertner, a Polish-born Belgian girl, who succeeded in involving several other friends in the project. These included Regina Sapir; the sisters Esther and Hanale Weisblum; Mala Weinstein; Leah Gutman; Fajga Segal, a proletarian leader from Vilna; and Hadassa Zlotnitzka-Talman, a courier in the Zionist Dror organization and a fighter in the Warsaw Ghetto uprising. Other girls who actively participated in the smuggling of explosive materials were Rochel Schwartz-Klarman, Rosalia Langsam-Zilberberg, Lusia Firstenberg, and Henia Hass.

The girls began to smuggle out minute amounts of gunpowder from the factory. They hid it in soup pots with double bottoms, in the knots of their kerchiefs, in the seams or folds of their dresses. It is a wonder that they succeeded, for all the munitions workers were checked from head to foot upon leaving the factory each day. It took the girls over a year to collect the necessary amount of explosive material.

The transference of the gunpowder took place in many ways and through varied hands. A key figure in this crucial linkage was Roza Robota of Ciechanow, Poland, who involved several of her landsmen in the project.

Roza had been born in Ciechanow in 1923 into a middle-class family. At sixteen she joined the local *Hashomer Hatzair* group, a socialist-Zionist organization, and became active in the ghetto underground. At the liquidation of the Ciechanow Jewish community in 1942, Roza was deported, along with all the Jews of the town, to Auschwitz. There she lost her entire family.

In Auschwitz she was selected to work in one of several units which examined and sorted the clothes of the crematoria victims. Active by nature and faithful to her ideals, she soon organized a rebellion among her fellow workers in the Clothing Kommando and maintained active contact with the Sonders and other units of the Birkenau underground.

When the explosives project got under way, the girls from the ammunition factory often handed over the powder to Roza directly. The clothing division where she worked was located near the high-voltage wire fence, which divided it from the crematoria square. Roza transferred the gunpowder to the Sonder men who worked in the crematoria, and they delivered it to Russian technicians who actually manufactured functional hand grenades and crude bombs from it. These homemade explosives were then stuffed into cans and buried by the Sonder workers in various pits around the area of the crematoria, to be saved until the proper time.

Other people who were involved in the explosives chain included Godl Zilber, a landsman of Roza's from Ciechanow, Yokl Wrobel in the Sonder, and two munitions workers named Israel Gutman and Yehuda Laufer. All of these people were in moment-to-moment danger of losing their lives.

In October 1944 the Sonderkommando recovered their hand-concocted explosives from the ground. Rabbi Aryeh Leib Langfus, who had been the judge of the Jewish Beis Din in Makow-Mazowieck, undertook the final step of the mission alone. With the explosives secreted on his body, he went into the crematoria and blew up the building, dying in the explosion.* The Sonder workers then severed the electrical wires surrounding the camp and tried to escape,♦ but the attempt was swiftly and easily crushed because there was no place to escape to. The fields behind the camp were mined, and all the escapees fell into the Germans' hands and were killed. People in other sections of the camp were aware of the emergency, for sirens began to shriek, and the workers in the Union factory were quickly moved to another block.

The explosion seriously damaged only one of the crematoria, which the Germans were able to restore to working order. After the revolt, the SS discovered a can of burn powder near the destroyed crematorium. This ruled out the use of other explosive materials such as petroleum or torches, which could have been brought in by outside personnel, and led to the investigation of the gunpowder pavilion in the Union factory. The Jewish workers in this pavilion were now the prime suspects. Two days

---

*There are varying accounts of this story. Other survivors report that in the general breakdown of communication that occurred during the revolt, Rabbi Langfus' plan did not materialize. He died instead a few days later when the Germans put to death all the Sonder workers who had been involved in the rebellion. It is clear, however, that in the uprising one of the crematoria was damaged.

♦Originally the Sonders had hoped to engineer a mass escape, but because of miscommunication among the underground factions, their plan fell through.

later, on October 9, 1944, the Political Division* arrested Ela Gertner, Regina Sapir, and Esther Weisblum. Why the Germans arrested these three only is not clear to this day; there was no evidence to point to a connection between these three girls and the Union underground or any other kommandos. The girls were held under torture, but they steadfastly denied any contact with the underground and did not disclose any names. The fact that they were released soon after the investigation was proof that the Germans had no previous knowledge of such a conspiracy. Even without clear evidence, the Germans could easily have put them to death; but now that they suspected the existence of the underground, they decided to release the girls instead in order to gain more information.

The head of the Auschwitz Gestapo recommended that the Political Division plant two spies in the Union factory, by the names of Koch and Schultz. Koch, a Slovakian half-Jew and an ex-Communist, became friendly with the girls and followed all their movements closely. The methods he used are unknown, but apparently he succeeded in gaining some information, for Ela Gertner was soon arrested again. There are conflicting reports about Ela's conduct during the interrogation; some say she broke down under torture and gave out some names, while others maintain that it was not Ela but another girl from the Union factory who betrayed the secret. In any case, the information brought about the subsequent arrests of Regina Sapir, Esther Weisblum, and Roza Robota. The four girls were incarcerated in Block 11, the notorious torture chamber of Auschwitz-1. They were tortured mercilessly but none of them gave in, and Ela Gertner did not release any more names (if indeed she had done so the first time). For the eventual price of their own young lives, they saved the lives of their friends.

To this day it remains a mystery why all the Jewish girls who worked in the explosives pavilion were not put to death. Instead they were punished with a vicious beating and were then forced to kneel for many hours. They suffered broken bones and other injuries, but remained strong enough to continue their underground work until the Germans finally withdrew in January 1945.

*The job of the Political Division was to handle political transgressors, Jewish and non-Jewish. Crimes included smuggling, radio construction, and any other activity that could be characterized as treason.

Close friends of the four imprisoned girls and other members of the underground tried to intervene on their behalf, even attempting to bribe some SS men, but they were unsuccessful. Roza's countrymen and fellow activists did manage, however, to smuggle one of their men, Noah Zablodowicz, into her cell with a bit of food and some clean underwear. Zablodowicz made contact with Jacob Kozhilaczik, the bunker Kapo, who had closest access to the cell, and by some powers of will managed to wrest from him a slim measure of solidarity. Some who knew Jacob Kozhilaczik have said that this was the only deed of kindness he performed in Auschwitz.

In the evening Kozhilaczik introduced Zablodowicz to the SS guard on duty as his good friend. Zablodowicz had brought with him a bottle of whiskey and a sausage, which he had obtained through contacts in one of the sorting kommandos, and the SS man soon became intoxicated. The Kapo then admitted Zablodowicz to Roza's cell and locked the door from the outside.

Noah Zablodowicz could hardly recognize Roza. Her face was lacerated and bruised beyond recognition. She told him of the sadistic methods the Political Division had used to force information from her and said that it had been very hard not to break down, but that she had not disclosed anyone. She was indifferent to Noah's consolation. "I know what I did," she said without pathos, "and I know what to expect. But you continue your work and don't let my fate stop you!" She accepted her lot and was ready to die.

No one knows what transpired in the last hours of the other three girls' lives. It is known, however, that they went to their deaths courageously. Two of the four were executed by hanging during the day, and the other two at night. All of the Jewish women in the barracks adjoining the execution square were released from work early that day and were forced to watch the first hanging. The two martyrs held their heads up high as they stood on the scaffold, and their last call was *"Zemsta!"**

The executions took place on January 6, 1945, only a few days before Auschwitz was liberated.

*"Revenge!"

THE PROTECTOR

Zlata Borenstein-Shnur-Gephart
Lodz, Poland

It is 5:00 p.m. The bell rings, the work in the camp stops, and the "dinner" is waiting — a kettle of black liquid called coffee. In spite of its sickening appearance it is warm, and its smell tears the nostrils and teases our empty stomachs.

As a Shtubowa, I had been put in charge of two hundred girls from the time I had come to Walden-Lust, and my responsibility was to keep order and quiet in my group. It was my job to haul the "coffee" and soup for my girls, and although my status was a bit higher than theirs, I was just as hungry as they were. And this was only because of my stupid pride.

On my way to the kitchen, I often noticed potato peels and sometimes even carrot peels in the garbage. My mouth always watered when I saw these scraps, and I would gladly have picked them up — if not for my pride.

Once I noticed some excellent pieces of potatoes, and even real slices of carrots! I was terribly hungry. I was about to bend down and grab them, but at the last minute I changed my mind. I told myself that I would rather die than fall so low, and walked away.

And yet I was angry with myself, for I was so very hungry. I knew that my pride was destroying me, and I was outraged. I promised myself that tomorrow I would do it. Then tomorrow came, and again . . . I could not do it! I could not stoop so low as to lift something from the garbage and eat it. Was I a dog? Was I to lose my human dignity because of hunger? No, not I!

But what about the others? What about my starving girls who weren't shackled by pride — why shouldn't *they* benefit from the food?

I could not bring myself to put my hand into that heap of refuse, but the next day, instead of fetching the coffee myself, I chose one of the girls to bring it. From then on I sent a different girl each day to haul the coffee. I never asked them about the scraps of food in the garbage cans, but I knew that they had found them.

The hunger in the lager was so vast that it could drive a normal person out of his mind. I remember how the Germans used to toy with the girls who watched them eating. When they wanted some entertainment, they would throw scraps of food in the direction of our barracks. It amused them to see a hundred starving girls fighting for one sandwich or a couple of potatoes. The scene gave them great pleasure, and they roared with laughter. Though I understood the girls, I cringed in shame and begged them not to run for the food. "For them it is a form of amusement!" I entreated them. "Do not satisfy their lust to see Jews turn into animals!" But nothing helped. The girls could not control themselves.

Once on their return from work, the girls noticed two unattended soup kettles on a wheelbarrow. They became wild, broke the column, and in a split second had attacked the kettles. Two girls pried open one of the lids, and with their palms they slushed out the soup and crammed it into their mouths. They fought and pushed until the kettles turned over, spilling their contents into the sand, and then they threw themselves down and began to lick the soup from the ground, licking up the sand with it. I watched them and my heart cried. They were totally dehumanized; they looked like a pack of dogs. I can still see this tragic scene in my mind . . . Whenever I close my eyes, I see the girls on their knees, licking the soup from the ground.

The Germans decided to punish the girls for this breach of conduct. However, since none of them admitted to the crime and none of the officials had witnessed it, the entire group was punished. We had to stand appel on *Fingerspitze*—on our toes. We stood for hours. It started to rain but we were not released. The rain turned to hail, and still we were standing . . . The SS guard changed every half hour, but we weren't permitted even to change our position. Anyone who tried was beaten with a truncheon.

Night fell. The Lagerfuhrer came and asked us again who had opened the kettles, but no one confessed. He threatened to punish all two hundred girls if we did not give up the "guilty" party, but we remained silent.

The hours dragged on. We stood freezing in the bitter cold; the guards continued to change every half hour. Each new guard demanded that we give up the culprit, and each time the demand was met with silence.

At one point I heard a murmur. Two sisters were whispering to each other: "Look at our Shtubowa. She saw who opened the kettles. Why doesn't she tell?"

"Let's tell him and get it over with," her sister whispered back.

"Hush! Let no voice be heard!" I hissed through my teeth.

I was angry, but I didn't blame them. They were tired, hungry, and cold, and they wanted desperately for the appel to end. They were right — but I knew that standing appel was only a temporary suffering. Disclosing a Jewish girl to the Germans was unthinkable to me. I would rather die than resort to such treachery.

Suddenly my name was called. I stepped out. The Lagerfuhrer demanded that I tell him the names of the girls who had attacked the kettles. I said I didn't know who had done it. He became furious, grabbed me by the neck, and lifted me up in the air. He pointed to a tree and hollered: *"Da virds du hangen!"**

He was literally choking me. After a few seconds he threw me to the ground but did not let go. Like a beast he roared: "You swine! You were there! You are responsible! You'll pay for them!"

I did not think. It is too risky to think in such moments. You cannot calculate or use logic — you have to do what your heart dictates. I remember only that I kept repeating, *"Ribono Shel Olam."*✦ But my mind was made up: I would rather die than disclose a hungry Jewish girl.

*"Here you will hang!"
✦Master of the World.

"Herr Lagerfuhrer, I did not see a thing," I said calmly, looking him straight in the eye. I got up and stood at attention in my paper-sack dress, torn wooden shoes, and shaven head, and I looked squarely at the SS officer in his polished, knee-high boots, his shining uniform and glittering helmet . . . but all I saw in my mind's eye were my hungry girls.

Suddenly an air-raid alarm sounded and the skies lit up with fire. In the blink of an eye all the SS men scattered, racing for the shelters, and the appel dissolved at last. With aching bodies we walked back to our barracks.

As a Shtubowa I was responsible for the girls' production. They had been set to work felling trees and bushes, and they had to produce a certain quantity each day, but unfortunately not all of them worked at the same speed. Some were too weak or too clumsy to finish their quota. Jadzia, for example, was totally uncoordinated. She had two left hands, and whatever she did came out wrong. Renia, on the other hand, was fast and produced well — and this too was hazardous. She wanted to find favor in the eyes of the German overseer.

"Renia, do not work so hard! At this speed you will not last long," I begged her.

"I'm hungry, and if I excel, they are bound to recognize it and give me additional soup," Renia reasoned.

"But Renia, they don't even notice you. And besides, you are setting a standard for the others. They will demand that all the other girls match your production. You're hurting them! They want to live!"

"I want to live too, but I cannot stand this terrible hunger! I want to eat my fill at least once, and then die! Zlata, can't you understand that?"

I did understand; but Renia died two months later.

Most of my girls were more rational and had a higher level of endurance than Renia. They worked diligently when the German overseer was watching, but when he turned around, they let go of their spades and told each other stories . . . stories in which they dreamed of a future, and of bread.

"I dream of a round bread, a drop of salt, and a knife," Basia said one day.

"Did you hear that, Zlata? Basia wants bread . . . ha, ha, ha! Why not fish for the Sabbath? Ha! And what's wrong with meat and *tzimmes*,* Zlata? . . ." interrupted Marysia, who had never lost her sense of humor.

"Zlata! *Zlata'she*! Just listen to them," Chana cut in. "Did you hear what they just said? . . . What they want is good. Even very good. But what's wrong with a roasted *katchkele*? They must have forgotten already how a roasted duckling tastes and smells, but not I! Do you believe me, Zlata?"

"I do believe you, Chana. But hold on to your spade, in case he turns around," I warned her, even while I burst into a hearty laughter.

"Zlata, you'll see — we will outlive them! Then I'll roast for you a *katchkele*, and you'll tell me how good it is and what a wonderful cook I am."

I was happy that the girls were in good enough spirits to joke, and while they talked I kept an eye on the German overseer. When I saw him begin to turn around, I would cough, and the girls would return to digging in the frozen earth. I protected them and they loved me for it; but the German knew this and held me responsible for them. He used to call me *Du traune* — good-for-nothing — and beat me up, because I would never tell him which girl had not done her work.

I was never angry at the girls when I was punished in their stead, for it was not a wasted suffering. They worked hard, and they were starving, cold, and exhausted. Sheltering them gave meaning to my wretched life, so that I didn't mind the physical abuse. In Egypt the Jewish foreman had also been beaten when his fellow Jews did not complete their production, for it was his responsibility to make them work faster.

I was not the only Shtubowa in the lager. The other one was Rela, and she drove the girls very hard. Sometimes I thought that she had lost her heart somewhere before she came to the camp. She pushed the girls around and yelled at them continually.

I asked her once why she added to their suffering.

"You are an idiot!" she retorted angrily. Rela had a weak character, and her fear of punishment obscured any compassion she still possessed.

Unfortunately she wasn't the only one of the Jewish supervisors who

*A traditional Jewish dish made of sweet potatoes and carrots.

had a mean streak; there was also Bashka. Bashka looked different from the rest of us. The hunger of the war seemed to have overlooked her completely; her body was full and her cheeks were pink. In the ghetto as well as here in the lager, she had always managed to be at the kettle, distributing soup — a position which carried great privileges. The distributor could choose "favorites" from among the girls and get them to do anything she wanted in exchange for the promise of extra soup. Bashka thought she held the world in her hands.

The unofficial prisoners' "law" required each portion of soup to have four chunks of potato in it, but Bashka held back the potatoes for her favorites and gave the others only one piece of potato in clear water. And on Sunday, when the girls received a farina soup, she did not mix the contents of the kettle. She ladled out the watery portion at the top, and when she reached the last fifth of the kettle she announced that there was no more soup left and shut the little window. The thick soup she reserved for her "special friends." I saw what was going on and was wounded to the core, but I could do nothing.

Once I saw a girl walking away from the soup window, crying. She showed me her soup; it was mere water. My blood began to boil. I walked over to the window and asked Bashka why she hadn't mixed the contents of the pot before she distributed the soup.

She burst out: "You glutton! You never have enough! And anyway, I am boss here and not you!"

"It's not for me! I just want some justice for the girls! They are dying of hunger . . ."

Bashka became enraged. She took a full ladle of soup and slung it into my face.

I never asked any favors, and I never took anything more for myself than what the girls received. The only exception was my corner. As a Shtubowa I had my own corner in the barracks. In the evenings and on Saturdays I used to invite the girls to my corner and tell them stories written by world-famous authors, as well as stories from the Midrash. My favorite subject, though, was Jewish history; I liked to portray for them the epochs of the Jewish judges, kings, and priests.

Some of the girls had never learned Jewish history and were completely ignorant of the things that I told them. Once when I was relating the story of King Solomon, I heard Bashka whispering: "I never knew the Jews had real kings . . ."

Curiously enough, Bashka became interested in my stories and never missed a session. She remembered that she had wronged me and was too shy to approach me personally, but she would often send a friend to urge me to give a talk on Jewish history.

I never held a grudge against Bashka. I could see that she felt awkward in my company, so I made the first move. I walked over to her and said: "Bashka, I know that you regret your outburst. Let's be friends."

Bashka burst out sobbing and begged me to forgive her.

"There is nothing to forgive. I was never angry with you . . ."

Later, when we were transferred to Bergen-Belsen, I once noticed a woman who looked very familiar lying on the floor. It was Rela, the other Shtubowa from my old barracks in Walden-Lust. She recognized me and motioned me to bend down.

"Zlata, I was wrong," she said, and closed her eyes forever.

Zlata Gephart came from the well-known Borenstein family of Lodz. She had been a student of Sara Schenirer, the renowned founder of the girls' seminary in Krakow, and from her rich education drew the stories and talks that inspired her young charges in the concentration camp. After the war she remained in Germany for two years to direct an orphanage and came to Israel in 1947. She is the founder of two Bais Yaakov schools, one in Chaifa and one in Kiryat Ata.

GLOSSARY

aktion (Polish, *akcja*) — a term used by the Germans to indicate an official roundup of Jews for death or deportation, accompanied by a curfew.

appel (G.) — roll call in the concentration camps.

Aryan — This term originally referred to the Indo-European languages and the peoples who spoke them. The Nazis used it to mean "a Caucasian of non-Jewish descent," although the word has no racial connotations. In this book, Aryan means "non-Jewish."

Aryan side — the non-Jewish side of a city, used after the formation of ghettos.

block — barracks; a building or unit of buildings in a concentration camp.

Blockelteste (G.) — block supervisor (similar to a Kapo; Jewish or non-Jewish).

bunker — a hiding place or hole, usually in the ghetto. Also refers to an air-raid shelter.

Gestapo — common name for the *Geheime Staatspolizei*, the German state police, organized in 1933 under the Nazi regime to monitor and destroy political opposition.

Hitler Yugend (G.) — Hitler youth movement.

Judenrat (G.) — the Jewish administration in the ghetto. These people were appointed by the Nazis to attend to all civil administrative tasks in the ghetto, including food distribution, housing, medical care, and sanitation. They were also expected to carry out all Nazi orders explicitly, including the roundup of given numbers of people for deportation. The Nazis in effect made the Judenrat agents against their own people.

Judenrein (G.) — literally, "cleansed of Jews." This was the German order for all Jews to evacuate the central portions of major cities by a given date.

Kapo (Italian, "head") — In the camps, a prisoner who was put in charge of a work group or a block. Kapos were male or female, Jewish or non-Jewish.

kommando — work gang.

Kripo — Office of the German criminal police station in some ghettos. Very few Jews emerged from it.

lager (G.)— concentration camp. Also refers to subdivisions within the camps.

Lagerfuhrer (G.) — camp chief.

Ordnungsdienst (G.) — the Jewish police force in the ghetto, who acted merely as puppets of the Nazis and were forced to impose German ordinances upon the Jews and to round them up for deportations.

"organize" — to acquire a needed item in the camps (e.g., a piece of bread, an item of clothing, medication) by whatever means possible. The word "steal" was never used by the Jews because all their possessions had been stolen by the Germans in the first place.

partisan — resistance workers during the war who operated from hiding places in the forest. The partisans were both Jewish and non-Jewish, but the Jewish partisans were not accepted by their gentile counterparts, who killed many of them.

pritsche (G.) — a plank of wood used as a bunk. Many people often shared one small pritsche.

revier (G.) — literally, hospital; in actuality, a building used as a dumping ground in the camps for those who were sick. Most of the sick people went to their deaths.

schnell (G.) — Quickly! Hurry!

Shtubowa (G.) — block overseer of lower status.

Sonder (G.) — literally, special. Refers to the group of men in the death camps who worked in the crematoria.

S.S. — *Schutzstaffel* (Defense Corps). This was the special security force drawn from the ranks of the SA, the military arm of the Nazi party. Its main role was to terrorize, murder, and otherwise enforce all Nazi edicts against the Jews. Heinreich Himmler transformed the SS into the primary instrument of the Final Solution.

Stubendeinst (G.) — the Blockelteste's assistant, Jewish or non-Jewish, who was required to carry out all of his or her orders.

Volksdeutsche (G.) — In Poland, the large minority of Polish-born German nationals who had immunity from Nazi law because of their birth.

Wehrmacht (G.) — the regular German army.

DEDICATIONS

**HANNELIESE
SCHUSHEIM
Nee Freudenthal — Cologne
Survivor Of The Riga Ghetto**

In Memory Of
JOHANNA/ERICH WOLF

Gertrude T. Wegner

In Blessed Memory Of
AUNT TOBINDA

Eleanor T. Nevins

In Honor Of My Mother
A Remarkable Survivor
Mrs. HELEN LEWIT

Mr. & Mrs. Jay Feder

DUBA STOLAVITSKY

Irving Smith

To My Beloved
THERESA

Randy Fishleder

We Will
Never Forget

**Mr. & Mrs. Morton
Schulman**

HEIDE SCHOENBROD

Helmut Schoenbrod

In Memory Of
My Beloved Husband
YEHUDA ROSENZWEIG

NEVER AGAIN

Argudin & Family

In Memory Of
MORDECHAI & RAYZL
LEDERMAN

Mrs. Annette Linzer

In Memory Of
RINTZI BAT SHLOIME
SHMAYE AND THE
STERN FAMILY

Mr. and Mrs.
Mitchell Rebhun

In Memory Of
ABRAHAM BARLAND
Father Of Pearl,
Sydell & Isadora

Harry Zlotowicz

In Memory Of
Mrs. CAROLINE
FREUDENTHAL
Nee Goldschmidt
Frankfurt, Cologne
Died In Auschwitz

In Memory Of
Mrs. ANNA
FREUDENTHAL
Nee Scweizer — Cologne
Deported to Riga, 1941
Died In Poland, 1944